In-Between

SUNY series, Philosophy and Race
───────────────
Robert Bernasconi and T. Denean Sharpley-Whiting, editors

In-Between

*Latina Feminist Phenomenology,
Multiplicity, and the Self*

MARIANA ORTEGA

Cover art: Mortega, *Multiple and One*, 2014. Corazones Fugitivos series. Acrylic and mixed media, 30 × 30 in.

Published by State University of New York Press, Albany

For information, contact State University of New York Press, Albany, NY
www.sunypress.edu

Production, Eileen Nizer
Marketing, Anne M. Valentine

Library of Congress Cataloging-in-Publication Data

Ortega, Mariana.
In-Between : Latina feminist phenomenology, multiplicity, and the self / Mariana
    Ortega.
        pages cm. — (SUNY series, philosophy and race)
    Includes bibliographical references and index.
    ISBN 978-1-4384-5977-6 (hc : alk. paper)—978-1-4384-5976-9 (pb : alk. paper)
    ISBN 978-1-4384-5978-3 (e-book)
    1. Hispanic American women.   2. Feminists—United States.   I. Title.

E184.S75O78 2015
305.48'868073—dc23   2015011074

10 9 8 7 6 5 4 3 2 1

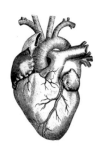

Para mis familias
Norma, Roberto, Olga, Luis, Brittan y Ed
y los de los mundos zurdos

Somos la orquídea de acero,
florecimos en la trinchera como el moho sobre el filo de la
espada,
somos una vegetación de sangre,
somos flores de carne que chorrean sangre . . .
somos la selva que avanza.
Somos la tierra presente . . .

—Joaquín Pasos

Voy,
vengo,
y luego pienso.

Que lo mismo
aquí que allá,
no hay
un lugar
conseguido. Que aquí,
como allá,
soy lo que
las gentes llaman
un extranjero.

Y como un extranjero
iré y vendré.
Hasta que aquí
como allá,
ni yo
ni nadie lo sea.

—Clementina Suárez

I remain who I am, multiple and one of the herd, yet not of it. I walk on the ground of my own being browned and hardened by the ages . . .

—Gloria Anzaldúa

I can take on the cloak of the detached universal, but it is an uncomfortable garment. It is not me, and I do not do my best work wearing it. I seek self-liberation when I write from my particular stance.

—Mary Matsuda

There is no other recourse but to destabilize and displace the subject of modernity from its conceptual throne and to sponsor alternative ways of relating and knowing that no longer shut out from "home" the realities of Latino, Asian, African, and other culturally marginalized peoples.

—Ofelia Schutte

Contents

Acknowledgments   xi

Introduction   1

Chapter 1   The New *Mestiza* and *La Nepantlera*   17

Chapter 2   Being-between-Worlds, Being-in-Worlds   49

Chapter 3   The Phenomenology of World-Traveling   87

Chapter 4   World-Traveling, Double Consciousness,
             and Resistance   119

Chapter 5   Multiplicitous Becomings: On Identity, Horizons,
             and Coalitions   145

Chapter 6   Social Location, Knowledge, and Multiplicity   173

Chapter 7   Hometactics   193

Afterword   215

Notes   221

Bibliography   255

Index   271

Acknowledgments

I am thankful to so many—students, scholars, friends—whose vision, intellectual labor, inspiration, and friendship have made this work possible.

Ellen Feder, thank you for giving me that paper on that curious notion of world traveling—you gave me a work that changed my own travels in philosophy. I remain touched and inspired by your philosophical acuity, your sharp explorations on race and sexuality, your quiet tenacity, as well as your kindness. Linda Martín Alcoff, thank you for being the first philosopher who encouraged me to write and to follow my vision; you philosophize not with a hammer but with a keen attunement to justice, depth, clarity, and philosophical insight that are just as strong—and thank you for that deep generosity that has helped me and other women-of-color philosophers walk on difficult terrains. María Lugones, mil gracias por sus peregrinajes que nos sacan de las penumbras; tanteando y tanteando ha encontrado un espacio filósofico lleno de seres largos y amplios que nos cuentan de teorías impuras, y posibilidades más allá de simples dicotomías y castillos en el aire; al igual que las callejeras que caminan en sus páginas, su trabajo filosófico es original, atrevido y siempre un paso por delante. Ofelia Schutte, thank you for leading the way, for vital work that put Latin American and Latina feminism on the map of academic philosophy; cómo aprecio saber que entiende la dolorosa pero transformadora nostalgia de los exiliados que siempre viven con un pie aquí y otro allá y con memorias difusas de lo que fue. Gail Weiss, thank you for your invaluable philosophical work on embodiment; your intelligence, wit, and zest for life are inspiring. Laura E. Pérez, thank you for understanding what I do with color, for sharing your deep spiritual sense of life; not only do you have a brilliant mind for theory, you also have a sharp eye for color, form, and what lies beneath them. I am so glad that you get Pasos's *Canto de Guerra de las Cosas*, a poem that is always walking on the corridors of my mind and body. Namrata Mitra, thank you for our many philosophical as well as personal conversations; I am constantly learning something new from your keen philosophical analyses and your incredible wit. Thank you, Gloría Anzaldúa, if you could hear my words, I would softly tell you gracias gracias gracias—your borderlands have alleviated the pain of so many of us whose journeys have taken us to lands in the middle; your courage to write yourself in the pages of your book and to defy conventions from all of your worlds continues to inspire and transform. Frederick Olafson is no longer with us, but I will always be thankful to him for teaching me Heideggerian phenomenology; I will always remain indebted to Judy Patel, a committed teacher who has helped so many learn a new language in a new land.

Amazing Latina feminists have helped me see phenomenology anew—thank you, Edwina Barvosa, Theresa Delgadillo, Carmen Lugo-Lugo, Jacqueline Martinez, Paula Moya, and Chela Sandoval. Meetings of the Roundtable on Latina Feminism, a small conference that I organize yearly and that is devoted solely to discussions on Latina feminist issues have been of the utmost importance for my intellect, for my soul, and for community building. Special thanks to Dianna Taylor in her role of Shula Chair in the John Carroll University Philosophy Department for her generous funding of the Roundtable. I thank all of the participants for their wonderful contributions, and for their spirit of cooperation. In Roundtable meetings I have gotten to know the new generation of Latina/o philosophers: Mariana Alessandri, Natalie Cisneros, Pedro DiPietro, Cynthia Paccacerqua, Andrea Pitts, Stephanie Rivera Berruz, Ernesto Rosen Velásquez, Elena Ruiz, and Gabriella Veronelli; I am impressed by their intelligence and encouraged by their commitment to justice. I look forward to reading more of their work. I am also indebted and inspired by the intelligence, strength, and perseverance of a group of women-of-color philosophers and scholars; it would indeed be very lonely without them: Alia Al Saji, Yoko Arisaka, Kristie Dotson, Kathryn T. Gines, Namita Goswami, V. Denise James, Emily S. Lee, Kyoo Lee, Donna-Dale Marcano, and Falguni A. Sheth. Whether through conversation, the printed word, or conference presentations, I have been fortunate to get to know and learn from a number of philosophers, including Emmanuela Bianchi, Alison Bailey, Talia Mae Bettcher, Robert Bernasconi, Helen Fielding, Jonathan Gunderson, David Kim, Eva Feder Kittay, Bonnie Mann, Jennifer McWeeny, José Medina, Kelly Oliver, Monique Roelofs, Ronald R. Sundstrom, Julie Sushystska, Paul C. Taylor, Cynthia Willet, and Kelli Zaytoun. Thanks to Dana Foote, Andrew Kenyon, and Eileen Nizer for helpful editorial advice. Mil gracias to Andrea Pitts for a great job with the index and to Elisabeth Paquette for her help with it. I thank John Carroll University for a generous Grauel Fellowship which helped me complete Chapter 6.

My friends provide constant support and joy. Thanks to Kate Catanese, Diana Chou, Kellee Davis, Catherine Gunderson, Karen Gygli, Bob Kolesar, María Marsilli, Jeannette Mohr, Adriana Novoa, Jessica Pfeifer, Salomon Rodezno, Nicolás León Ruiz, Lisa Salamon-Handel, Sara Schiavoni, Gloria Vaquera, Regina Webb, and Paula Woods. The Sistah Sinema crowd is an amazing group of queer women of color who are smart, creative, defiant, and loving. Thank you Karla Anhalt, Kaylan Baxter, Kirby Broadnax, Shaundra Cunningham, Nicole Harris, Lisa Hopps, Mo Jackson, Carmen Lane, Jessica Lewis, Deidre McPherson, Gabi Mirelez, Maudisa Meroe, Mercedes Noble-Reyes, Senoria Page, and Phyllis Seven Harris.

I am grateful to my family, whose constant love sustains me. Norma, Roberto, Olga, Luis, Hugo, Hugo Roberto, and Ronald—you are in Miami and Los Angeles, but I always carry you with me; I admire your endurance and your courage. I am so, so grateful for your love. I have many good memories of those in California and Managua whom I do not see often but are part of me: Nohelia, Gabriela, Celeste, Nohelita, Martha, Mario, Roberto José, Mario, and Cristiana. Edward Alix, you are now part of the Ortegas. I cannot thank you enough for all you have done to make life easier as I sat in front of the computer for long periods of time. I am charged by your positive energy, love of Euclid, kindness, and incredible humor. Lastly, I would like to thank my partner, Brittan Davis, whose strength, intelligence, and perseverance always leaves me in awe. Our conversations on psychology, philosophy, feminism, and art, as well as our moments of joy nourish me; your love and support have nourished this book as well—my love to you and our Kokoro.

Earlier versions of parts of chapters 2 and 3 were previously published as " 'New Mestizas,' 'World-Travelers,' and *Dasein*: Phenomenology and the Multivoiced Multicultural Self." *Hypatia* 16(3) (Summer): 1–29. A version of chapter 7 has been previously published in *Living Alterities: Phenomenology, Embodiment, and Race*, ed. Emily Lee, 133–172. Albany, NY: State University of New York Press.

Introduction

I want, I need, mestiza theories, in the flesh and in ink, holding the disparate, the incommensurable, opening different worlds. Flesh and blood beings live in the borderlands, struggling, surviving, creating, transforming, resisting. Borderlands in our minds, in our words, in the printed page. They are an invitation—to explore, to see anew, to transform. Come in.

Feeling comfortable in the world of philosophy has not been easy for me. This book is my *hometactic*, my attempt at finding a sense of belonging and ease within a discipline that forgets the contributions of those regarded as "others." If philosophy remembers them, it does so with piercing abstraction and condescension. Yet, as theory, as praxis, this so-called love of wisdom can also offer a different, empowering possibility—that of disclosing selves that have been relegated to the margins, whose ways of knowing and being have been covered over; philosophy can regard their thinking, their words, and their experiences as valuable and as worthy of further analysis. Philosophy can make these selves matter—and they can tell it many a story, enriching it, expanding it, not letting it linger in narrowness and delusions of fairness and neutrality.

Preoccupied with questions of selfhood, subjectivity, and personal identity, philosophers have looked for general explanations over particular discussions describing selves as embodied and marked by race, sex, gender, ability, and other identities.[1] It is not that long since Maurice Merleau-Ponty, one of the most important figures of the phenomenological movement, brought to light the importance of the body in philosophical investigations of the self—but even he remained silent about the particularities of that body.[2] People of color, immigrants, exiles, border dwellers, those at the margins, have paid attention to those particularities and have told their stories and described their struggles; they have offered gifts of words arising from their lived experiences. It would be good for philosophy and philosophers

1

to listen to these stories and to recognize how important they are for the development of richer philosophical theories. The danger, some will say, is that what these voices tell us is not philosophy but merely personal stories, digressions. Sara Ahmed asks, "But why call the personal a digression? Why is it that the personal too often enters writing as if we are being led astray from a proper course" (Ahmed 2006, 22)?

The "proper course" of philosophy on the question of selfhood has moved us away from personal stories by these gendered and racialized selves to metaphysical inquiries as to the nature of selfhood and subjecthood in general. Even existential phenomenological accounts that profess to do justice to lived experience avoid personal descriptions informed by particular social identities, staying within the confines of general categories of existence. Strong dichotomies have been set up, separating the general and the particular, theory and practice, prescription and description. First-person narratives have been relegated to the realm of literature, as if this were a less important realm. Consider Italian writer Italo Calvino's discussion of the alleged difference between philosophy and literature:

> The eyes of philosophers see through the opaqueness of the world, eliminate the flesh of it, reduce the variety of existing things to a spider's web of relationships between general ideas. . . . Along come the writers and replace the abstract chessmen with kings and queens, knights and castles, all with a name, a particular shape. (1986, 39)

This problematic understanding of the difference between philosophy and literature continues to inform views about what constitutes the proper task of philosophy. But why not follow the so-called digressions to see where they lead, to see how they can transform our visions of ourselves and of philosophy itself?

At a time when I was fascinated with questions regarding the nature of selfhood, choice, and death as studied by existential phenomenology, I digressed. I found words written by Gloria Anzaldúa, María Lugones, Audre Lorde, Ofelia Schutte, and other women of color whose writing is not constrained by disciplinary borders, whose writing constitutes both self-explorations and offerings, invitations to their lived experiences.[3] I still remember the first time I encountered voices of fleshy Latina selves explaining their experiences in difficult terrains, baring it all, triumphs as well as defeats, satisfactions as well as fears, moments of paralysis and of transformation. Lugones's now famous world-traveling essay (Lugones 2003, ch. 4) pulled me in a way that not many other philosophical discussions had—and I, having come to the United States due to war, from a rude awakening and introduction to existential questions at an early age, *had* been moved by the existential account of *Dasein* with its discussion of temporality, anxiety, and death. Philosophy let me explore questions about the meaning of life at a time when meaning seemed to have vanished. Yet, I related to Lugones's discussion in a more intimate and powerful way. I had found an essay written by a Latina philosopher describing experiences familiar to me as well as to other Latinas and other women of color as we navigate unwelcoming worlds. I *had* to digress. Doing so has brought me to this book, this project with which I fearfully but defiantly attempt to cross borders and to offer, following Anzaldúa, a *mestiza* theory—if *mestizaje* can be said of a group of words.

The *mestiza* theory that I present in this book is a theory of *multiplicitous selfhood*, of selves characterized by *being-between-worlds, being-in-worlds, and becoming-with*. It is a view primarily inspired by my excursions into what I refer to as Latina feminist phenomenology, especially the work of Anzaldúa and Lugones, and into existential phenomenology, primarily the work of Martin Heidegger. My account takes into consideration not only the multiplicity of the self in general, the multiple positions that we all inhabit, but also the experiences of selves in borderlands, in *nepantla* or in-betweenness. These are selves that Anzaldúa describes as living in *El Mundo Zurdo* (the left-handed world), selves that constantly travel worlds—immigrants, exiles, multicultural beings, those that Anzaldúa daringly calls *los atravesados*:

> A borderland is a vague and undetermined place created by the emotional residue of an unnatural boundary. It is in a constant state of transition. The prohibited and forbidden are its inhabitants. *Los atravesados* live here: the squint-eyed, the perverse, the queer, the troublesome, the mongrel, the mulato, the half-breed, the half dead; in short, those who cross over, pass over, or go through the confines of the "normal." (1987, 3)

Crossing borders is not always easy or possible, and in many moments one might become paralyzed, discouraged, before the crossing; one enters, as Anzaldúa calls it, the *Coatlicue* state, and feels the blocks, the fear, not knowing where to go (Anzaldúa 1987, 41–51, 74). And I should be frank: I have become paralyzed for long periods of time while engaging in this project—stopping, doubting it, becoming fearful of not having the right words or a worthwhile theory or a contribution to make in this territory of philosophy that I feel I precariously inhabit. Anzaldúa says,

> Writing produces anxiety. Looking inside myself and my experience, looking at my conflicts, engenders anxiety in me. Being a writer feels very much like being a Chicana, or being queer—a lot squirming, coming up against all sorts of walls. . . . Living in a state of psychic unrest, in a Borderland, is what makes poets write and artists create. It is like a cactus needle embedded in the flesh. (1987, 73)

I have felt the needles of this project and have let them inside me. I have stopped writing, putting my words away, being paralyzed, only to come back, to pluck the words out again.

I have been fearful in part because I am fully aware as to how diligently disciplinary borders are patrolled and how strongly disciplinary affiliations are felt. Given the current academic state of compartmentalization of disciplines and even of subjects within disciplines, it is not surprising that Latina feminists—with the notable exception of Jacqueline Martinez, who proposes a phenomenology of Chicana experience (2000, 2011, 2014)—do not appeal to existential phenomenological accounts, especially that of Heidegger, whose political engagement with National Socialism is inexcusable.[4] It is also not surprising that the work of Latina feminist theorists is not considered in most philosophical camps. Feminist philosophers have paid more attention to the work of Latina feminists, although even within feminism the work of Latina feminist theorists remains understudied, underanalyzed, and tokenized in order to satisfy the demands of inclusiveness and pluralism associated with feminist theory. If not undervalued, writings by Latina feminists are completely ignored within feminist theorizing. As Martinez notes:

> One of the reasons it is so seemingly easy for some feminists in the Anglo-American academy to overlook the contributions of Anzaldúa, Moraga, and other feminists of color is that they retain a rootedness in communities through which they retain an intersubjectively confirmed completeness, comfort, and assertiveness within their own position and all of the normative conditions carried therein. They can, in other words, take their intersubjective position for granted and thereby make their own sense of the world into a total world, even while making claims to the contrary. (2014, 229)

Thus, providing an account that makes use of the work of Latina feminist theorists as well as the work of canonical existential phenomenologists such as Heidegger is not an easy task and might not be welcomed by purists or by those interested in studying only accepted or canonical texts within the various movements in philosophy.

My intertwining of Latina feminism and Heideggerian existential phenomenology might be problematic not only for purists but for those who are aware of the terrible political views held and defended by Heidegger. I am aware that engaging Latina feminism with his account of human beings might consequently not be considered to be the politically correct choice. Yet my use of Heideggerian phenomenology as I develop my view of multiplicitous selfhood does not constitute an endorsement of his political or personal views but rather an engagement with valuable phenomenological insights from his description of the self as *Dasein*.[5] It is also a rethinking, a reorientation of his work. Heidegger's introduction of the notion of *Dasein* in his existential analysis stands as one of the most important philosophical critiques of the highly regarded epistemic subject. As such, it has had great influence in Western philosophical thinking. I thus engage with the Heideggerian account so as to make a positive contribution that makes use of some elements of Heidegger's important analysis of selfhood. I do not wish to defend his politics or provide an in-depth analysis and commentary of *Dasein*. My aim is to use Heidegger's work constructively and to introduce a notion of selfhood that retains some important Heideggerian elements but, with the help of recent Latina feminist phenomenology, also takes this account beyond Heidegger's characterization of the self.[6] I have jokingly said to friends who ask me why I pay attention to Heidegger at all that I wish to shatter Heidegger's account of *Dasein*—to see all the different directions in which Heidegger's view can be taken rather than staying confined within the borders set up by Heidegger's text and those who interpret it—but I am serious.

Having learned from Anzaldúa and Lugones about the inaccessibility of purity, I venture into an analysis of the self that does not uphold disciplinary boundaries. I do so defiantly because, after encountering theories by women of color, I refuse to ignore them, as is continually done in philosophical circles, and as I have witnessed young students of philosophy prompted to do in order to satisfy a canonical and narrow vision of what texts count as philosophical and what thinkers count as philosophers.[7] After encountering existential phenomenological views of self that attempt to go beyond the unitary, epistemic subject, and the transcendental ego, and realizing that they do not do justice to the lived experience of the selves that

Anzaldúa and Lugones so powerfully describe, I cannot accept them as they are. Existential phenomenological accounts of self stand to gain from the insights offered by Latina feminists, whose intimate and compelling *autohistoria-teorias*, Anzaldúa's term for personal, biographical essays that theorize, constitute powerful phenomenological accounts, which themselves stand to benefit from the insights of the more traditional phenomenological views.

As this work will show, both Latina feminist phenomenological accounts of the self and existential phenomenological accounts have various similarities, the most important being the commitment to provide an account of selfhood that does justice to lived experience. This commitment, as well as other features that I describe below, have led me to understand Latina feminist views as phenomenologies, although I am aware that Latina feminists themselves might not categorize their work as part of the phenomenological tradition as understood in the discipline of philosophy and that they do not use traditional phenomenological methods.[8] In fact, many Latinas do not endorse the label of feminism, either, since they do not see themselves in white women's feminist accounts.[9] My intention here is not to conform or reduce these writers' work into the framework of a more classical and accepted phenomenology so as to make them more palatable or to legitimize them within academic philosophy. I do not wish to suggest that Latina feminists' discussions of selfhood are important only insofar as they fit the framework of Heideggerian existential phenomenology or a more systematic phenomenology or that we reduce the latter to a Latina feminist framework. Such an understanding of this project would be mistaken and would miss the sense of *mestizaje* introduced here. Besides similarities, there are tremendous differences between traditional philosophical phenomenological accounts and writings by Latina theorists in terms of goals, scope, vision, audience, and politics. These differences cannot be forgotten or ignored.

My aim is to think together with Anzaldúa, Lugones, other Latina feminists, and to some extent with Heidegger, so as to open new possibilities for understanding ourselves, so as to disclose an account of self that takes into consideration recent work by Latinas urging us to think about the multiplicity in our selves. In my view, this multiplicity has been buried in philosophy given its quest for not only more traditional, unitary, accounts of selfhood but also for notions of selfhood that bypass particularities of our raced, gendered, and classed everyday existence. I invite you, then, to bypass preconceptions about what kinds of theories and philosophies belong together and to pay attention to the intricate ways in which Latina feminist phenomenology and Heideggerian existential phenomenology cross paths so as to disclose the self's multiplicity.

On the Concept of Experience

A key feature of the theory of multiplicitous selves that I introduce here is that it has been inspired by the work of Latina feminists such as Anzaldúa and Lugones, whose writings are deeply informed by their lived experience, specifically by their experience of marginalization and oppression as well as their experience of resistance. My methodology is thus one that takes seriously the ways in which Latina feminists reappropriate the concept of experience. I see Latinas' appeals to this concept as some of the most significant moments in recent feminism because they provide theories and descriptions of selves that are ignored even within feminism, offer rich descriptions of Latinas' lives that point to the complexity and multiplicity or their experience, and illustrate the range and depth of Latina feminist theorizing. Works not just by Anzaldúa and Lugones but also by Norma Alarcón, Linda Martín Alcoff, Edwina Barvosa, Cristina Beltrán, Aimee Carrillo-Rowe, Jacqueline Martinez, Cherríe Moraga, Paula Moya, Juana María Rodriguez, Chela Sandoval, Ofelia Schutte, and others discuss the lived experience of Latinas/os in the United States and provide much-needed interventions in the study of selfhood and identity. That the concept of experience is being reclaimed, in this case by Latina feminist theorists, is not surprising. In their attempt to make their voices known, women of color have appealed to their experiences and have offered powerful narratives and intersectional analyses of their condition and of their struggle to survive as well as to resist in worlds that have not been welcoming. As documented by African American feminists Patricia Hill Collins and Kathryn Gines, women of color have theorized from their own standpoint from very early on, providing intersectional analyses of their condition well before Kimberlé Crenshaw coined the term and Collins made it key in her influential account of "black feminist thought" (Crenshaw 1989; Collins 2008; Gines 2011, 2014).[10] Their appeal to experience is, in my view, a disclosure, a making visible, audible, a making perceptible, those beings in marginalized and nondominant positions whose histories have been previously erased, ignored, or covered up.

The "elusive master concept of experience," as Clifford Geertz (1986) describes it, has a long and complicated history (Jay 2005), including Edmund Husserl's famous appeal to the primacy of experience (1982), feminist views that take the concept as a necessary starting point for theorizing (Harding 2004), and poststructuralist critiques that have viewed appeals and reconstructions of experience as problematic given their view that subjects do not simply have experience but are constructed by it (Butler 1988;

Scott 1991; Perpich 2010). As Shari Stone-Mediatore reminds us in her sharp analysis of the concept, both empiricist and poststructural critiques of the appeal to experience fail as one elevates experience to the realm of indubitable evidence and the other reduces it to a prediscursive domain. For Stone-Mediatore, the key is to understand experience not as indubitable evidence but as a resource for critical reflection, a "resource for confronting and renarrating the complex forces that constitute experience" and to understand marginalized experiences as "creative responses to socially situated, multilayered, only partly ideologically constituted experiences" (2003, 123–124). The appeal to experience, then, needs to be understood as a complex process encompassing disclosure, memory, interpretation, and reinterpretation of experiences rather than as simply the exposition of indubitable evidence.

Writings by Anzaldúa and Lugones that appeal to experience in general and more specifically to marginalized experience should not be taken to describe unquestionable evidence as to what constitutes being a Latina. Nor should they be taken as discourse without connection to real, material, systemic societal conditions. I take seriously the view that telling one's story is part of a multilayered exercise that includes many facets: narrating one's story in order to make sense of it, processing with ink and paper what one feels through the skin, providing narratives so that others like us can hear our stories, and developing accounts that have the potential for critical engagement with and resistance to dominant norms. So I keep in mind Mohanty's wise words:

> The mere proliferation of third world women's texts, in the West at least, owes as much to the relations of the marketplace as to the conviction to "testify" or "bear witness." Thus, the existence of third world women's narratives in itself is not evidence of decentering hegemonic histories and subjectivities. It is the way in which they are read, understood, and located institutionally which is of paramount importance. (1991, 34)

I appeal to the words of Anzaldúa, Lugones, and other Latina theorists not to make grand claims about what it means to be a Latina in the United States or to create a set of categories that one must satisfy to be the "right" kind of Latina. It is important to remember the tremendous heterogeneity within the umbrella category of "Latina" identity, which includes *mestizas* (Indigenous and European), *mulatas* (African and European), Latinas born in the United States, immigrants, exiles from Latin America, and so on, thus avoiding what Carmen Lugo-Lugo describes as "racial and ethnic clumping" and the "Chicanas and Latinas' Syndrome" or the development of views about Chicana experience and their application to all other Latinas (Lugo-Lugo 2008, 3, 8). Anzaldúa's, Lugones's, and other Latinas' words have inspired me to see the philosophical discussion of the self differently—that is, their words have opened up a new set of possibilities for thinking about the self together with them and existential phenomenology. They have *reoriented* me to a different way of doing philosophy that does not ignore the voices of women of color in the name of a supposedly neutral, objective philosophizing (Ahmed 2006).[11] Their voices need to be heard, and their words, read, reinterpreted, and included in philosophical investigations.

Yet, I am not interested in these Latina voices merely because of my philosophical curiosity about the question of selfhood. I appeal to Latina feminist voices and to a methodology that does not adhere strictly to using works traditionally categorized as philosophical because I have been deeply, personally moved by their accounts. They redirected my practice of philosophy to the point that I cannot carry out a philosophical investigation of selfhood without considering them. I have been wounded by Latina feminst voices in the sense that they call me to become more engaged with them. They offer a *punctum*—what for Roland Barthes was that aspect of the photograph that wakes us and alerts us to look further, investigate, understand, and care—that aspect of the work that pierces us (Ortega 2008, 237). My own experience of being pierced by the words of Latina feminists like Anzaldúa and Lugones thus informs this investigation and my desire to offer an account of multiplicitous, in-between selves in which Latina feminist phenomenology and classical existential phenomenology meet in order to develop a view of self that does justice to experience, including the experience of marginalized, in-between selves whose lives have been mostly ignored by standard philosophical views of selfhood.

Latina Feminist Phenomenology

As noted, the Latina theorists who have inspired me and reoriented my philosophical thinking would not count themselves among the ranks of feminists or phenomenologists. As aware as I am of the possible problems associated with views that appeal to the concept of experience, I am also aware of the complicated process of naming, of assigning labels to works so as to make them fit particular movements. Again, I would like to reiterate that it is not my wish to set disciplinary boundaries around the views of Latina theorists studied here or to reduce their views by placing them in ready-made categories. Yet I believe that it is important to note certain characteristics that a number of works written by Latina theorists share. Such characteristics may be understood as part of a more general development that I describe here as Latina feminist phenomenology. In the following I outline some features that I believe works by Anzaldúa, Lugones, and others share and that makes it possible for these works to be loosely understood as Latina feminist phenomenology, with awareness that such phenomenology is in process, does not have rigid boundaries, does not use traditional phenomenological methodology, and does not always offer systematic investigations.

Following previous work by feminist phenomenologists, I propose some of the defining characteristics for what constitutes what I am here calling Latina feminist phenomenology: (1) attention to the lived experience of Latinas/os in the United States, including those born here or in Latin America and the Caribbean; (2) emphasis on concrete, embodied *everyday* experience; (3) attention to the intersection or, as Lugones describes it, the intermeshedness of race, sex, gender, class, sexual orientation, ability, age, ethnicity, and so on; (4) disclosure of the way in which the gendered or racialized (*mestizaje/mulataje*) aspect of Latina/o experience is covered up in traditional philosophical discussions that take white male experience as the norm; (5) attunement to historical and cultural processes that recognizes the heterogeneity of Latinas/os; and (6) critical deployment of experiential knowledge in order to contest or reimagine established notions of *Latinidad*. The writings of Latina feminists that have inspired this work share many if not all of these features and thus offer phenomenologies of Latina experience that are helpful as we attempt to provide more inclusive theories of selfhood.

A Note on the "Ontic" and the "Ontological"

Given my appeal to Heideggerian phenomenology, it is important to understand Heidegger's key distinction between the ontological and the ontic. In his existential description of the human being, "ontological" refers to ways of being, whereas "ontic" refers to entities or particular facts regarding those entities. This distinction is tricky and may be confusing for those not trained in Heideggerian philosophy. While I do not engage with these terms in depth, I have chosen to include in my account of the multiplicitous self some notions inspired by Heidegger's work, such as *being-between-worlds, being-in-worlds, being-at-ease,* and *becoming-with.* It is important to note from the outset that when I appeal to such notions I am not appealing to categories of existence that stand outside experience or in some otherworldly realm. I am appealing to ways of being or faring in the world or worlds that are always connected to concrete, particular aspects of existence. In Heideggerian terms, this means that such notions always carry with them an ontic element and are not to be understood as detached from concrete experience. We are always living our lives in specific situations and contexts, and thus being-between-worlds, being-in-worlds, being-at-ease, and becoming-with are to be understood as happening within those situations and contexts. Following Heidegger's early existential phenomenological explanation, I take being always to be connected to beings or entities, the ontological as always connected to the ontic. As Heidegger claims in *Being and Time*, there is a "relatedness backwards and forward" between the ontic and the ontological (1962, 28 [8]).[12]

Moreover, the reason for my appeal to these notions stems from my view that the Heideggerian explanation of human beings, while lacking in terms of its ethics and politics, does capture something important about us, that life is not about the entities we encounter or particular facts about them or ourselves. It is about the intertwining of the world and us. Our experience as well as our sense of existing or being cannot be simply reduced to the material. Our lived experience reveals a sense of being, a sense of how we *are*, how we fare, that is connected to material circumstances and entities. I cannot presume to know what being in general is, but I have a sense of how I *am* as I live this life and traverse the complex terrain of the borderlands and the many worlds in which I find myself and to which I travel by necessity or by desire—I am thus deeply interested in the existential dimension of our lives as multiplicitous selves.

Overview

Chapter 1 pays tribute to one of the key figures inspiring this work: Gloria Anzaldúa. I discuss Anzaldúa's quest to find a satisfactory account of self and her different visions of selfhood; these range from the celebrated account of the new *mestiza* that is greatly informed by Anzaldúa's own embodied and lived experience in the US-Mexico border to her elaboration of *la nepantlera*, a view of self that does not rely on external forms of identification. I engage with Anzaldúa's struggle as she attempts to explain the sense in which the new *mestiza* is both an individual self and a plurality. I offer a reading of the new *mestiza* as a *mestizaje* of multiplicity and oneness. Such a *mestizaje* of multiplicity and oneness informs the account of multiplicitous selfhood elaborated in chapter 2.

Chapter 2 constitutes a thinking together with Anzaldúa, Lugones, and Heidegger with the aim of introducing the notion of multiplicitous selfhood as being-between-worlds and being-in-worlds. While I discuss important similarities between Heidegger's existential phenomenological view of *Dasein* and Latina feminists' accounts, I also explain a key difference between Latina feminists' views and Heidegger's. This difference has to do with the fact that multiplicitous selves in the margins are constantly experiencing disruptions in their everyday being-in-worlds or instances of what I describe as not-being-at-ease. It points to a problem in Heidegger's discussion—namely, that Heidegger's existential analytic does not fully capture the lived experience of marginalized selves highlighted by Latina feminists. I elaborate on the notions of being-between-worlds and being-in-worlds. My view of multiplicitous selfhood is yet another type of *mestizaje* inspired by Anzaldúa's *mestizaje* of multiplicity and oneness, Lugones's account of world-traveling, and Heidegger's account of being-in-the-world. In addition to analyzing ontological features such as being-in-worlds and being-between-worlds, I discuss the multiplicitous self's flexibility, decenteredness, and intersectionality. I also explain this self's continuity by way of the notions of temporality and mineness.

Chapter 3 analyzes in detail the experience of world-traveling, a term coined by María Lugones and a practice that is key to the multiplicitous self. I begin with an explanation of Lugones's characterization of world-traveling. I aim to show that even though Lugones's concept of world-traveling is central for her view of multiple selves, her account is problematic given her definition of world-traveling as a shift of self in different worlds. I also discuss Lugones's additional characterizations of selfhood, the curdled, *mestizo* self, and active subjectivity. Ultimately, I propose a view of world-traveling as having access to an opening to different worlds in which different aspects of the self are highlighted or animated depending on the power relations at work in different worlds. I argue that world-travelers are not different selves in different worlds; they are multiplicitous selves constantly negotiating different social identities and positionalities. Rather than appealing to *ontological pluralism*, as Lugones does, I appeal to *existential pluralism*, a view that captures both the existential sense of being an "I" as well as the multiplicity of the self while being-in-worlds.

Chapter 4 emphasizes the political aspect of world-traveling in terms of fostering possibilities of resistance. I analyze world-traveling as resonant with the Du Boisian notion of "double-consciousness," but I ultimately maintain that the multiplicitous self has a multiplicitous consciousness that is helpful in opening up resistant practices. I point out that even though world-traveling can indeed be a liberatory practice, it can nonetheless itself become part of the status quo, thus limiting its possibilities as a resistant practice. I thus provide a discussion of world-traveling vis-à-vis the Heideggerian concept of *the they* (*das Man*) to show the ways in which world-traveling can be subject to social pressure to conform to everyday norms. Finally, I provide a discussion of problems that arise in world-traveling as practiced by members of dominant groups. I ultimately suggest the need for a practice of *critical* world-traveling that needs to be employed by members of nondominant and dominant groups as they travel across worlds.

Chapter 5 discusses the relationality of the multiplicitous self by way of an analysis of the notions of identity and identity politics in light of recent reconstructions of these notions by Linda Martín Alcoff and Allison Weir. I explain Martín Alcoff's understanding of the philosophical critique of identity and introduce her reconstruction of identity as interpretive horizon. I aim to show that the account of the multiplicitous self benefits from a vision of identity as horizon that highlights the inextricable link between self and other. At the same time, I point to the need for a stronger consideration of multiplicity in Martín Alcoff's account. Moreover, with the help of Weir's view of identity politics, I discuss the need to rethink identity politics beyond the framework of category and oppositional identity and propose a view of coalitional politics informed by both location and relations with others. In this vision of coalitional politics, I appeal to *becoming-with*—the possibility that my relations with others with whom I fight oppression is an experience that stands to change both who I am and my understanding of worlds.

Chapter 6 engages the relationships among social location, knowledge, and multiplicity. I analyze the postpositive realist view of social identity (PPRI) as proposed by Paula Moya. My aim is to show that a view that takes into consideration social location for a theory of identity and wishes to do justice to the experience of multiplicitous selves must accept the complexity of multiplicity. I first briefly discuss PPRI's claims regarding identity, social location, and epistemic privilege. Moya's account of a shift in her understanding of herself from "Spanish girl" to "Chicana"—a shift toward what Moya considers a truer identity—provides an example to explore PPR's commitment to lived experience and multiplicity. I refer to Moya's model as "the forward-moving truer identity model," the view that selves are better off as linearly progressing toward a truer identity. My analysis of this model points to PPRI's problematic view of the temporality of multiplicitous

selves, its preference for synthesis and integration, and an undercutting of
the positive, constructive aspects that arise even in the difficult experiences
of the multiplicitous self.

Chapter 7 examines the notion of *home* given an appeal to the multiplicity of the self. As constant exclusions in and outside of the academy have
prompted me to reflect on the question belonging, I discuss this important
notion of home by way of an analysis of a politics of location, the notion of
belonging that accompanies such a politics, and the view of multiplicitous
selfhood. In this chapter's first section, I discuss how "home" becomes constitutive of a politics of location that reaffirms so-called authentic identities
and serves to exalt those identities by way of a negation of those who do
not belong. I also carry out an analysis of the notion of belonging in light
of multiplicitous selfhood. We shall see that, given the multiplicity of the
self, the notions of home and belonging need to be reinterpreted. Following Michel de Certeau's view of tactics, in the second section of chapter 7,
I introduce the notion of "hometactics," an everyday praxis that allows for
a sense of familiarity and a thin sense of belonging that captures both the
positive aspects related with home while avoiding its restrictive, exclusive
elements.

I conclude with a brief personal reflection on what prompted this work
and with an invitation to develop a praxis of intersectional philosophy that
can help us move away from philosophy as a love of exclusion toward a real
love for wisdom, toward a new and more inclusive vision of philosophy that
does not cover up, undermine, or make invisible the lives and thoughts of
those who are in-between worlds and who continually travel worlds—those
who can also teach us to be wiser.

A theory in the flesh means one where the physical realities of our lives—our skin color, the land or concrete we grew up on, our sexual longings—all fuse to create a politic born out of necessity. Here, we attempt to bridge the contradictions in our experience. We are the colored in a white feminist movement. We are the feminists among the people of our culture. We are often the lesbians among the straight. We do this bridging by naming our selves and by telling our stories in our own words.

—Cherríe Moraga

1

The New *Mestiza* and *La Nepantlera*

Borders—barbed-wire, wooden, sometimes invisible—separating, con-straining, restricting. Seeing, sensing anew. Borderlands—where cultures, ideas, norms, selves are remade, reconfigured, where pain mingles with uncertainty, fear, anxiety, creativity, and new possibilities. The new mestiza lives there. The shadow beast is her strong will, unfreezing her so she can take a stance, so she can change. The new mestiza is the shadow that walks hand in hand with the words on these pages, leading us away from tidy, unified selves. It is good company.

In this chapter, I discuss Gloria Anzaldúa's explorations of selfhood, in particular her account of the new *mestiza*,[1] one of Anzaldúa's most important contributions in her celebrated text *Borderlands/La Frontera: The New Mestiza*, a deeply intersectional text that has been influential in various disciplines, including border studies, literary studies, women's studies, queer studies, and many others (Anzaldúa 1987).[2] Given this text's tremendous appeal, the force of the ideas in it, and the fact that it has become canonical in some circles, it is important for me to approach it with caution as I wish to remain respectful of Anzaldúa's words but also to have a reflective, critical edge as I engage with them.[3]

My first reading of *Borderlands/La Frontera* was a powerful experience. Anzaldúa's words touched me deeply; they moved me in a way that few texts had done before. Her profound awareness of the intersecting, inter-meshed nature of her multiple oppressions and her moving *autohistoria*, what I would call her lived-theory, pierced me.[4] Reading about her struggles in the borderlands struck me intellectually and viscerally, given my own experience as a Latina who felt displaced and who often wondered about the question of home ever since revolution transformed my life, and many other Nicaraguans' daily lives in the summer of 1979. My family and I thus traveled to a new land, to new worlds, without economic means and without the ability to speak English—not knowing that we would not step on the familiar streets of Managua for a long, long time.

Along with so many others who experience life at the borderlands, not just geographically but also culturally and metaphorically, I find myself in the words that Anzaldúa so vividly crafts. Reading *Borderlands/La Frontera* felt like reading my own story, my struggles as I felt myself caught between the Nicaraguan and US worlds, between a language that sounded sweet—yes, sweet like the wonderful tropical fruit such as *nancites* and *jocotes* that I could no longer have—and a language that erased me because it was not mine. Anzaldúa's powerful writing, filled with pain but also with possibilities for personal, political, and spiritual transformation, has inspired so many inhabitants of the borderlands—it is no wonder that there are altars made in her honor.[5] She transforms the border, what limits and constrains, to the borderlands, an in-between space of possibilities and creation. I read all those words—about edges of barbed wire, cultural clashes, homeland, movements of rebellion, blood sacrifices—and found them magnetic, pulling me toward deeper reflection and sensation about what it means to reside in a liminal space. Her work had and continues to have a tremendous impact on me emotionally and intellectually, both opening and healing wounds and also granting me new possibilities of theorizing.

In this chapter I pay particular attention to Anzaldúa's understanding of selfhood. In the first section I discuss her various characterizations of the self, including those in *Borderlands/La Frontera* and in later writings. While Anzaldúa offers various descriptions of selfhood, the new *mestiza* became representative of her view despite her and her critics' recognition of the problems associated with her choice of *mestizaje* as the leading metaphor for the self in *Borderlands/La Frontera*.[6] This section points out some key characteristics of the new *mestiza*, including her embodiment and situatedness in an in-between space, what Anzaldúa described as borderlands and *nepantla*, and her tolerance for ambiguity and contradiction. It also notes some of the criticisms of this important notion of the self. In the chapter's second section I engage with Anzaldúa's texts so as to show the tremendous struggle that Anzaldúa goes through as she tries to explain both the multiplicity and oneness of the self.[7] I conclude the chapter by pointing to the fact that Anzaldúa offers a *mestizaje* of both multiplicity and oneness, a paradoxical position that acknowledges that the self has a lived experience that encompasses multiplicity in terms of her various social identities and oneness in the sense of being an "I." Although perplexing, this position captures Anzaldúa's complex vision of the self in the borderlands. It also inspires my own view of multiplicitous selfhood that, as we will see, attempts to capture the individual and existential sense of oneness of the self as well as the self's multiplicity given her social locations and her being-in-worlds.

She Seeks New Images of Identity

The path of Gloria Anzaldúa's explorations on selfhood and identity is difficult to grasp because her understanding of these notions goes through various reconfigurations and transformations.[8] While she is most known for her view of the new *mestiza*, she also explains other visions of self, such as *la nepantlera*, new tribalism, *nos/otras*, geography of selves, and *la naguala*. Some months before Anzaldúa passed away from diabetes complications, she wrote,

> I'd like to create a different sense of self (la nepantlera) that does not rest on external forms of identifications (of family, race, gender, sexuality, class, nationality), or attachments to power, privilege, and control, or romanticized self-images. But can we talk about ourselves in ways that do not rest on some notion of identity when identity is the means by which we (both individuals and groups) attempt to create a sense of security and belonging in the midst of a fast paced, ever-changing world? (Anzaldúa 2009, 302)

In this passage, Anzaldúa refers to one of her later visions of selfhood, *la nepantlera*. Anzaldúa defines *nepantleras* as "boundary-crossers, thresholders who initiate others in rites of passage, activistas who, from a listening, receptive, spiritual stance, rise to their own visions and shift into acting them out, haciendo mundo Nuevo (introducing change)" (Anzaldúa & Keating 2002, 571). She describes a self that lives on the borders but that can cross them and facilitate passages across worlds, a self that does not form self-understandings based on race, sex, gender, or other forms of what Anzaldúa describes as external forms of identification, a self that acknowledges an unmapped common ground: the humanity of the other" (Anzaldúa & Keating 2002, 570).

An important aspect of this later description of self is Anzaldúa's rejection of what she calls an "oppositional form of identity politics." Anzaldúa regrets the manner in which identity politics becomes dependent on forging political alliances by virtue of a shared identity, be it race, class, gender, sexual orientation, ability, and so forth. In her view, the oppositional aspect of such identity politics stems from the fact that binaries are created in the process of forging identities—for example, us/them, gay/straight, able/disabled, and so on—and groups find themselves opposing the other side of the binary. Anzaldúa rejects this establishment of binaries and notes that identity politics sets itself up for failure. Rather than transforming institutions, it tries to reclaim power only from the very institutions that made it powerless in the first place. Given Anzaldúa's concern for a more inclusive understanding of identity, an "interconnectivity," especially in her later writings, she is wary of oppositional identity politics (Anzaldúa & Keating 2002, 569).

Yet, as Martín Alcoff notes, identity politics is a complex notion that has had multiple meanings. While a common understanding of it, especially by critics, sees identity politics as appealing to homogeneity within a group as well as to separatism, this is a mistaken understanding of the notion. Martín Alcoff takes the Combahee River Collective's "A Black Feminist Statement" as the locus classicus of identity politics and points out that according to the writers of the statement identity politics is connected to the general relevance of identity in politics (Martín Alcoff 2006, 15; Combahee River Collective 1979). They do not assume that groups are homogenous, and they do not call for a separatist stance. Rather, they wish to underscore the importance of identity in their personal experiences of doing political work. Keating also points out the complexity of the collective's statement and the fact that it calls for a multipronged approach against racial, sexual, and class oppression, a complexity that, according to Keating, is missing in some of the more recent versions of identity politics (2013, 92–93). As understood by early proponents, identity politics is complex and not the narrow politics that appeals to homogeneity and calls for separatism.[9] In her understanding of identity politics, Anzaldúa herself falls for this problematic understanding, and thus tries to forge an altogether different vision of identity not based on specific external forms of identification.

However, despite her appeal to a new understanding of selfhood that does not rely on external forms of identification, in the same passage Anzaldúa recognizes the need to appeal to identity so as to get a sense of security and belonging in this "fast-paced, ever-changing world." The passage illustrates Anzaldúa's struggle regarding selfhood and identification, a struggle that can be seen throughout her writings. Anzaldúa recognizes the importance that claiming her Chicana identity, her queerness, and her other social identities has had for her as she attempted to find some sense of comfort in the midst of the "intimate terrorism" caused by life at the borderlands (Anzaldúa 1987, 20). At the same time, she recognizes the narrowness and confining nature of what she calls "identity boxes" and thus calls for a radical shift, what she calls "a different story (of mestizaje) enabling you to rethink yourself in more global-spiritual terms instead of conventional categories of color, class, career" (Anzaldúa & Keating 2002, 561) and appeals to a "new tribalism" and a "retribalizing of mestizaje" (2002, 560).[10]

Interestingly, a great deal of the power of the notion of the new *mestiza*, one of Anzaldúa's most important contributions and her most celebrated account of self as described in *Borderlands/La Frontera*, is that it is derived from Anzaldúa's lived experience in what she calls the *herida abierta*, the open wound, of the US-Mexico border, an experience that is defined in terms of identity based on race, gender, class, and sexuality, as well as opposition to whites, Mexicans, and Mexican Americans and their norms. Anzaldúa's writing in the *Borderlands/La Frontera* period, what Keating calls Anzaldúa's "middle writings" (2009, 11), highlights oppositional identity in terms of the way in which Anzaldúa understands herself in opposition to the traditional norms held by these groups. Her work in the early and late periods contests such identifications and calls for more inclusive visions of self and identity, such as *la nepantlera* as well as a "new tribalism,"[11] what she describes as an "expanded identity" (Anzaldúa 2009, 283).[12] When describing this new tribalism in her later piece, "(Un)natural bridges, (Un) safe spaces," Anzaldúa states,

> Our goal is not to use differences to separate us from others, but neither is it to gloss over them. Many of us identify with groups and social positions not limited to our ethnic, racial, religious, class, gender, or national classifications. Though most people self-define by what they exclude, we define who we are by what we include—what I call the new tribalism. (Anzaldúa and Keating 2002, 3)

In the later writings Anzaldúa also appeals to the wider notion of *nos/otras*, a play on the Spanish word *nosotras*, which means "us." Anzaldúa inserts a slash between *nos* and *otras*; while *nos*, Spanish for the feminine "we," underscores our coming together or "us," *otras* refers to otherness. Anzaldúa states in a 1996 interview,

> We are mutually complicitous—us and them, white and colored, straight and queer, Christian and Jew, self and Other, oppressor and oppressed. We all find ourselves in the position of being

simultaneously insider/outsider. . . . Hopefully sometime in the future we may become nosotras without the slash. Perhaps geography will no longer separate us. We're becoming a geography of selves—of different cities or countries who stand at the threshold of numeros mundos. (Anzaldúa 2000, 254–255)[13]

Nos/otras, then, signifies an understanding of ourselves as insider/outsider. It appeals to the possibility of our being together while at the same time recognizing differences. As Keating notes, *nos/otras* affirms collectivity, while at the same time it recognizes difference and divisiveness and also allows for the possibility of healing by understanding that "we contain the others, the others contain us" (Keating 2006, 10).[14]

According to Keating, in her later work Anzaldúa proposes this more "expansive" theory of subjectivity by appealing to the notions of new tribalism and *nos/otras* that move beyond oppositional identity categories, thus problematizing her appeals to identity in *Borderlands/La Frontera*. In a 1983 interview Anzaldúa states,

I use labels because we haven't gotten beyond race or class or other differences yet. When I don't assert certain aspects of my identity like the spiritual part of my queerness, they get overlooked and I'm diminished. When we come to a time when I don't have to say, "Look, I'm a dyke," or "I'm spiritual," or "I'm intellectual," I'll stop using labels. That's what I want to work towards. But until we come to that time, if you lay your body down and don't declare certain facets of yourself, they get stepped on. (Anzaldúa 2000, 77)

In 2002 she writes,

Today categories of race and gender are more permeable and flexible than they were for those of us growing up prior to the 1980s. *This bridge we call home* invites us to move beyond separate and easy identifications, creating bridges that cross race and other classifications among different groups via intergenerational dialogue. Rather than legislating and restricting racial identities, it tries to make them more pliant. (Anzaldúa & Keating 2002, 2)

We can see that Anzaldúa is constantly struggling with the idea of social identities as it is clear that she recognizes their importance in our political struggles, but she also considers them as labels that lead to exclusion. In addition, Anzaldúa wavers from appeals to a radical transformation in which there will be no room for identity categories at all to appeals for a reconfiguration of previous labels, what she calls "separate and easy identifications" and oppositional identities, to a more "pliant" sense of identity—in other words, there are different ways in which *nos/otras* becomes *nosotras*.[15]

While I understand Anzaldúa's concern regarding the narrowing, essentializing, and homogenizing aspect of identity categories, I wonder about her desire for a time when we do not have to appeal to our racial identities or other types of identities.[16] Will this vision promote a belief in race neutrality when such neutrality is not really in effect? After the US election of President Obama, much has been said about race neutrality and a postracial time. However, pervasive racial oppression remains, and this oppression needs to be acknowledged rather than covered over by rhetoric about race neutrality. When discussing what she considers a dangerous postracialism, Crenshaw states,

> It is a trick room whose welcoming spaciousness belies the gradual closing of the four walls, a closing that represents a synthesis between colorblindness that simply denied the structural reproduction of racial power and post-racialism that seeks to minimize its effects. Escape seems impossible until an off switch can be found. (2011, 1347)

Where do we find an off switch? Is the notion of new tribalism or *nos/otras* that will lead to a new "geography of selves" part of this switch?

It is interesting to note that even in one of her earlier writings, "La Prieta," Anzaldúa had an inclusive vision that she called *El Mundo Zurdo,* or the Left-Handed World, an inclusive community in which members of different groups are able to form coalitions regardless of their different ideologies and affinities (Keating & González López 2011, 14). This world is, according to Anzaldúa, "a network of kindred spirits, a kind of family" that works for change (Moraga & Anzaldúa 1983, 209). What allows them to form alliances is their condition of not fitting in society or being the "queer groups" that don't belong anywhere.[17] As she notes,

> We are the queer groups, the people that don't belong anywhere, not in the dominant world nor completely within our own respective cultures. Combined we cover so many oppressions. But the overwhelming oppression is the collective fact that we

do not fit, and because we do not fit we are a threat. Not all of us have the same oppressions, but we empathize and identify with each other's oppressions. . . . In El Mundo Zurdo I with my own affinities and my people with theirs can live together and transform the planet. (Moraga & Anzaldúa 1983, 209)

Anzaldúa's account of self and identity is complex and in process—it progresses, evolves, circles, and encompasses various related visions of self-hood such as the new *mestiza*, *la nepantlera*, new tribalism, and *nos/otras*. Her recognition of the importance of identity categories for political purposes and her desire to have an altogether different kind of self and identity that does not rely on external forms of identifications (e.g., race, sexuality, etc.) create a productive tension in her discussions of selfhood.[18] The trajectory of Anzaldúa's understanding of self is not simply linear, as if it were possible to neatly arrange the trajectory from new *mestiza* to *la nepantlera* to new tribalism. A more inclusionary account of self was already at work in the early writings (Anzaldúa 2009, 11). As pointed out previously, Anzaldúa's recognition of the importance of identity categories is also a concern even in the later writings.

The New *Mestiza* in *Nepantla*

Anzaldúa is acutely aware of the difficulty of the task of providing an account of self that captures the complexities of her lived experience in the borderlands. While cognizant that in her later work she emphasizes a much more expansive vision of selfhood, here I would like to highlight some main characteristics of the new *mestiza*, because I consider these features to be of great importance when attempting to provide an account of selfhood that goes beyond traditional accounts that emphasize unity and undermine the multiplicity of the self. Anzaldúa's discussion of the new *mestiza* includes an appeal to identity, but not an identity that is easily categorized as oppo-sitional. As noted earlier, *Borderlands/La Frontera* includes an oppositional sense of identity as Anzaldúa situates herself against the norms of Chicanos, whites, and Mexicans. She also wishes to find the "true" Chicana faces, a desire that places her dangerously close to an essentialist view of identity (1987, 87). However, as Elena Ruiz-Aho notes, Anzaldúa writes about her own concrete lived-experience, and other *mestizas* may or may not relate to it (Ruiz-Aho 2011, 357). Moreover, in the very same account of the new *mestiza*, Anzaldúa already provides a more expansive, inclusive view since she highlights the new *mestiza*'s ability to be on "both shores at once" or to "cross the border into a wholly new and separate territory" (Anzaldúa 1987, 78–79). As she says, "I seek new images of identity, new beliefs about ourselves, our humanity and worth no longer in question" (1987, 87). Despite her seemingly essentialist remarks about the new *mestiza*, Anzaldúa is already working with elements for a more expansive identity.[19] It is thus important to keep in mind the tensions regarding identity that run through Anzaldúa's work.

In this section, I first explain some of the main features of the new *mestiza,* such as her situatedness, her state of in-betweenness or being in the borderlands and *nepantla*, and her tolerance for ambiguity and contradiction. These tensions are helpful in understanding alternatives to traditional understandings of selfhood and subjectivity that miss the importance of the multiplicity of the self. I also discuss the way in which these three characteristics of the new *mestiza*, characteristics that are also part of Anzaldúa's later visions of selfhood such as *la nepantlera*, are key for transformation and resistance to oppression.

As a lover of the written word as well as images, Anzaldúa appeals to myths and metaphors that might perhaps disclose what overly theoretical accounts of self that rely on traditional ways of thinking about self, identity, and subjectivity cannot even begin to capture—thus Anzaldúa forms a vision of a new self, the new *mestiza*, that is to reveal the agonizing but also rewarding struggle of life in the borderlands. *Mestizaje*, or race-mixing, particularly between Europeans and Amerindians, has a long history, from its early uses when the Spanish arrived in the New World to José Vasconcelos's understanding of it as he developed the idea of a *raza cósmica* to Chicano contemporary understandings of a "critical *mestizaje*," a *mestizaje* that understands itself as "embedded in a legacy of colonial struggle and moving through new configurations of resistant identities" (Pérez-Torres 2006, 45).

Even though *mestizaje* is generally understood in terms of racial mixing, Anzaldúa's use of the concept is not one that prioritizes this racial dimension. For Anzaldúa, the "new *mestiza*" is a notion that is more inclusive than racial *mestizaje* (Anzaldúa 2009, 205; 2013, 104). Interpreting the term as primarily signifying a racial identity is problematic because that would suggest that Anzaldúa's notion captures only the *mestiza* identity of Chicanas. While her account of the new *mestiza* is anchored in her lived experience as a Chicana living on the US-Mexico border and prioritizes this experience—one must not overlook the material, economic (Saldívar 1991, 83), and geographic conditions of the new *mestiza*—Anzaldúa's account captures both material as well as metaphorical aspects of a life in the borderlands. The metaphorical and theoretical aspects of Anzaldúa's account, however, cannot be considered as the most important ones, either, as they might lead to theories that lack specificity and materiality, thus allowing for the erasure of the importance of the actual conditions of those who inhabit the borderlands.

The new *mestiza* is a self inhabiting the borderlands, a self in-between the United States and Mexico, who experiences a lived struggle because she is split between cultures, races, languages, and genders, all tugging at her, pulling her to one side or the other, demanding alliances or setting down rules, continually pushing her to choose one or the other, to suffer from "an absolute despot duality" (Anzaldúa 1987, 19). Anzaldúa rejects such dualities and binaries and, instead, finds that in the borderlands the new *mestiza* occupies another space, a liminal space of *nepantla* or in-betweenness.[20] According to Keating, *nepantla* is an extension or elaboration of her theory of the borderlands and the *Coatlicue* state, the state in which the new *mestiza* becomes paralyzed but that is also necessary for transformation and change (Keating 2006, 8). She quotes Anzaldúa's discussion as to why she chooses to use *nepantla* instead of "borderlands":

> I found that people were using "Borderlands" in a more limited sense than I had meant it. So to elaborate on the psychic and emotional borderlands I'm now using "nepantla." . . . With the nepantla paradigm I try to theorize unarticulated dimensions of the experience of the mestizas living in between overlapping and layered spaces of different cultures and social and geographic locations, of events and realities—psychological, sociological, political, spiritual, historical, creative, imagined. (Qtd. in Keating 2006, 8)

Nepantla is an unstable, precarious, and unpredictable space, "*tierra desconocida*" (unknown land) and a "bewildering transitional state" that is disorienting and displacing and leads to dissociation of identity (Anzaldúa 2009, 243,180). It is a space of constant displacement that leads to an uncomfortable and alarming feeling but that is also the "home" of the *new mestiza* (Anzaldúa 2009, 243). As such, it is also a space of healing and meaning-making that encompasses spirituality and political activism (Román-Odio 2013, 54). While being in this space, the new *mestiza* develops a *mestiza* consciousness that, according to Anzaldúa, can reflect critically and see from different perspectives. Consequently, it is a space rich with possibilities not only of critique but also of transformation. It is a space in which new identities can be forged:

> Nepantla is the Náhuatl word for an in-between state, that uncertain terrain one crosses when moving from one place to another, when changing from one class, race, or sexual position to another, when traveling from the present identity into a new identity. (Anzaldúa 2009, 180)

In *nepantla*, the new *mestiza* experiences "Coatlicue states," what Anzaldúa describes as ruptures in the everyday world that include a double movement, including moments of fear and inability to move but also moments of creativity and transformation, of crossing and acquiring a new identity. In these crossings, the new *mestiza* acquires a *mestiza* consciousness, or a "consciousness of the Borderlands" (Anzaldúa 1987, 77). *Mestiza* consciousness is a "plural consciousness," as it requires the negotiation of multiple ideas and knowledges (Mohanty 2003, 80). Thus for Anzaldúa such consciousness implies a "multiplicity that is transformational" (Anzaldúa 2009, 246). *Nepantla* is both the space that makes possible the new *mestiza* consciousness as well as the space that becomes "home" to the new *mestiza*, in which she can further develop her critical abilities and continue to transform herself. *Nepantla* represents actual borderlands, a theoretical space, but also "states of mind." As Anzaldúa says, "I associate *nepantla* with states of mind that question old ideas and beliefs, acquire new perspectives, change worldviews, and shift from one world to another" (Anzaldúa 2009, 248).

As a liminal subject that lives in *nepantla* between cultures, races, languages, and genders—as a subject with various in-betweens—the new *mestiza* can question, mediate, translate, negotiate, and navigate these different locations and thus be able to form a critical stance. Such a critical stance allows for the possibility that the new *mestiza* will become resistant. Commentators such as Lugones rightly point out that *nepantla* constitutes a theoretical space for resistance (Lugones 1992, 31). Key to her ability to be critical and thus resistant and to her ability to transform herself is the new *mestiza* consciousness's tolerance for both contradiction and ambiguity:

> Because I, a *mestiza*,
> Continually walk out of one culture
> and into another,
> because I am in all cultures at the same time,
> alma entre dos mundos, tres, cuatro,
> me zumba la cabeza con lo contradictorio.
> Estoy norteada por todas las voces que me hablan
> Simultáneamente. . . .

The *new mestiza* copes by developing a tolerance for contradic-
tions, a tolerance for ambiguity. She learns to be an Indian in
Mexican culture, to be Mexican from an Anglo point of view.
She learns to juggle cultures. . . . Not only does she sustain
contradictions, she turns the ambivalence into something else.
(Anzaldúa 1987, 77, 79)

The tolerance for ambiguity and contradictions is for Anzaldúa abso-
lutely necessary for the new *mestiza*'s possibility for transformation and resistance. The interesting question is how the experience of contradiction and
ambiguity leads to transformation and even resistance rather than keeping
the new *mestiza* in a state of intimate terrorism, without the possibility of
change. Different interpreters provide different explanations for the formation of the new *mestiza*'s critical stance. Edwina Barvosa, for example, finds
that the critical abilities of the new *mestiza* are generated by the intersections of her multiple identities and worlds. Such overlaps are, according to
Barvosa, the basis for inner tensions and critical vantage points in the sense
that the new *mestiza* can analyze her knowledge and identities vis-à-vis each
other as she goes back and forth between her social spheres (2008, 89–96).[21]

Lugones sees the possibility for resistance arising out of the new *mestiza*'s tolerance for ambiguity and contradiction but also from her transgres-
sion of rigid conceptual boundaries and her breaking of the unitary aspect of
new and old paradigms that lead her to create a new value system through
the uprooting of dualistic thinking (1992, 34). As opposed to other commentators who see the new *mestiza*'s resistance as social, Lugones points
out that, for Anzaldúa, crossing-over is a solitary act, "an act of solitary
rebellion," that emphasizes the inner life of the self and the psychology of
oppression and liberation rather than a "sociality of resistance" (Lugones
1992, 36). Such a sociality of resistance, which, in Lugones's view can be
developed from Anzaldúa's text, is of the utmost importance since "unless
resistance is a social activity, the resister is doomed to failure in the creation
of a new universe of meaning, a new identity, *a raza mestiza*" (Lugones 1992,
36). While I agree with Lugones that there is an emphasis on the individual
character of Anzaldúa's voyage of resistance and transformation, I also see
the social as playing an important role in Anzaldúa's account. Both the
individual and the social are linked in her development of resistant practices.

Lugones and Barvosa rightly capture the connection between the possibility of acquiring a critical stance derived from a life in *nepantla* and
the possibility of transformation and resistance. It is in the cracks between
worlds in which meanings and ideas overlap that the new *mestiza* can inter-

pret these meanings vis-à-vis each other and find points of commonality and divergence that might help her provide a more critical interpretation than if she just had access to knowledge and meanings in separate spheres. As Anzaldúa states in a 1996 interview, "Navigating the cracks between the worlds is difficult and painful, like going through the process of reconstructing a new life, a new identity. Both are necessary for survival and growth" (Anzaldúa 2000, 255).

Situatedness, in-betweenness, and tolerance for ambiguity and contradiction remain crucial in Anzaldúa's account of the new *mestiza* and in her later characterizations of self. They attest to the deeply phenomenological aspect of her account as they capture her lived experience in the borderlands or *nepantla*. Through a passionate engagement with her own experience of inhabiting the US-Mexico border, her deep sense of being liminal, and her recognition of the ambiguous and contradictory aspects of her life that produce intimate terrorism as well as transformation, Anzaldúa offers a moving Latina feminist phenomenological account. This account serves as an inspiration for those who wish to move beyond traditional understandings of the subject or of selfhood that do not take into consideration the importance of situatedness, liminality, ambiguity, and plurality. Even philosophical phenomenological views of self that take into consideration situatedness and ambiguity can benefit from Anzaldúa's vision so as to do justice to the lived experience of those who inhabit the borderlands.

The Perils of *Mestizaje*

While Anzaldúa's account of the new *mestiza* is extremely helpful in providing possibilities for accounts of selfhood that are more attuned to situatedness and multiplicity, it is important to remember that the term, as well as Anzaldúa's use of it, might be problematic. For example, Debra A. Castillo and María Socorro Tabuenca Córdoba criticize Anzaldúa for providing an account of the borderlands that is overly metaphorical and is defined and narrated from a "first world" perspective (Castillo & Tabuenca Córdoba 2002). While Castillo and Tabuenca Córdoba's critique picks up on possible pitfalls of Anzaldúa's account given the importance of the metaphorical there, the new *mestiza* needs to be understood as anchored in specific material conditions, as a situated, embodied being. Anzaldúa's Latina feminist phenomenology is at its best when describing her embodied experience in situated contexts in the precarious life of the borderlands. Anzaldúa's descriptions emphasize the new *mestiza*'s struggle in the US-Mexican borderlands as it is felt in the flesh rather than as an intellectual exercise:

Wind tugging at my sleeve
feet sinking into the sand
I stand at the edge where earth touches ocean
where the two overlap
a gentle coming together
at other times and places a violent clash. . . .

      I walk   through the hole in the fence
          to the other side.
   Under my fingers I feel the gritty wire
      rusted by 139 years
         of the salty breath of the sea. . . .

this "Tortilla Curtain" turning into *el río Grande*
    flowing down to the flatlands
        of the Magic Valley of South Texas
    its mouth emptying into the Gulf.

1,950 mile-long open wound
         dividing a pueblo, a culture,
           running down the length of my body,
            staking fence rods in my flesh,
          splits me splits me
           me raja me raja. . . .

In our very flesh, (r)evolution works out the clash of cultures.
  (Anzaldúa 1987, 1–2, 81).

As Jacqueline Martinez reminds us, readings and applications of Anzaldúa's account of the new *mestiza* cannot overlook this struggle in the flesh that Anzaldúa describes, the "gut-wrenching struggle" from which her theory of the new *mestiza* arises (Martinez 2000, 81). Indeed, the account of the new *mestiza* is a "theory in the flesh" (Moraga & Anzaldúa 1983, 23). It is a theory in the flesh that is mindful of the intersecting or intermeshed nature of social identities such as gender, race, sexuality, class, nationality, religion, and other identities. Castillo and Tabuenca Córdova's critique underscores the metaphorical import of the notion of *mestizaje* in Anzaldúa's work and undertheorizes the various ways in which Anzaldúa's account is not just metaphorical but explicitly appeals to embodied, material experience.

The second criticism, the view that Anzaldúa's *Borderlands* is narrated from a "first world" perspective, carries more weight—and this is a reason why Anzaldúa's discussion is criticized for being overly metaphorical. It is indeed the case that if we think about the border from the perspective of those who are on the Mexican side, it is impossible to miss the specific material geopolitical situation Mexicans face. From the point of view of the United States, however, it becomes more possible to minimize this geopolitical situation and underscore the metaphorical aspect of the border; it becomes easier to think abstractly about the border (Castillo & Tabuenca Córdoba 2002, 16). After all, a number of academics residing in the United States and occupying spaces in academic institutions informed by and promoting privilege do not need to actually cross the border to survive, to get educated, to sell goods, and so on. In this sense, Anzaldúa's narrative has elements that can be understood as deriving from a "first world" perspective; for example, the very fact that Anzaldúa writes and publishes on her experience at the borderlands is a sign of privilege. Not only that— Anzaldúa's own understanding of her spatial location is informed by her identity as a Mexican American residing in the United States. Moreover, as Mexican scholar Tabuenca Córdoba notes, Anzaldúa herself does not appeal to Mexican writers or provide a perspective from the Mexican side (Tabuenca Córdoba 1995–1996).

As readers and admirers of Anzaldúa's work, we need to be aware of this "first world" point of view that informs Anzaldúa's depiction of that open wound that is the US-Mexico border. It is important that we do not ignore the problematic issues in Anzaldúa's account. We are not in the business of creating gods, or goddesses, here—at least I hope not—or of excusing our favorite thinkers' missteps or mistakes.[22] We should thus be keenly aware of the manner in which her writing betrays a "first world" point of view. Nonetheless, when considering this particular criticism, it is important that we remain attuned to the way in which a point of view from "the first world" does not unquestionably point to privilege. That is, to be a Chicana residing on the border confers certain privileges and points of view or horizons through which experience is understood. However, this perspective is also one that has a glimpse, and if not a glimpse, a deep, vivid perception of what it means not to be privileged, of what it means to be marginalized. I consequently take seriously Anzaldúa's description of the borderlands and her description of her many puzzling, painful, but also transformative experiences, with the understanding that her discussion is in need of the inclusion of a point of view from the other side of the border.

In addition to the criticism that Anzaldúa's account is overly meta-phorical and narrated from a "first world" perspective, her choice of meta-phor is also criticized, even by Anzaldúa herself. In a late 1980s interview she states,

> Identity is sort of like a river. It's one and it's flowing and it's a process. By giving different names to different parts of a single mountain range or different parts of a river, we're doing that entity a disservice. We are fragmenting it. I'm struggling with how to name without cutting up. . . . I was trying to do that with the *new mestiza*. I was trying to get away from just think-ing in terms of blood—you know, the *mestiza* as being of mixed blood. The *new mestiza* is a mixture of all these identities and has the ability, the flexibility, the malleability, the amorphous quality of being able to stretch, and to go this way and that way, add new labels or names which would mix with the others and they would also be malleable. But it's hard to articulate. I am trying to find metaphors—like the mountain range, the river, the *mestiza*—but they're not quite what I want. (Anzaldúa 2000, 132–133)

Unfortunately, the metaphors fail to capture Anzaldúa's vision and lead to various complications. Yarbro-Bejarano rightly points to the importance of the tension found in *Borderlands/La Frontera* between "*mestiza* conscious-ness as an activity or process of the non-unitary subject and the crystallized production of the 'name' *mestiza* consciousness" (Yarbro-Bejarano 1994, 17). Once named, this self is given boundaries, specific interpretations that limit it, when in fact it needs to be understood in terms of its being a process that is in the making and that is open to numerous possibilities for creating and reinterpreting itself. Hence Anzaldúa compares the new *mestiza* to a *nagual*, a Nahuatl term for a shape-shifter. As she notes, "We shift around to do the work we have to do, to create identities we need to live up to our potential" (Anzaldúa 2009, 211). However, the new *mestiza*, what Anzaldúa considered a term more inclusive than the racial *mestizaje*, becomes the most prominent metaphor for the self in *Borderlands/La Frontera*.

In my view, this choice of *mestizaje* as the leading metaphor for her primary account of self in *Borderlands/La Frontera* is both highly problem-atic and constructive. That there is a contradictory aspect to Anzaldúa's account of self is not surprising, as the notion of contradiction plays a cru-cial role in Anzaldúa's view of the new *mestiza*. Contradictions can be used productively—I have learned from Nietzsche as well as Anzaldúa on this matter. Nevertheless, another criticism of Anzaldúa is worrisome. According to Saldaña-Portillo, a serious problem with Anzaldúa's appeal to the new *mestiza* and her connection to Aztec goddesses is that while it romanticizes the indigenous past, it actually silences present indigenous peoples and their concerns, ultimately keeping aspects of indigenous culture as "ornamentation" (Saldaña-Portillo 2001, 420). This is a serious charge, indeed, that cannot be ignored. I still remember that, when reading Anzaldúa for the first time and being incredibly moved by her analysis of a life pulled in multiple directions, I was sometimes perplexed by her references to indigenous deities from which I was far removed except for the occasional Mexican history lesson in high school. It was not clear to me how her appeal to Aztec goddesses connected to me, to present-day Chicanas/os, and to indigenous peoples in the United States and Latin America. Yet, I would like to suggest that taking seriously Anzaldúa's view of the new *mestiza* does not preclude the possibility of understanding present indigenous populations or of activism denouncing the numerous problems and afflictions of these populations. It does mean, however, that we must be vigilant about the ways in which her position might undermine such populations and leave us with a romanticized vision of indigenous identity. It is necessary to keep a critical, reflective stance when appealing to Anzaldúa's account of *mestizaje*.

Furthermore, this critical stance needs to take into consideration Cristina Beltrán's strong critique that *mestizaje* should not be seen as always yielding an antiessentialist, liberatory, transgressive identity. She points out that in order for Anzaldúa's notion of the new *mestiza* to replace the overly nationalistic rhetoric of the early Chicano movement's appeal to Aztlán, to move from homeland to borderland, Anzaldúa needs to maintain a "hierarchy of hybridity" (Beltrán 2004, 600). That is, Anzaldúa needs to exalt the importance of the indigenous heritage in opposition to whites/Westerners and to privilege the indigenous side of *mestiza* identity. According to Beltrán, Anzaldúa's project of offering a notion of multiple, fluid subjectivity fails. As she states,

> Anzaldúa's theory celebrates ambiguity and the tearing down of dichotomies, yet she continually constructs a dominant narrative of subjectivity in which some subjects represent multiplicity and insight while others signify unenlightened singularity. . . . Chicano hybridity is created in opposition to the unquestioned existence of autonomous self-contained subjects. (Beltrán 2004, 604–605)

Beltrán thus claims that for Anzaldúa's theory to work, she must posit a vision of white, Western Europeans as monolithic.

I agree with Beltrán's claim that a *mestiza*, or what she calls a hybrid identity, should not necessarily be regarded as always progressive and liberatory. Liminality is not a sufficient condition for liberation. Given the role that marginalization plays in Anzaldúa's understanding of the development of *la facultad*, the epistemic privilege conferred to the new *mestiza* should not be seen as automatically deriving from the experience of liminality or from sharing an indigenous heritage. We are already familiar with the pitfalls of early standpoint theories that in effect essentialize the marginalized and reify their epistemic privilege (Harding 2004). Anzaldúa herself makes comments regarding Chicanas/os and the new *mestiza* that do have an essentialist tone, despite the fact that the very notion of the new *mestiza* in *nepantla* counters simple dichotomies and essentialisms. This is one of the obvious tensions in the text that, in my view, illustrates Anzaldúa's struggle as she recognized both the political import of claiming an identity and the essentializing, homogenizing impulse brought about by such claims. As noted earlier, Anzaldúa's own vision of identity politics can be rather narrow.

Beltrán is rightly attuned to the oppositional aspect of Anzaldúa's account. Yet I wonder if she is correct in stating that in Anzaldúa's vision those who are on the other side are Western whites. Anzaldúa questions not only norms, practices, and epistemologies arising from the US or European white tradition but also from Mexican and indigenous tradition (as she retells and refashions indigenous myths). Beltrán, however, wishes to show that Anzaldúa's version of *mestizaje* is ultimately dependent on a narrow vision of whites, which allows her to portray the *mestizo/a* identity as fluid, multiple, and resistant. Ultimately, according to Beltrán, Anzaldúa essentializes Chicanos as well. Again, there are passages in *Borderlands* that support this criticism. Yet, as noted earlier, Anzaldúa's project is much more complex. Reading her descriptions of the new *mestiza* in *Borderlands* along with her 2002 account of *conocimiento* shows just how difficult it is for the new *mestiza* to cross or to become a "bridge" to the other side (Anzaldúa & Keating 2002, 540–578). It is not the case that Anzaldúa unproblematically confers epistemic privilege to the new *mestiza*.

Anzaldúa herself comments that she was not born in Tenochtitlan in the ancient past or in a contemporary Aztec village and states, "Beware of el romance del *mestizaje*, I hear myself saying silently. Puede ser una ficción . . . but I and other writers/artists have invested ourselves in it" (Anzaldúa 2009, 181). While Saldaña-Portillo's critique must be kept in mind, as well as other criticisms of Anzaldúa's view such as Sáenz's accusation of an unacceptable nostalgia for old gods (Sáenz 1997), it is important to understand, as Anzaldúa notes, the investment that Chicanas and other Latinas have in the notion of the new *mestiza*. This investment is due to the numerous possibilities of transformation that the notion of the new *mestiza* offers. As noted, Anzaldúa's *mestiza* consciousness is "a multiplicity that is transformational" (Anzaldúa 2009, 246). It is both transformational personally for the *mestiza* herself and for readers, scholars, and followers as they struggle to understand the experience of marginalization and possibilities of transformation and resistance. I thus embrace Anzaldúa's visions of selfhood while taking into consideration the complexity and multiplicity of her text and her quest to understand herself from her location in the borderlands and while also being aware of the dangers of her choice of *mestizaje* in creating and representing Latina subjectivity. As Gregory Velazco y Trianosky notes, the central challenge for those advocating a theory of identity on the notion of *mestizaje*, is "to do so without being drawn into the essentialist quagmire (Velazco y Trianosky 2009, 286).

La Nepantlera Way: Later Visions of Selfhood and Transformation

The possibility of transformation runs not only through Anzaldúa's vision of the new *mestiza* but also through the visions of self that, as discussed previously, are associated more with her later writings, such as *la nepantlera*. In the later 2002 essay, "now let us shift . . . the path of conocimiento . . . inner work, public acts," Anzaldúa emphasizes the work of *las nepantleras*:

> Las nepantleras must alter their mode of interaction—make it more inclusive, open. In a to-and-fro motion they shift from their customary position to the reality of the first one group then the other. Though tempted to retreat behind racial lines and hide behind simplistic walls of identity, las nepantleras know their work lies in positioning themselves—exposed and raw—in the crack between these worlds, and in revealing current categories as unworkable . . .
>
> When you're in the place between worldviews (nepantla) you're able to slip between realities to a neutral perception. A decision made in the in-between place becomes a turning point initiating psychological and spiritual transformations, making

other kinds of experiences possible. (Anzaldúa & Keating 2002, 567, 569)

Like the *new mestiza*, it is in the cracks between worlds that *la nepantlera* forms a more critical stance that may lead to transformation.

In this same 2002 text, Anzaldúa tackles the questions of how one acquires *conocimiento*, her term for a particular kind of intuitive knowing or "spiritual inquiry" that prompts one to action and transformation (Anzaldúa & Keating 2002, 542).[23] She also emphasizes spiritual activism and the personal or inner struggle connected to the possibility for change:

> When and how does transformation happen? When a change occurs in your consciousness (awareness of your sense of self and your response to self, others, and surroundings) becomes cognizant that it has a point of view and the ability to act from choice. When you shift attention from your customary point of view (the ego) to that of la naguala. . . . When you include the complexity of feeling two or more ways about a person/issue. When you're in the place between worldviews (nepantla) you're able to slip between realities to a neutral perception. A decision made in the in-between place becomes a turning point initiating psychological and spiritual transformations, making other kinds of experiences possible. (Anzaldúa & Keating 2002, 568–569)

Despite her awareness of the relational aspect of identity, of the fact that identity doesn't depend on individuals alone but on those with whom one interacts (Anzaldúa 2000, 242), when discussing the question of transformation, Anzaldúa emphasizes the personal, inner journey that in her view is necessary for other types of transformation. As she says, "The struggle has always been inner, and is played out in the outer terrains. . . . Nothing happens in the 'real' world unless it first happens in the images in our heads" (Anzaldúa 1987, 87). Her interest and emphasis on inner transformation, however, should not be interpreted as one sided or as precluding a sociality of resistance. While Anzaldúa highlights personal, inner struggle—this is one of the most powerful aspects of her writing—she is deeply committed to social change. Possibility of collective transformation, reconfiguration, and creation of norms that defy oppression runs through her work. As Keating explains,

> Anzaldúa develops a holistic worldview that synergistically combines social activism with spiritual vision, creating what she calls

"spiritual activism." . . . Spiritual activism is spirituality for social
change, spirituality that recognizes the many differences among
us yet insists on our commonalities and uses these commonalities
as catalysts for transformation. . . . For Anzaldúa self change (or
what some might call "personal growth") is never an end in itself
but instead must be part of a larger process requiring back-and-
forth action on individual and collective levels. (2006, 11–12)

An important aspect of this later explanation of the inner account of transformation that Anzaldúa offers is the notion of the *naguala*. As noted earlier,
according to Anzaldúa, in order for change to happen you have to shift
your consciousness from your customary or ego-related point of view to
that of *la naguala*. She defines the *naguala* as the feminine form of *nagual*,
the indigenous term for a shaman who shifts shapes. In Anzaldúa's view,
the *naguala* has to do with an aspect of the self that is unconscious; it is
"a creative, dreamlike consciousness able to make broader associations and
connections than waking consciousness" (Anzaldúa & Keating 2002, 577).
But how does this shift to the *naguala* occur? Does it happen automatically
as one inhabits the borderlands, *nepantla*?

In my view, the *naguala* is connected to Anzaldúa's account of *la
facultad* in *Borderlands/La Frontera*. *La facultad* is, according to Anzaldúa,
an "instant sensing . . . a quick perception arrived at without conscious
reasoning . . . an acute awareness mediated by the part of the psyche that
does not speak, that communicates in images and symbols" (1987, 38).
It is a survival tactic that according to Anzaldúa is latent in all of us but
that is particularly honed by border dwellers that constantly face difficult
situations or those who do not feel psychologically or physically safe in the
world. It constitutes what Anzaldúa calls a shift in perception that deepens
our awareness and vision of everyday objects and people.

This shift in perception is triggered by both fear and by experiences
that come into our everyday mode of perception and cause a break in one's
defenses and resistance. As Anzaldúa says, "Confronting anything that tears
the fabric of our everyday mode of consciousness and that thrusts us into
a less literal and more psychic sense of reality increases awareness and la
facultad" (1987, 39). This unconscious sense for what dangers lurk around
us, for what is friendly or threatening, is for Anzaldúa a mark of the inhabitants of the borderlands, of the new *mestiza*. This notion of *la facultad*
becomes more complex in the account of the *naguala* as *la nepantlera* is
capable of having this sense and awareness as she shifts from one perspective to the other. Through shifting and being able to see multiple views

or perspectives and comparing them, *la nepantlera* is thus more capable of transformation, and of developing alternative interpretations that are key to forging a critical stance.

Anzaldúa is clearly appealing to the marginalized lived experience of border-dwellers and conferring epistemic privilege on them, although the knowledge, or *conocimiento,* that she is bringing to light is not always reflective or conscious. It can clearly become thematized later, but it is also connected to *la facultad.* Thus the fear and experiences that threaten our resistance and thus hone *la facultad* are preliminaries to the shift to the *naguala* that, in turn, opens the possibility for personal and other types of transformation. Even in *Borderlands/La Frontera* Anzaldúa has a view as to who is most apt to develop *la facultad,* namely, *los atravesados*: women, homosexuals of all races, the dark skinned, the outcast, the persecuted, the marginalized, and the foreign. As she puts it, "When we're up against the wall, when we have all sorts of oppressions coming at us, we are forced to develop this faculty so that we'll know when the next person is going to slap us or lock us away" (Anzaldúa 1987, 39).

Although she sometimes seems to claim that all of those who have multiple oppressions develop this skill, it is best to interpret her as offering a view that claims that those in the margins are more likely to develop *la facultad,* but not all of them do. In her later writings she is closer to this position as she suggests that not all border-dwellers can become *nepantleras,* that *nepantleras* are more aware new *mestizas* as they can not only cross over worlds but also facilitate crossings. The standpoint of the new *mestiza* or *nepantlera,* then, is not to be seen as one that comes by virtue of her inhabiting the borderlands but one that is arrived through gut-wrenching personal struggle, a struggle that, as Mohanty states, is "born of history and geography" (2003, 81).

As we have learned from various feminists who analyze the status of experience and critique attempts to provide an account of group experience, say women's experience or Latinas' experience, it is important not to homogenize or essentialize the experience of the marginalized and the oppressed; that is, we need to remember that it is not the case that all oppressed people share the same set of characteristics.[24] It is also important not to consider Anzaldúa's discussion of her and other Latinas' oppression and marginalization as indubitable evidence. Following Mohanty and Stone-Mediatore, we should look at Anzaldúa's appeal to the experience of marginalized Latinas as a resource for critical reflection (Mohanty 2003, ch.2; Stone-Mediatore 2003, ch.5). As Stone-Mediatore points out,

> By highlighting phenomena that condition her borderlands exis-
> tence but that are omitted from ruling narratives of "Mexican
> American," Anzaldúa shows how her poverty and mental anguish
> are not as "natural" as they may seem but are, rather, an effect of
> the social and cultural hierarchies that position Mexican American
> women in North American society. (Stone-Mediatore 2003, 144)

Once the relations between the meaning of "Mexican American" and such
social and cultural hierarchies are revealed, there are more possibilities and
openings for renarrating this identity and for resistance to these hierarchies.

Like the new *mestiza, la nepantlera* remains a complex self whose
capability to deal effectively with the many contradictions and ambiguities of a life in *nepantla* makes her incredibly strong and tremendously
flexible. While Anzaldúa's account of the new *mestiza* highlights her inner
struggle, Anzaldúa's elaboration of *la nepantlera* in her later work highlights
the question of collective transformation and resistance, since, as noted, she
makes suggestions as to how *la nepantlera* can guide and facilitate crossings for others (Anzaldúa & Keating 2002, 568–574). Yet, the desire for
transformation and collective change is already part of the story of the
new *mestiza*; and the deeply personal and inner aspect of her account that
is key to her Latina feminist phenomenology is also present in the later
writings. Anzaldúa's struggle between finding a satisfactory account of self
that recognizes the political import of identity but that does not appeal to
external categories, and finding an altogether different way to understand
ourselves also remains.

A *Mestizaje* of Multiplicity and Oneness

As Anzaldúa struggles to find an appropriate characterization of the self
throughout her writings, wavering from more oppositional accounts to more
inclusive views that do not rely on external modes of identification, she also
struggles to do justice to a lived experience that includes both multiplicity
and a sense of oneness—an experience that is also philosophically interesting as we struggle to provide theories of selves that are phenomenologically
rich and capture this existential sense of oneness. In this section I engage
Anzaldúa's work in light of philosophical questions regarding the oneness
and the multiplicity of the self. We will see that there is an additional
tension found in Anzaldúa's explorations on selfhood as she attempts to
explain the existential sense of being one self, an "I," and her recognition

of the importance of her multiplicity. Nevertheless, this tension remains productive and leads to an understanding of her view as providing what I call a *mestizaje* of multiplicity and oneness, a *mestizaje* that defies the logic of duality by its refusal to choose oneness over multiplicity or vice versa. This *mestizaje* of multiplicity and oneness captures both one's existential sense of being a continuous self as well as the recognition and importance of one's various social identities. This *mestizaje* points to alternative visions of self that go beyond the traditional, unified epistemic subject as well as beyond phenomenological views of subjectivity.

I cannot overemphasize the enormous influence that Anzaldúa's work in general, and her notion of the *new mestiza* specifically, has had on various theorists in many disciplines. As Chela Sandoval notes in her influential piece "*Mestiza*je as Method: Feminists-of-Color Challenge the Canon," no other Chicana deployment of feminism has been as recognized, exchanged, or influential as Anzaldúa's "Chicana *Mestiza*je," a *mestiza*je capable of reforming disciplinary canons (Sandoval 1998, 352–353). While the concept of the new *mestiza* described here is valuable for the way it has influenced numerous disciplines and has inspired important discussions on the possibility of resistance to oppression and marginalization, it is also philosophically interesting for many reasons, including the fact that it provides a new way of looking at identity, one that does not rely on the notion of the unified subject, whether in its Cartesian or Kantian versions. It is also an interesting alternative to existential, phenomenological, and pragmatist philosophical views of identity that, while pointing out the pitfalls of the accounts of modern subjectivity, are problematic themselves due to their omission of the lived experience of selves in the borderlands or in-betweenness. Looking at Anzaldúa's account might be helpful for philosophers as we strive to provide accounts of self that can capture the complex experience of the selves in the borderlands.[25]

At first glance, Anzaldúa's account of the new *mestiza* seems to describe a being with a dual personality, since she is both a Chicana and an American living in the US-Mexico borderlands. The new *mestiza* can also be seen as a hybrid identity, a being that is a combination or mixture of two specific identities, her being Mexican and American, or her being male and female. Anzaldúa also explains that in her encounter with opposite elements, the new *mestiza* works out a synthesis and thus adds a "third element." Moreover, in her account of *nepantla*, Anzaldúa highlights the fact that the new *mestiza* is more than one person: "In this liminal transitional space, suspended between shifts, you're two people, split between before and after (Anzaldúa & Keating 2002, 544). She also says, "I, like other queer people, am two in one body" (Anzaldúa 1987, 19). Interestingly, the new *mestiza* can fit all of these descriptions. She is like Coatlicue, the Aztec earth goddess, creator of heaven and earth as well as destroyer, who inspires Anzaldúa and whom she describes as follows: "Simultaneously, depending on the person, she represents: duality in life, a synthesis of duality, and a third perspective—something more than mere duality or a synthesis of duality" (Anzaldúa 1987, 46).

Anzaldúa often refers to the new *mestiza*'s multiple or "plural" personality that operates in a pluralistic mode (1987, 78, 79). The new *mestiza* is a plurality, and *mestiza* consciousness is, as noted previously, "a multiplicity that is transformational" (Anzaldúa 2009, 246). But how does Anzaldúa understand this multiplicity? Just as her account of the new *mestiza* is not clear—given the fact that Anzaldúa wants the concept to go beyond oppositional identity politics but that a great deal of the strength of the account is connected to her being Chicana—her discussion of multiplicity is at times confusing. Again, this confusing, sometimes contradictory, aspect of her account might not necessarily be damning. It reflects the complexity of the self that Anzaldúa is trying to explain. As readers of Anzaldúa's text, we are being challenged to deal with the contradictory, ambiguous, and transformative aspects of not only the new *mestiza* but also of Anzaldúa's text itself.

In an earlier 1983 interview Anzaldúa states, "I don't believe you have to slay the ego. I believe you have to leave it and incorporate all the pieces you have cut off, not give the ego such a limelight but give some of the other parts a limelight" (Anzaldúa 2009, 88). Later in *Borderlands/La Frontera*, despite having described the new *mestiza* as a self with a plural personality, she makes the following statements that suggest a sense of "oneness," not a unified ego but what seems like an integrative, joining force of the self:

> I've always been aware that there is a greater power than the conscious I. That power is my inner self, the entity that is the sum total of all my reincarnations, the godwoman in me I call *Antigua*, mi *Diosa*, the divine within, *Coatlicue-Cihuacoatl-Tlazolteotl-Tonantzin-Coatlalopeuh-Guadalupe*—they are one. . . .
>   And suddenly I feel everything rushing to a center, a nucleus. All the lost pieces of myself come flying from the deserts and the mountains and the valleys, magnetized toward that center. *Completa.* (Anzaldúa 1987, 50, 51)

In these comments, Anzaldúa appeals to a unifying sense for the new *mestiza*. She even writes about her "total self" (1987, 73) and the possibility of the end of the inner struggle that one has while living in the borderlands, an experience of "true integration" (1987, 63). In most sections of *Borderlands/La Frontera*, however, she emphasizes the duality or plurality of the new *mestiza*, leaving us to wonder about the importance of her occasional comments regarding the unity, integration, and totality of the self. Are these comments the product of Anzaldúa's wishful thinking at precarious moments when the psychic restlessness and intimate terrorism of the life at the borders or borderlands seems too much to bear? Or do they point to her view that despite the plurality and multiplicity of the new *mestiza*, Anzaldúa hopes for some sort of unifying principle or integration of the self's multiple aspects? This unity, however, cannot be thought in the traditional sense. As Anzaldúa notes, "I fear a unity that leaves out parts of me, that colonizes me, that violates my integrity, my wholeness and chips away at my autonomy" (1998, 268).[26]

In the aforementioned comments and other writings, Anzaldúa not only discusses the "unity" of the self but also the self's plurality or multiplicity in terms of the idea of layered selves, as well as the ideas of personas and reincarnations. It is thus difficult to fully grasp Anzaldúa's view. While at times she writes about the new *mestiza* as having many selves and thus her identity being always in flux and in the making, and at times she appeals to the new *mestiza*'s total self, at other times she seems to be discussing what I would call a multiplicitous self. But as we shall see in the next chapter, this self, though it has many social identities and occupies multiple positionalities, is one self.

What makes the self one or "total" is not always clear in Anzaldúa's writings. Yet she sometimes appeals to a spiritual component when calling for unity, wholeness, and totality, not just for herself but for the relationship between all the parts of herself and the world. In some instances, she appeals to her "soul" as the main element of herself, one that gives her a sense of totality as well as a sense of unity with her environment (Anzaldúa 2009, 91). This appeal to spirituality or to a spiritual element that unifies or integrates her is not surprising, since Anzaldúa's respect for spirituality and the spirit world is shown explicitly throughout her works and in interviews. Commentators such as Theresa Delgadillo find this spiritual element in Anzaldúa's work to be key in *Borderlands/La Frontera*, so much so that she finds spirituality informing "every aspect of the work that *Borderlands* performs with respect to subjectivity, epistemology, and transformation, including its consideration of inherited and invented practices honoring the sacred" (Delgadillo 2011, 6). Keating also considers the spiritual dimension of Anzaldúa's work as crucial and sees Anzaldúa's "spiritual activism" as "the most comprehensive of her theories because it could be said to contain them all" (2006 11). However, it is also an aspect of her work that is not always discussed by commentators, given that many academics have been seduced by a solely rationalist paradigm that undermines and undervalues or simply does not accept explanations that appeal to the world beyond the material or to experiences that are not based on rationality. As Anzaldúa states in a 1998–1999 interview, "This whole society is premised on the reality described by the scientific mode of observable phenomenon, while whatever is imagined or subjectively lived doesn't have any credence. Spirituality is subjective experience" (Anzaldúa 2000, 282).

This spiritual aspect of her vision must not be forgotten as we attempt to grasp her understanding of selfhood. It might be the case that the sense of "oneness" and totality that Anzaldúa experiences and brings into her discussion of self may be seen as a product of a deeply personal, spiritual inner experience that cannot be easily described or readily understood by someone else, especially those who do not accept spirituality or a spirit world. As she says,

> Some greater self or total self is guiding me to be a certain way; it has instructions for how I should live my life, instructions that the "little me" subselves don't know. Now I'm trying to get information on which way to go, I'm trying to listen more to my inner voice because before diabetes I was too much out in the world. (Anzaldúa 1987, 289)

This total self can represent a larger force of the universe, the divine, but also the sense that the "I" feels in being interconnected with all aspects of oneself, the universe, and the spiritual world. There is always a deep connection between one's sense of self and the material and spiritual worlds.

In comments and writings after *Borderlands/La Frontera*, Anzaldúa also appeals to a sense of oneness and totality of the self while at the same time recognizing its plurality or multiplicity. Consider the following statement from a 1991 interview: "I think the different personas that we are—the you that's with me right now has one face, the you that's going to be with other people tomorrow will have a slightly different one, but basically there's the you" (Anzaldúa 2000, 161). Here Anzaldúa seems to appeal to an almost essential aspect of the self beyond all specific self presentations or to a substance that is beyond all properties. Yet, in my view, she might be appealing to a sense of oneness, of being an "I," that is both attuned to the multiplicity of the self and to relations with others. For Anzaldúa, being an "I" is always connected to other selves and to the rest of the world in its material and spiritual manifestations.[27] Anzaldúa thus describes the "total self" as a tree, whose roots are always connected to the world and to nature. She states,

> We all have many different selves or subpersonalities, little "I's": This self may be very good at running the house, taking care of the writing as a business, making a living from the writing, and figuring out expenses. This other self is very emotional and this other self is the public figure who goes out, does speeches and teaches. Whatever subpersonalities you have (and some are antagonistic to others)—they all make up el árbol, which is the total self, and it's embedded in this ground which is the world and nature. So it's all relational. . . . Every few years you pull up the roots, get on the train, and move. Some of it changes pero las raíces como culture, race, class—some of that stays . . . you always pick up your roots and take them with you. (Anzaldúa 2000, 242)

She points not only to the sense of oneness of the self but also to this self's plurality by appealing to a "geography of selves," or a vision in which identity is comprised by a cluster or layering of various social identities:

> I think identity is an arrangement or series of clusters, a kind of stacking or layering of selves, horizontal and vertical layers, the geography of selves made up of the different communities you inhabit. When I give my talks I use an overhead projector with a transparency of a little stick figure con un pie en un mundo y otro pie en otro mundo y todos estos mundos overlap: this is your race, your sexual orientation, here you're a Jew Chicana, here an academic, here an artist, there a blue-collar worker. Where these spaces overlap is nepantla, the Borderlands. Identity is a process-in-the-making. You're not born a Chicana, you become a Chicana because of the culture that's caught in you. (Anzaldúa 2000, 238)

As noted, in her later writings and interviews, Anzaldúa emphasizes the multiplicity of the self and explains that her identity is "always in flux" (Anzaldúa 2009, 209), that identity is a "changing cluster of components" and a "shape-shifting activity," describing a person who changes identities as a *nagual*, the Nahuatl term meaning "shapeshifter" (Anzaldúa 2009, 212). This shapeshifting of identities can be considered tactical or strategic, as Anzaldúa describes them as responses to particular embodied situations that she encounters. Thus she writes that at a conference the intellectual Gloria takes the center stage; at a meeting with Chicanos, the ethnic Gloria comes out; and so forth (Anzaldúa 2009, 211). She notes,

> As a mestiza, I have many true faces, depending upon the kind of audience or the area I find myself. . . . We shift around to do the work we have to do, to create identities we need to live up to our potential. (Anzaldúa 2009, 211–212)

This strategic understanding of identity is a position later taken up and expanded by theorists such as Chela Sandoval in her important account of oppositional, "differential consciousness" (Sandoval 2000).

Anzaldúa's understanding of identity as a shape-shifting process that is continually in flux is not meant to be a call for the view that the new *mestiza* may choose any identity she wishes, as if she were only the product of discourse, as if the new *mestiza* could choose identities like articles of clothing. As noted previously, the new *mestiza* is one in which the *mestiza* is embodied and situated in a particular space where particular economic, cultural, and historical circumstances crisscross. Again, while there is certainly a metaphorical aspect in Anzaldúa's account of *mestizaje*, and thus the borderlands might not always refer to actual locations, we cannot fail to take into account the materiality of her position. The identities that the new *mestiza* tactically "chooses" remain grounded in particular social and geographic locations—she always picks up her roots and takes them with her (Anzaldúa 2000, 242).

Anzaldúa's account of self remains multiple as her writing shape-shifts and presents different or transformed visions of self and identity, sometimes emphasizing multiplicity and other times oneness and totality—sometimes appealing to oppositional identity, while at the same time criticizing such an account. As noted, Anzaldúa is inspired by the goddess Coatlicue, and like Coatlicue, her treatment of selfhood represents "duality in life, a synthesis of duality, and a third perspective—something more than mere duality or a synthesis of duality" (Anzaldúa 1987, 46). Anzaldúa's difficult and sometimes confusing quest toward an understanding of self and identity is a phenomenological exercise—an examination of her own experience that not surprisingly points to both multiplicity and oneness due to her situatedness in the difficult terrain of the borderlands. What arises out of this exercise is also a notion of the self that is paradoxical but meant to capture the lived experience of border-dwellers—a self best understood as a *mestizaje* of both multiplicity and oneness. As multiple, the self has various social identities; as one, the self has a sense of being an "I," an existential sense of ownness but also a sense of being a totality. This totality can be understood through what Anzaldúa describes as the Coyolxauhqui imperative (Anzaldúa 2005).

Coyolxauhqui is the Aztec moon goddess who was decapitated and dismembered by her brother Huitzilopochtlí. Anzaldúa appeals to this myth in order to bring to light the situation of contemporary women, their split between body, mind, spirit, and soul (2005, 11). She recognizes the many different ways in which she and others are split and thus rendered power-less. She consequently calls for healing. Keating sees this call for healing as connected to Anzaldúa's spiritual activism, which aims to effect "material-spiritual" change (Anzaldúa 2000, 11). She quotes Anzaldúa:

> When you take a person and divide her up, you disempower her. She's no longer a threat. My whole struggle in writing, in this anticolonial struggle, has been to . . . put us back together again. To connect up the body with the soul and the mind with the spirit. (Anzaldúa 2000, 11)

The Coyolxauhqui imperative, then, symbolizes healing and integration. For Anzaldúa it is "a necessary process of dismemberment and fragmentation, of seeing that self or the situations you're embroiled in differently. It is also a symbol for reconstruction and reframing, one that allows for putting the pieces together in a new way" (Anzaldúa 2005, 122). This imperative not only represents Anzaldúa's spiritual activism but also her view of the complexity of the self residing in *nepantla*, a self that has various inter-secting social identities but that can be fragmented by oppressive norms and practices of dominant culture, a self that has a sense of being an "I" existentially and spiritually, the possibility of being a whole, of healing and "integration"—a self that remains multiple and one.

An identity is sort of like a river. It's one and it's flowing and it's a process. . . . Soy amasamiento, I am an act of kneading, of uniting and joining that not only has produced both a creature of darkness and a creature of light, but also a creature that questions the definitions of light and dark and gives them new meanings.

—Gloria Anzaldúa

2

Being-between-Worlds, Being-in-Worlds

I am multiplicitous. Multiple and one. Psychic restlessness. Intimate ter-rorism. Cactus needles embedded in my skin and in my words. Latina, de las otras, daughter, sister, lover, student, teacher, philosopher. English. Spanish. Other languages, but not of words. Of worlds, many of them. IN—confusion, pain, paralysis, creation, transformation—BETWEEN.

Anzaldúa walks the difficult paths of her life in the borderlands with eyes wide open in order to disclose moments of anguish and grief but also moments of creativity and renewal. She struggles to find a satisfactory account of selfhood that can do justice to her complex lived experience. This deep exploration of her everyday life and, by extension, of the experi-ence of others who traverse the difficult terrains of the borderlands consti-tutes a powerful, moving phenomenology. Interestingly, her Latina feminist phenomenological account of the new *mestiza* shares characteristics with the Heideggerian existential phenomenological description of *Dasein*, Hei-degger's term for human beings.

In this chapter, I would like to think Anzaldúa, Lugones, and Hei-degger together. Thinking of Anzaldúa's account of *mestizaje* with its move-ment of both multiplicity and oneness in light of Lugones's description of world-traveling and Heidegger's account of *Dasein* as being-in-the-world leads me to a notion of multiplicitous selfhood as *amasamiento*, an act of kneading very different visions of self from different traditions—yet anoth-er instance of *mestizaje*. While the Heideggerian view of *Dasein* offers an important explanation of selfhood, it nevertheless does not always capture the experience of marginalized, in-between selves that Latina feminist phe-nomenological descriptions so powerfully depict. Examining these three thinkers together discloses important similarities and differences between their visions of self. The view of multiplicitous selfhood that arises out of this thinking is meant to capture a general sense of selfhood, but, at the same time, it emphasizes the lived experience of selves in the margins. Following Anzaldúa, Lugones, and Heidegger, I describe the multiplicitous self as being-between-worlds and being-in-worlds—the multiplicitous self is thus an in-between self.

In the first part of this chapter I briefly describe some elements shared by both the Heideggerian explanation of *Dasein* and the notion of the new *mestiza* and other selves described by Latina feminists. I also point to a key difference between the Heideggerian view and Latina feminists' visions of self—namely, that the self in the borderlands, or the self that world-travels, constantly experiences ruptures in her everyday experiences that lead to a more thematic or reflective orientation toward activities. Phenomenologists such as Heidegger, Sartre, and Merleau-Ponty, however, depict a self that has a primarily practical, nonreflective orientation in the world. Understanding this difference is helpful, especially as we broaden philosophical accounts so as to include the lived experience of selves at the margins. Traditional phenomenological views thus stand to benefit from taking into consideration Latina feminist phenomenological descriptions of selfhood.

In the second section of this chapter I return to the idea of a *mestizaje* of multiplicity and oneness and introduce the notion of multiplicitous self-hood as being-between-worlds and being-in-worlds. I also bring to light the intersectionality and flexibility of this self. I explain the multiplicity and oneness of the multiplicitous self, neither elevating the sense of multiplicity such that the sense of being one self disappears, nor prioritizing oneness such that multiplicity is sacrificed or erased. Being-between-worlds and being-in-worlds are notions that disclose this self's multiplicity. In order to capture the sense of "oneness" of the multiplicitous self, I provide an explanation of the self's continuity of experience by way of the notions of temporal-ity and *mineness*. We will see that while the multiplicitous self undergoes moments of contradiction, ambiguity, and what I refer to as a *thick* sense of not being-at-ease, this self still experiences a continuity of experience, an *existential continuity* that makes possible the self's sense of being an "I."

While the account of multiplicitous selfhood offered here is to be understood as a general account of self—that is, all of us are multiplicitous selves—this work pays particular attention to those multiplicitous selves whose experience is marked by oppression and marginalization due to their social identities, those selves that have not figured prominently in the pages of philosophical discourses. Even though all of us are multiplicitous, some multiplicitous selves—those who are multicultural, queer, border dwellers, and whom Anzaldúa names *los atravesados*—experience more of what she describes as "psychic restlessness" and "intimate terrorism" due to their marginalization and oppression. That is, these selves' multiplicity is sharper, sometimes piercing, thus leading to a sense of alienation and *Unheimlichkeit,* or uncanniness, that makes their lives more vulnerable to injustice. Through engagement with the work of Anzaldúa and Lugones, I would like to draw attention to the experience of these *atravesados.* I am aware, however, that different social locations yield different ways of understanding one's marginalization or belonging. There is not a simple dichotomy between marginalized/nonmarginalized or oppressed/oppressor. Selves need to be understood in their complexity and in terms of the different roles they play in the matrix of power relations such that each of us can be understood variously as oppressors, oppressed, or resisting (Lugones 2003, 200).[1] It is my hope that the intertwining of Latina feminism and Heideggerian phenomenology discloses a better understanding of the complexity of the experience of these selves who remain at the margins not only of traditional philosophical investigations but also of society.

Latina Feminist Phenomenology and Heideggerian Existential Phenomenology

Crisscrossings

One of the most important philosophical contributions made by Heidegger in his groundbreaking work *Being and Time* and other early works is his elaboration of a self that must be conceived in terms of *being-in-the-world* rather than in terms of being an epistemic substance. That is, in the Heideggerian account, the self has a practical involvement with a nexus of equipment found in the world. This Heideggerian account of self as being-in-the-world, of a self that is "there," a *Dasein* (therebeing), constitutes a critique against Cartesian epistemic subjectivity, in which the subject is understood as a substance or a thinking thing, and the primary relationship to the world is via mental representations of things that stand outside the sphere of the subject's mind. Heidegger's "existential analytic," or description of the different ways of being of *Dasein*, is indeed considered a key critique to traditional substantial and epistemic understandings of subjectivity. As such, it stands as one of the most important contributions to philosophy in general, and to the philosophy of selfhood specifically, inspiring noted continental philosophers that include Sartre, Arendt, Merleau-Ponty, Ortega y Gasset, and Derrida.[2]

Because of its important critique against established traditional, epistemic, and substantial conceptions of subjectivity and its elaboration of a situated, temporal, existential self, I have chosen to engage Heideggerian phenomenology with Latina feminist phenomenology. Despite the fact that Anzaldúa and Heidegger are writing from very different perspectives and political views, and with different aims—Anzaldúa's writing is a deeply personal act and has an interdisciplinary orientation, while Heidegger's writing is connected to a systematic, philosophical attempt at carrying out an ontological investigation—Anzaldúa's notion of the new *mestiza* shares some important elements with Heidegger's description of *Dasein*. Rather than providing an in-depth explanation of Heideggerian existential characteristics, in the following I revisit and expand on some of the various characteristics that I have previously noted as shared by both Heidegger's existential analytic and Latina feminist conceptions of self (Ortega 2001). While there is not a one-to-one correspondence between Heidegger's work and work by writers such as Anzaldúa and Lugones, there are significant crisscrossings.

Like the new *mestiza* discussed in the previous chapter, the self that Heidegger proposes is one *in the making* rather than a substantial self. When describing *Dasein* in *Being and Time*, Heidegger claims that "the 'essence' of this entity lies in its "to be"" (Heidegger 1962, 67 [42]). In other words, human beings do not have an essence but make themselves through living, through making choices. As he puts it in *The Basic Problems of Phenomenology*, "In everyday terms, we understand ourselves and our existence by way of the activities we pursue and the things we take care of" (Heidegger 1982, 160). Rather than accepting the traditional understanding of selfhood as a substance in which a number of set properties inhere, Heidegger understands the self as always *in process, in the making*.

A key structure of this existential self in process, which is connected to the self's understanding and ability to make choices while moving toward the future, is the notion of projection (Heidegger 1962, 185 [145]). According to Heidegger, projection is what we all do by virtue of being human— that is, to exist is to project ourselves toward future possibilities. Neither *Dasein* nor the new *mestiza* are substantial entities; they are existential selves that make themselves through their choices. While Heidegger emphasizes that projection is not always thematic or reflective, Anzaldúa's account does not. In fact, as we shall see later in this chapter, the life of the new *mestiza* is not always as nonreflective as that of *Dasein*'s. However, both thinkers agree that the self is always in process. They are deeply aware that the self is defined through choice and is thus not some entity whose possibilities and characteristics are preset, as one may provide a list of properties of a chair or a pen. *Dasein* is always projecting itself upon possibilities; the new *mestiza* is deeply aware of the possibilities for change and transformation that life at the borderlands offers. Heidegger, Anzaldúa, and other Latina feminists also share a view of the self as *thrown*.[3] They understand the self as always already in the world. As opposed to a view such as Descartes's, in which there arises the possibility for doubting the external world as well as other minds, a thrown self is always already existing in the world and practically engaging with objects.

While Heidegger painstakingly explains major ontological, existential characteristics of a self that is *thrown*, he unfortunately does not explain the specific ontic situations that are of concern for the self that is "there" and that dwells in the world. His primary interest remains in fundamental ontology, in finding general ontological characteristics of human beings, even if it is an ontology that is always connected to the ontic or specific characteristics of humans. Anzaldúa and other Latina feminists, however, underscore the ontic, the specific material characteristics and conditions of human beings. Latina feminists concentrate on the particular power relations informing specific economic, cultural, and societal "theres." As we have seen, one of Anzaldúa's great contributions is her powerful and detailed description of the new *mestiza* as a being who is thrown in the US-Mexico borderlands and has to negotiate her various social identities in this complex in-between territory.

Characteristic of a self that is thrown and defines itself by making choices is the mood of anxiety (*Angst*), a mood that Heidegger connects to *Dasein*'s potential for living authentically. Heidegger says, "Anxiety is anxious about naked Dasein as something that has been thrown into uncanniness. It brings one back to the pure 'that-it-is' of one's ownmost individualized throwness" (394 [343]). In the Heideggerian account, anxiety is connected to the self's possibility for what Heidegger calls resoluteness or authentic or proper existence (*Eigentlichkeit*) as opposed to being under the mode of the "they" (*das Man*), or what Heidegger describes as the everyday being of the self. Similar to the Kierkegaardian notion of "the public," the "they" refers to the anonymity and generality implicit in everyday interaction. It serves as a guide to everyday social interaction in the sense that when we are in this mode we basically follow the norms and practices in our culture or society. This way of being of everydayness, however, also leads to *Dasein*'s loss of responsibility for its actions, since it blindly follows prescribed norms and practices.[4] Despite the fact that anxiety is the mood that presents the uncanny in the world, that makes *Dasein* not feel at home, it is also the mood that allows for the possibility of self-awareness and a life in which the self understands and accepts the responsibility for making choices. Through anxiety, then, *Dasein* can begin to take up authentic existence, which, in this account, has to do with building one's own ground by way of choices that are not merely dictated under the mode of the "they." Ultimately, for Heidegger, anxiety is not always necessarily negative. Rather, it is a mood that discloses the possibilities of being-in-the-world and the individual aspects of the self.

In Anzaldúa's account, a sense of anxiety also permeates the life of the new *mestiza*. In this instance, anxiety is also connected to the possibility of choice, to the fact that the new *mestiza* has, as Anzaldúa says, to cross—to cross worlds, borders, ways of life. Since the new *mestiza* constantly occupies liminal spaces, she has to make difficult choices. As described in the previous chapter, the new *mestiza* experiences *Coatlicue* states that include moments of utter despair and sometimes paralysis, an inability to make choices:

> It is her reluctance to cross over, to make a hole in the fence and walk across, to cross the river, to take that flying leap into the dark, that drives her to escape, that forces her into the fecund cave of her imagination where she is cradled in the arms of Coatlicue, who will never let her go. If she doesn't change her ways, she will remain a stone forever. *No hay más que cambiar.* (Anzaldúa 1987, 49)

In my view, here Anzaldúa describes an existential crisis based on the anxiety that arises when she faces extremely difficult choices given her multiple positionalities. This terrible anxiety can turn into moments of paralysis. While, in the Heideggerian view, anxiety discloses a self not at home in the world, in the Anzaldúan story, anxiety is connected with paralysis and an inability to make choices. Methodologically, however, anxiety plays similar roles in these two accounts, since it is through anxiety that the self becomes capable of ultimately making choices that are not expected or prescribed. In a sense, anxiety is part and parcel of being human and of recognizing that familiar existential call for creating one's own "essence" through one's own choices. Both the sense of uncanniness and the paralysis of the *Coatlicue* state are preludes, as Anzaldúa would say, to crossing, to becoming oneself by disrupting the influence of the "they" or by literally and figuratively crossing borders and making decisions that are not dependent on cultural impositions.

In addition to understanding the self as in process, as thrown, and as anxious, Heidegger and Anzaldúa strongly reject the subject/object dichotomy. This dichotomy posits a clear separation between the subject generally conceived in terms of an inner domain and the object understood as standing outside or apart from the subject. Since Heidegger rejects the notion of a substantial core and believes that the human being is a being-in-the-world that is defined in terms of dwelling in the world, he rejects the divide between subject and object (Heidegger 1962, §§12 & 13). In his view, a philosophical account that posits this dichotomy does not accurately capture the way in which the self exists in the world. Moreover, it allows for the possibility of the self to doubt the existence of the outside world—that is, since the self has access to objects in the world via representations of those objects that are held in the inner domain of consciousness, it becomes possible to question both the existence of the external world and the existence of other minds. Yet Heidegger rejects this dichotomy and from the outset offers a conception of a self that already stands "outside," that is always in the world. Understanding that world does not consist in primarily epistemic, reflective relationship to the world; rather, understanding is based on a practical engagement with objects found in the world. The self does not need to move from the inside of his consciousness to the outside world and back inside. As opposed to an epistemic subject, *Dasein* does not go *out* to the world in order to capture representations of objects that are then placed *in* the "cabinet" of consciousness (Heidegger 1962, 89 [62]).

Similarly to Heidegger, Anzaldúa strongly rejects the subject/object dichotomy, but her criticism against it stems not from an explicit desire to overturn a substantialist, primarily epistemic account of the subject but from the personal and political circumstances that arise when one is in a situation that calls for an endorsement of the subject/object and other dichotomies. Anzaldúa as well as other Latina feminists, such as Lugones, are staunch critics of dichotomous views and the worlds that arise out of such views, worlds that are always arranged in terms of dualities. As Anzaldúa states,

> The work of *mestiza* consciousness is to break down the subject-object duality that keeps her a prisoner and to show in the flesh and through the images in her work how duality is transcended. The answer to the problem between the white race and the colored, between males and females, lies in healing the split that originates in the very foundation of our lives, our culture, our languages, our thoughts. (Anzaldúa 1987, 80)

Anzaldúa claims that one of the consequences of dualistic, dichotomous thinking is the narrowing of possibilities. That is, we are led to choose one side of the duality or the other rather than appreciating the ways in which both sides are interrelated, and whether there are more than just two sides to an issue. Both Heidegger and Anzaldúa are cognizant of the dangers of the dichotomy between subject and object—Heidegger appreciating how such a dichotomy misses the intimate relationship between self and world, and Anzaldúa warning us of the reductive aspect of dichotomous thinking, not just in terms of our selfhood but also in terms of our political possibilities.

Given the critique of the subject/object duality, both Heidegger and Anzaldúa are deeply attuned to the interrelatedness between self and world, including the relationship among selves. Thus, sociality is a key element in these descriptions of self. Not only does Heidegger understand the self as already in the world, he also explains the self as always connected to others or as having the possibility of connecting to others. As a being-in-the-world, *Dasein* has being-with (*Mitsein*), the ontological characteristic that makes it possible for *Dasein* to be with others (Heidegger 1962, §26). The very name of the self, *Dasein*, or therebeing, captures the interrelatedness between self and world. *Dasein* is always situated in particular contexts and finds others at work, at play, and in other circumstances. According to Heidegger, even when there is no other self around, *Dasein* always has being-with. In this account the self is not an isolated subject, a *solus ipse*. Yet Heidegger concentrates on this social aspect of the self in terms of the notion of the "they," which, as we have seen, is the everyday way of being in which the self follows prescribed norms and practices and does not accept responsibility for choices. In fact, one of the most important aspects of the life dominated by the "they" is that the self follows everyday norms and practices in such a way that adherence to these practices creates a sense of comfort in the world, what we may call being-at-ease. The everyday mode of the "they" allows for familiarity and thus the transparency of norms and practices.

Like Heidegger's, Anzaldúa's account highlights the importance of situatedness and sociality, not only in specific moments of the new *mestiza*'s existence—for example, Anzaldúa's own experience in what she calls the *herida abierta*, the open wound, of the US-Mexico border—but also in specific histories and cultural myths that inform her experience. Anzaldúa's account goes far beyond Heidegger's because he does not consider the multiplicity of particular histories. Heidegger discusses the importance of *Dasein* being a historical being that interprets itself in specific environments, but he does not describe or engage with those environments. Anzaldúa's attention to the self's situatedness also includes consideration of the self's connection to others and to the specific histories connected to those others. While Heidegger offers a more general account of *Mitsein*, or being-with, and historicality, Anzaldúa's emphasizes the history of the United States and Mexico as well as the history of the Aztec people and their mythology. Consider Anzaldúa's remarks about her relationship with the customs, beliefs, and history of her people:

> This very minute I sense the presence of the spirits of my ancestors in my room. And I think *la Jila* is *Cihuacoatl,* Snake Woman; she is la *Llorona,* Daughter of Night, traveling the dark terrains of the unknown searching for the lost parts of herself. I remember la Jila following me once, remember her eerie lament. I'd like to think that she was crying for her lost children, los Chicanos/*mexicanos . . .*
>
> Raza india Mexicana norteamericana, . . . I am fully formed carved by the hands of the ancients, drenched with the stench of today's headlines . . . (Anzaldúa 1987, 38, 173)

Both Heidegger and Anzaldúa, then, include a consideration of the importance of situatedness and history in their work. While Heidegger highlights the fact that *Dasein* is a historical being by virtue of being temporal, Anzaldúa is interested in resurrecting and reinterpreting the ancient history and myths that have informed Mexican and Mexican American culture.

Finally, a very important characteristic that is shared by Latina feminist phenomenologists and more traditional phenomenological accounts such as Heidegger's is the interpretative or hermeneutic dimension of the self. In the Heideggerian text, this hermeneutic dimension is of utmost importance and manifests itself in terms of what is understood as a hermeneutic circle. While in the early hermeneutic tradition, such as Schleiermacher's, the hermeneutic circle concerns the interpretation of texts, in the Heideggerian existential description of *Dasein* it represents the fact that the self already has a sense of the answer to the question of the meaning of being (a preontological understanding of being) and thus can ask the question in the first place. In other words, we as humans already have a sense of what the meaning of being is, and this sense is always guiding our investigation on the question of the meaning of being, leading us to find general characteristics of our existence. In Heidegger's writings, the hermeneutic circle ultimately points to the self's situatedness in specific contexts and how these contexts can themselves be interpreted anew. Rather than entailing a vicious circularity, it is representative of the intimate connection between temporal lived experience and understanding.

This hermeneutic dimension of existence is also a compelling driving force in the work of writers such as Anzaldúa and Lugones. It can be seen in the manner in which the new *mestiza* interprets and reinterprets herself,

taking cues from a situation that involves not only geographical spaces but
historical and cultural processes. It is also present in the way in which the
new *mestiza* proposes to rethink and reinterpret the meaning of those very
spaces that have helped her become who she is. In that "open wound" of
the US-Mexico border, the new *mestiza* feels the "intimate terrorism," the
violence and fear of the life of in-betweenness, but it is here that she also
develops her *movimientos de rebeldía*—strategies of resistance that allow her
to reinterpret herself and her cultures. In Lugones, the hermeneutic dimension of the world-traveler self is also evident, as this self that travels worlds is
constantly interpreting and reinterpreting these worlds and finding resistance
against the dominant logic pervasive in these worlds. More recently, Latina
feminist Linda Martín Alcoff draws attention to the hermeneutic aspect
of human existence by providing an account of visible social identity as
interpretative horizon inspired in part by Hans-Georg Gadamer's historical hermeneutics and by Merleau-Ponty's phenomenology of embodiment.[5]

A Key Difference: Not Being-at-Ease

Despite there being some significant similarities between the accounts of
self provided by Heidegger and Latina feminist phenomenologists such as
Anzaldúa and others, it is necessary to keep in mind that there are important differences as well. Such differences make it particularly difficult for
theorists to engage the Heideggerian existential analytic with writings by
Latina theorists, and vice versa. No difference is greater than the political
stances of the writers I am discussing here, Heidegger having chosen to
support an unforgivable political position, and Latina feminists choosing
to write in defense of those who are marginalized. This difference alone
might be enough for some to reject a project such as the present one or to
claim that we should not engage such disparate theorists. However, I hold
on to the view that examining the work of Latina feminists together with
Heidegger's account of the self might prove to be helpful, since Heideggerian
and existential phenomenology in general need to take into consideration
the lived experience of those in the margins. Not doing so would leave us
with existential accounts of self that go beyond the substantial, epistemic
subject and all the problems that such a view of the subject entails but
that, nevertheless, do not do justice to the lived experience of those who
are marginalized.

Yet another crucial difference is that, as we have seen, writers such as
Anzaldúa, Lugones, and other Latina feminists fully engage with the situatedness and particularities of the self. Instead of providing a general account

of the self's existential structures, as Heidegger does, Latina feminists find themselves fully engaged with concrete and particular aspects of the self's existence, what Heidegger regards as ontic characteristics that, despite playing an important role in his account, do not hold as much interest for him as ontological characteristics do. It is this full recognition, engagement, and elaboration of the situatedness of the self that make these accounts such powerful theories "in the flesh," as Moraga would say.

In my view, one of the reasons for the great power of Latina feminist phenomenologies is their description of the painful and conflicting moments of a life in-between. Here, rather than providing a list of all the differences between the two views, I would like to revisit a point that I made previously regarding a crucial difference between the accounts of selves described by Latina feminist phenomenologists and those of existential phenomenologists such as Heidegger, Sartre, and Merleau-Ponty: the selves described by Latina feminist phenomenologists do not find themselves "in-the-world" with the ease that traditional existential phenomenologists describe (Ortega 2001, 9).

Recall Anzaldúa's description of *la facultad* discussed in chapter 1. *La facultad* is the unconscious sense of what is helpful or hurtful in the environment, of what is behind everyday phenomena. According to Anzaldúa, it is an ability that is honed by marginalized selves given the continuous experience of fear, danger, and what she calls tears in the fabric of the everyday mode of consciousness that threaten one's freedom and resistance (Anzaldúa 1987, 39). A life of fear and danger at the borderlands, then, gives rise to a "sixth sense," the survival practice of *la facultad* (Anzaldúa 1987, 39). Paradoxically, while a life at the borderlands can give rise to this unconscious capacity, it can also lead to a more reflective everyday existence due to these everyday tears or ruptures of norms and practices. One of the main sources of anguish for the new *mestiza* is precisely that, unlike Heidegger's *Dasein*, she does not have a nonreflective, nonthematic sense of all the norms and practices of the spaces or worlds she inhabits. Thus, she does not always navigate her daily existence primarily in terms of know-how, as we have seen that Heidegger claims *Dasein* does. While she might indeed have a sense of norms from one culture, she may not have a sense of the norms across borders, thus having a very different experience than that described by phenomenologists such as Heidegger.[6]

Considering the fact that the multiplicitous self occupies various social locations and is immersed in various cultures, she might hold contradictory norms. In the case of someone who has crossed over to another culture, she might have an understanding of the norms and practices of the context with which she identifies, but not of those customary of her new surroundings.

She might consequently not feel at ease. "Ease" is the term that Lugones uses to explain the sense of familiarity the self has when fluent in the language, norms, and practices of her culture. This ease is the result of a shared history with others (Lugones 2003, 90). If we recall Anzaldúa's account of the new *mestiza*, it is clear that she is not at ease. Rather, a great deal of her experience in the borderlands is one of discomfort, distress, pain, and sometimes paralysis. Thinking about the experience of the new *mestiza* together with the Heideggerian description of *Dasein* reveals an important difference between the *new mestiza*'s experience and *Dasein*'s. The ruptures in her everyday existence, given her multiple social, cultural, and spatial locations, prompt her to become more reflective of her activities and her existence, what we may describe as a life of not being-at-ease.[7] While all selves may experience not being-at-ease occasionally, multiplicitous selves at the margins experience it continuously.

To illustrate the way in which norms and practices might be altered as one moves from one culture to another or as one crosses borders, I have previously used the everyday example of norms regarding utensils. While in Nicaragua, I followed the practice of eating cake with a spoon; this practice was disrupted in the United States, where I was expected to eat cake with a fork, thus causing me to be more reflective about this action (Ortega 2001, 10). There are numerous other examples of ruptures of everyday norms and practices that I experienced in the wake of my relocation to the United States.[8] Two other "everyday" examples that were nevertheless significant to me come to mind: greeting people by kissing them on the cheek and standing up to greet teachers as they enter the classroom. In the US cultural context to which I arrived, the aforementioned practices were not expected of me. As I was given a fork to eat cake, as I got looks of surprise or even uncomfortable and unfriendly looks when I approached people to kiss their cheek, and as I was looked at with mocking or confused glances while I stood up to greet teachers, I stopped relating to the world in terms of a practical orientation or know-how that, according to Heidegger, is the primary way in which the self is in the world. Suddenly, having to think about using a fork rather than a spoon to eat cake, having quickly to move my body away from people whom I was greeting, and quickly sitting down and realizing that I had not done what was expected of me brought about a host of reflections about my actions. I became more engaged in a mode of "knowing-that" and didn't feel familiarity with my environment, thus I was not being-at-ease.

In my view, then, being-at-ease is a function of one's ability to be nonreflective about everyday norms in the sense that Heidegger indicates and of having familiarity with the language, as well as sharing a history with people in the sense that Lugones describes. However, there are different senses of not being-at-ease, including what I regard a *thin* sense of not being-at-ease, the experience of minimal ruptures of everyday practices, and a *thick* sense of not being-at-ease, the experience of a deeper sense of not being familiar with norms, practices, and the resulting contradictory feelings about who we are given our experience in the different worlds we inhabit and whether those worlds are welcoming or threatening.

As noted earlier, I interpret the Heideggerian account of a practical, nonthematic everyday orientation to the world as indicating a sense of being-at-ease. This is not to say that in the Heideggerian account human beings are always being-at-ease. Heidegger provides an important account of instances when equipment breaks down and the self engages in a more thematic and reflective stance (Heidegger 1962, 102–107 [72–76]). In addition to providing discussions related to the breaking down of equipment, he provides elaborate descriptions of more existentially profound moments that include anxiety, being-toward-death, and resoluteness. My point, however, is to note that the experiences of the selves described by Anzaldúa, Lugones, and other Latina theorists include a lived experience of constantly not being-at-ease due to the numerous ruptures or tears of everyday norms and practices, the numerous deeper existential moments that they experience, the confusions and contradictions about their selves, and the unwelcoming, threatening nature of their experiences given their race, class, gender, sexual orientation, ability, ethnicity, and other social identities.

The anxiety that Heidegger describes can itself be considered a rupture in the sense that Anzaldúa describes—anxiety disrupts *Dasein*'s existence under the mode of the "they"—and thus we can see the importance of this type of experience in both the Heideggerian and the Anzaldúan accounts. Yet the experience of the selves described by Latina feminists shows a life of constant ruptures and a persistent breaking down of equipment, both in terms of everyday norms and practices and in terms of deeper existential and societal issues. While Heidegger does consider the disruption of everyday practices and existential moments prompted by anxiety, his account would be enhanced by the recognition of and engagement with the experiences in a life of constant ruptures prompted by marginalization and a life at the borders and borderlands—ruptures that Anzaldúa, Lugones, and other Latina feminists so vividly describe.

The selves described by Latina feminists continually experience not being-at-ease or tears in the fabric of everyday experience while performing practices that for the dominant group are, for the most part, nonreflective, customary, and readily available—what Heidegger calls "ready-to-hand."[9] *Los atravesados* are constantly having such ruptures, as well as deeper experiences of alienation, of not feeling at home, of questioning their very sense of self. Existentialist phenomenological accounts such as Heidegger's, Sartre's, and Merleau-Ponty's do not fully capture their everyday experience.[10] While existential phenomenologists have not written extensively about the importance of the kind of knowledge that arises out of such conditions of alienation and marginalization, writers such as Anzaldúa connect this life experience of the marginalized with *la facultad*.[11]

Even though it is necessary to realize the importance of the fact that multiplicitous selves continually experience a life of not being-at-ease, it should be noted that a life of complete being-at-ease is not necessarily what writers such as Anzaldúa, Lugones, and Heidegger would find desirable. It would be completely misguided to suggest that a life of being-at-ease is the goal of these thinkers. We have already seen that even Heidegger, who provides an analysis of being-in as a nonreflective orientation in the world connected to our practical use of equipment, is deeply interested in bringing to light the way in which the "they," or the everyday mode of *Dasein* that provides familiarity with one's environment, is problematic. Heidegger is thus interested in the possibilities of modifying that everyday mode so as to include a life that allows for authentic choice.

Despite her gripping, sorrowful descriptions of the difficulties of life in the borderlands, Anzaldúa recognizes the creative potential of a life of not being-at-ease. Lugones agrees with Anzaldúa, since complete being-at ease "tends to produce people who have no inclination to travel across 'worlds' or no experience of 'world' traveling" (Lugones 2003, 90). Lugones does not endorse such a life because of her belief in the importance of the experience of world-traveling in its connection to self-understanding and possibilities of resistance. Similarly, Heidegger sees this life as an impediment to authentic existence.[12] As we shall see in chapters that follow, an in-depth analysis of Lugones's view of world-traveling reveals not only challenging issues regarding the status of the self that travels worlds but also of the ways in which world-traveling itself might be subject to the negative characteristics associated with the "they," or the everyday way of being of *Dasein*.

Considering insights from the Heideggerian phenomenological view of self along with Latina feminist phenomenological accounts reveals a number of intersections between these views—a self in the making, a sense of "throwness," the importance of the mood of anxiety, a rejection of the subject/object dichotomy, and a strong sense of situatedness and sociality. There are also important differences related to the ontological as well as political scopes of these writers' projects. The difference that I have emphasized here, however, is that selves like the new *mestiza* and others described by Latina feminists are constantly experiencing ruptures of everydayness or disruptions in the fabric of their daily lives and do not inhabit the world in a nonthematic or nonreflective way; these selves are continually not being-at-ease. A *thin* sense of not being-at-ease is the result of ruptures of everyday norms of practices that are usually transparent and taken for granted by those familiar with the culture and environment, while a *thick* sense of not being-at-ease arises from ruptures in everyday norms, practices, and experiences that are more meaningful for the self and thus lead to existential crises regarding identity and other features of the self. This *thick* sense of not-being-at-ease becomes even more pronounced when the self is in a condition of marginalization and oppression. A recognition of both the similarities and differences between these phenomenological accounts of self is of great importance in order not only to provide a comparative analysis of phenomenological views but also to provide more robust phenomenological descriptions of selfhood that are better attuned to issues of multiplicity and marginalization.

Multiplicitous Selfhood as Being-between-Worlds and Being-in-Worlds

The points of convergence and the key difference between the selves described by Latina feminists and the Heideggerian phenomenological account of *Dasein* are helpful in developing a richer phenomenological conception of selfhood. Following the insights from Latina feminists and Heidegger's view of self, I propose a conception of in-between, multiplicitous selfhood. Like the new *mestiza* and *Dasein*, the multiplicitous self is a self in process or in the making. This self is situated in specific material circumstances that include particular histories, occupies multiple positionalities or social identities, and, like the new *mestiza*, is an in-between self.

Consider Anzaldúa's description of the new *mestiza*:

Being a mestiza queer person, una de las otras is having and living in a lot of worlds, some of which overlap. One is immersed in all the worlds at the same time while also traversing from one to the other. The mestiza queer is mobile, constantly on the move, a traveler, callejera, a cortacalles. Moving at the blink of an eye, from one space, one world, to another, each world with its own peculiar and distinct inhabitants, not comfortable in any one of them, none of them "home," yet none of them "not home" either. (Keating 2009, 141)

And Lugones's description of the "outsider," which echoes Anzaldúa:

> The outsider has necessarily acquired flexibility in shifting from the mainstream construction of life where she is constructed as an outsider to other constructions of life where she is more or less "at home". . . . One can travel between these "worlds" and one can inhabit more than one of these "worlds" at the same time. I think that most of us who are outside the mainstream of, for example, the United States dominant construction or organization of life are "world" travelers as a matter of necessity and of survival. It seems to me that inhabiting more than one "world" at the same time and traveling between "worlds" is part and parcel of our experience and our situation. (Lugones 2003, 77, 88)

What stands out in these descriptions of selves is their condition of liminality, their in-betweenness. They inhabit more than one world and have to travel constantly across worlds.[13] The intertwining of insights from Latina feminists and Heidegger leads me to think of the multiplicitous self as being-between-worlds and being-in-worlds, terms meant to capture the ontological and existential dimension of Heidegger's understanding of the self, the multiplicity underscored by Latina feminists' descriptions of selves at the borders and borderlands, as well as what I have here referred to as Anzaldúa's *mestizaje* of multiplicity and oneness.

Multiplicity

Being-in-worlds is to be understood as a key existential characteristic of the multiplicitous self and is meant to capture this self's complexity. While Anzaldúa employs both the terms "plurality" and "multiplicity," I prefer multiplicity and use the term in its adjectival form, thus referring to a multiplicitous self. What I regard as a possible distinction between the terms "multiplicity" and "plurality" informs different ways of interpreting the self. In my view, the term "plurality" suggests multiple selves, while the term "multiplicity" suggests a complexity associated with one self. In an effort to follow what I have here called Anzaldúa's *mestizaje* of multiplicity and oneness, I appeal to a multiplicitous self as being-in-worlds and being-between-worlds, a singular self occupying multiple social locations and a condition of in-betweenness.

To say that being-in-worlds is an existential characteristic of the multiplicitous self is to say that the multiplicitous self has a sense of how she fares in worlds—it constitutes an existential dimension of this self. Here I do not mean to provide a list of all the existential or ontological characteristics of the multiplicitous self in the way Heidegger does with *Dasein*. Rather, I would like to underscore the existential dimension of the life of the multiplicitous self by rethinking Lugones's idea of "world" with the aid of Heideggerian existential phenomenology. I also wish to enhance Heidegger's ontological project by way of both Anzaldúa's and Lugones's thinking. Thus, while the multiplicitous self inhabits one world in the traditional sense (the collection of entities in the world), this self is in many worlds, worlds understood in light of both Lugones's view of "world" and Heidegger's understanding of being-in.

For Lugones, a "world," a term that she writes in quotes in order to differentiate her definition of the notion from the traditional meaning of it, refers to an actual world rather than a possible world.[14] In her view, it does not mean the totality of things in the world, a worldview, or a culture. In Lugones's sense, "world" can be understood as a place inhabited by "flesh and blood people"; an actual society, given its dominant or nondominant culture's description and construction of life in terms of the relationships of production, gender, race, sexuality, class, politics, and so forth; a construction of a small portion of society; an incomplete, visionary, non-utopian construction of life; a traditional construction of life (Lugones 2003, 87); or at the very least "a community of meaning" (144) in which meanings are a result of what Lugones calls an "ongoing transculturation, interworld influencing and interworld relations of control and resistance to control" rather than determined by ossified cultural codes (Lugones 2003, 26). A world in this sense is thus incomplete, and it is not monistic, homogeneous, or autonomous (Lugones 2003, 26). Worlds are intertwined and stand in relation to powers with each other (Lugones 2003, 21). As I understand Lugones's notion of "world," worlds are always open to interpretation and reinterpretation. She does not provide a fixed definition of the term but attempts to give us a sense of its various meanings.

Adding an ontological dimension to Lugones's understanding of "world" by way of Heidegger's account of being-in-the-world brings to light the fact that the world understood as an actual society given dominant or nondominant construction of life, constructions of a small portion of society, visionary constructions of life, communities of meaning, and so forth, is inextricably linked to the self and vice versa. That is, when we think about worlds—here I do not place quotation marks around the term although I agree with Lugones that the term does not refer to the collection of all things—we have to think about the ways in which such worlds are connected to the self and the ways in which the self *is* in them, the way in which the self fares in them. Losing this connection allows for the possibility of not only understanding the self as apart from worlds but also of providing theories that are not connected to lived experience. Given the importance of lived experience for writers such as Anzaldúa and Lugones, I would like to underscore the existential and ontological dimension of the self. Being-in-worlds captures such a dimension as well as the multiplicity of the self that both of these writers have brought to light.

As multiplicitous, the self has various social identities and the possibility of being in various worlds. For example, as multiplicitous, I am in many worlds—the Latino world, the Nicaraguan world, the lesbian world, the Latina lesbian world, the Spanish-speaking world, the academic world, among others, these worlds crisscrossing and overlapping in my many experiences. While I am in specific spaces, say the university where I work, I am being-in-worlds in the sense that I have a sense of how I, as a Latina, fare in that space. Moreover, I am also in the world of middle-class white Clevelanders, the world of primarily white students, the world of teachers, and so forth. As noted previously, for Anzaldúa the self is in various worlds while, at the same time, traveling from world to world. The multiplicitous self is thus also being-between-worlds and is deeply aware of the experience of liminality. These notions of being-in-worlds and being-between-worlds are not to be understood as being static or excluding one another. I can be in various worlds and at the same time be in-between-worlds. I might be in some worlds at a particular time in my experience and then have travel to other worlds. Yet I constantly remain in-between some worlds. How long I stay in worlds and how much world-traveling I engage in is contingent not only on my choices but also on my particular social identities and locations and the social, cultural, historical, and economic relations that influence those locations and my experience of them. From a Foucauldian perspective, we could say that the life of the multiplicitous self as she inhabits some worlds and travels to others is always permeated with relations of power that subject her and discipline her.

Going back to the example of my workplace, I feel deeply this being-between-worlds as I occupy a space and participate in norms that are part of a world of primarily middle-class whites who might not have any sense of the Latino world in general. Consequently, I might occupy the same spatial location but have different ways of being in that location because I have access to different worlds. As a Latin American born in Nicaragua, I occupy this location differently than a white US-born citizen does. My experience might include apprehension or worries about not understanding the norms and practices associated with the particular location. I might experience different senses of not being-at-ease.[15] My experiences while being a teacher in a primarily white environment not only include ruptures of everyday practices of teaching and norms and conventions associated to life in the Midwest but also experiences connected to racism, sexism, and homophobia that deeply disrupt my sense of self and well-being.

Since there is overlapping between worlds, some of these worlds will share norms, meanings, and points of view, while in other cases there will be minimal overlapping. Power relations at work in these various worlds are established differently and construct the multiplicitous self in various ways. They will also inform whether the self has to world-travel constantly. Even when "crossing," when traveling to another world, the multiplicitous self is in-between. Moreover, as Ofelia Schutte writes in her powerful essay on cultural alterity and North-South cross-cultural communication, there will be cases in which there will be incommensurability, and some elements will be lost in cross-cultural communication (Schutte 1998). In other words, something might be lost or misunderstood as we travel from world to world. Complete translation is not possible, and the multiplicitous self will in some sense always be an outsider.

Occupying certain spatial locations connects the multiplicitous self to different worlds. Yet spatial location is not the main element involved in being-in-worlds. As I have noted, the sense of "world" that I am appealing to is informed by Lugones's definition as well as the Heideggerian understanding of the term that, as we will see, is connected to the idea of dwelling and existing. It is not merely concerned with ontic material conditions but extends to the ontological or ways of being of the self. That is, dwelling has both an ontological and ontic dimension and thus conveys a sense of how the self *is* and a sense of the self's connection to specific material conditions. Consequently, I might not be actually residing in a particular place or experiencing a specific culture, say Managua and aspects of Nicaraguan culture, to have access to the world of Nicaraguans, but I might have access to this world given my previous experience with it. Or I might have access to the world of Latinas given that being Latina is one of my social identities.[16] Being-in-worlds is meant to convey the condition of the multiplicitous self as being able to inhabit as well as access various worlds. It is also intimately connected to being-between-worlds, given that this self is not always in one world or another and, instead, can be in-between worlds to different degrees, sometimes ready to cross over—but even while crossing, remaining in in-betweenness and liminality. For many multiplicitous selves, being-between-worlds is in fact an everyday way of being, as the borderlands, according to Anzaldúa, can become a "home" to the new *mestiza*. In other words, for many multiplicitous selves, their condition of in-betweenness is highlighted and felt acutely given different conditions of marginalization. It might also be highlighted through what I regard as geographic ruptures—sudden movements to other lands because of economic, cultural, or political conditions, movements that might turn multiplicitous, in-between selves into fugitive selves, exilic selves, wounded selves—selves marked primarily by these geographic ruptures that, of course, are not merely related to the land and earth but to our flesh and blood, to our very being. Multiplicitous selves, then, are being-between-worlds and being-in-worlds in different ways. In what follows I would like to elaborate on the notion of *being-in-worlds* vis-à-vis Heideggerian phenomenology.[17]

Being-in-Worlds and Heidegger's Phenomenology

Since in my description of the multiplicity of the self I use terminology inspired by the Heideggerian notion of being-in-the-world, I would like to differentiate my position of being-in-worlds from Heidegger's famous concept of being-in-the-world, as my reading of Latina feminist phenomenology has influenced the way in which I approach this concept. For Heidegger, being-in-the-world is a rich concept encompassing the characteristics of "worldhood," "being-in," as well as the entity that is "in-the-world." Being-in-the-world is not simply an aggregate of these elements but what Heidegger considers a unitary phenomenon that stands as another name for human being, or *Dasein* (Heidegger 1962, 78 [53]). This phenomenon is supposed to capture the rich experience of *Dasein* as a whole. Heidegger, however, breaks it down and provides an explanation of the separate elements of worldhood, world, and being-in.

"World" in the Heideggerian sense does not mean the totality of things in the world that are objectively there and not as functional equipment (ontic sense). It does not mean the being of entities that one may find in a particular world—such as the world of the mathematician, the world of the teacher (ontological sense). "World" in the Heideggerian sense is to be understood in yet another ontic sense as "that 'wherein' a factical Dasein as such can be said to live" (1962, 93 [65]), an understanding that captures the interrelatedness between self and world. Thus, "world" does not simply signify an objective world.[18] According to Heidegger, "world" is where *Dasein* dwells. In other words, the term "world" already involves the sense of the way in which human beings exist in the world by way of their activities and choices, and the sense of how they fare in the world that arises from such activities and choices.

I see this Heideggerian understanding of world as dwelling, which captures the crucial relatedness of self and world, as connected to the way in which Latina feminists such as Lugones and Anzaldúa understand the notion, given that they are also interested in giving an account of a relational, situated self. As Heidegger says, " 'world' may stand for the 'public' we-world, or one's 'own' closest (domestic) environment" (1962, 93 [65]). Lugones and other Latina feminists, however, are more specific as to what these domestic environments are, and they add particularities and political considerations to them. As we have seen, Lugones considers worlds as actual societies and communities of meaning connected to the production of and the relationship between gender, race, sexuality, class, politics, and so forth. I think it is helpful to read Heidegger through Lugones here. That is, when engaging with Heidegger's account of dwelling in the world with Lugones's philosophy in mind, we need to consider specific issues connected to the intersection or intermeshedness of gender, race, sexuality, class, politics, ability, and so on, and how such social locations inform the way we *are* in worlds.

Another element that is encompassed by the Heideggerian account of being-in-the-world is being-in. With this understanding of being-with, Heidegger is moving beyond the dichotomy of subject and object, leaving the account of an isolated substantial I, as well as providing a novel way of understanding the way human beings are in the world. Rather than occupying space the way a book does inside a bag or tables do inside a room, being-in is connected to the self's activities when existing in the world, activities that, as previously noted, have a nonreflective or nonthematic practical orientation toward objects in the world (Heidegger 1962, 107 [77]). Heidegger states,

> Being-in is not a 'property' which Dasein sometimes has and sometimes does not have, and *without* which it could be just as well as it could with it. It is not the case that man 'is' and then has, by way of an extra, a relationship-of-Being towards the 'world'—a world with which he provides himself occasionally. . . . Because Dasein is essentially an entity with Being-in, it can explicitly discover those entities which it encounters

> environmentally, it can know them, it can avail itself of them,
> it can *have* the 'world' (84 [56]) . . .
>
> Being-in-the-world has always dispersed itself or even split
> itself up into definite ways of Being-in. The multiplicity of
> these is indicated by the following examples: having to do with
> something, producing something, attending to something and
> looking after it, making use of something, giving something up
> and letting it go, undertaking it, accomplishing, evincing, inter-
> rogating, considering, discussing determining. . . . All these ways
> of Being-in have concern as their kind of Being . . . (83 [57])

Heidegger thus effectively redefines what being *in* the world means for
humans. We are not objects standing next to other objects inside a room—
rather, as humans, we are always situated, living our lives through a series
of choices and practical interactions with things that are available to us and
interacting with other people.

This Heideggerian sense of being-in is integral to my conception of
being-in-worlds, since I understand multiplicitous selves as always connected
to things and in relation with selves in the world. I also take multiplicitous
selves as having a practical orientation toward objects. Nevertheless, as noted
earlier, selves as described by Anzaldúa, Lugones, and other Latina feminists—multiplicitous selves that are marginalized—might not find themselves primarily nonreflectively and practically oriented toward objects in
the way that Heidegger describes. His understanding of being-in does not
fully capture their experience, an experience of recurrent thin and thick
senses of not being-at-ease due to constant ruptures of everydayness. While
Heidegger's description of *Dasein* highlights a sense of being-at-ease resulting
from a practical orientation in the world guided by the nonreflective use
of equipment that is "ready-to-hand," multiplicitous selves such as the new
mestiza and the world-traveler experience an arduous life of not being-at-ease
in the worlds that they travel to. Inspired by Heidegger, I describe these
selves as experiencing multiple instances of un-readiness-to-hand and a certain not-being-with or an inability to have encounters with others or to be
recognized by others. However, not being-at-ease might be constructive as it
prompts traveling to other worlds and thus can lead to richer experiences. As
noted earlier, even the Heideggerian account that explains *Dasein* as having
familiarity with the environment includes a discussion of the way in which
anxiety plays a crucial role in *Dasein's* existence by serving as a wake-up
call from a life of being-at-ease under the mode of the "they." Being-at-ease
might be a welcomed way of life, but it is also an avoidance of change and

transformation. A self that is being-between-worlds and being-in-worlds might experience different levels of being-at-ease depending on the many worlds that she is in, the different degrees to which such worlds intersect, the power relations organizing personal and structural components affecting the self's experiences, and the reception of the self's various social identities.

The extent to which a multiplicitous self is being-at-ease in the different worlds is deeply important. Even though all of us are multiplicitous selves, our experiences are greatly affected by relations of power influencing the construction, understanding, and regulation of our various social identities. Not all of us will experience the type of "intimate terrorism" that Anzaldúa describes. Even though all of us are being-between-worlds and being-in-worlds, our experiences in various worlds will differ. We cannot forget the disparity in the experience of a multiplicitous self that occupies dominant social locations and that of a multiplicitous self who is at the margins and is oppressed. While it is certainly the case that all of us will experience breaks in our everyday practices—we will feel uneasiness, anxiety, and even "intimate terrorism" at some point in our lives—there are multiplicitous selves whose lives are marked by these feelings given various economic, global, cultural power disparities and given the key fact that they remain in-between worlds.

Intersectional, Flexible, and Tactical Selfhood

So far I have described the multiplicitous self in terms of being-in-worlds and being-between-worlds. In this section, I describe this self in light of the important notion of intersectionality introduced by women-of-color writers. Recognition of the multiplicity of the self requires an understanding of the complex ways in which the self's various social identities intersect or intermesh, recognizing the manner in which different axes of oppression are intertwined, and considering this self's flexibility. The multiplicitous self is intersectional, flexible, and tactical, and needs to be understood by way of an intersectional approach.

Intersectionality has a rich history even before the 1980s, when Kimberlé Crenshaw coined the term and Patricia Hill Collins made it key in her influential account of black feminist thought, a group-based collective standpoint theory inspired by the lived experience, forms of knowledge, and appeals to justice of African American women (Gines 2011, 2014; Crenshaw 1989; Collins 2008). Although not identified by its current name, intersectionality, the way in which experience is informed by the intersection of multiple axes of oppression (e.g., gender, race, sex, class, etc.)

is at the heart of various black women's speeches and writings. Consider the words of Sojourner Truth, Ana Julia Cooper, and later writers such as Frances Beale, who discusses her "double jeopardy" as black and female, and Deborah King, who examines her "multiple jeopardy" (Beale 1995; King 1995). Intersectional approaches are also found in various writings by Latinas, including early works by Chicanas (García 1997), essays by contributors from the influential anthology *This Bridge Called My Back, Writings by Radical Women of Color* (Moraga and Anzaldúa 1983), and *Anzaldúa's Borderlands/La Frontera* (1987). In my view, Anzaldúa's discussion of her lived experience in the borderlands stands as one of the most important intersectional analysis offered by a Latina feminist. Yet we are in need of more research on intersectional approaches in early Latina feminist writings so as to acknowledge their important contributions in this area.

While various women of color write about their lived experience guided by an intersectional approach, Crenshaw coined the term. Her early analysis of antidiscrimination law and feminist and antiracist activism brings to light the way in which women of color become invisible due to a reliance on a "single axis" approach (Crenshaw 1989, 1995). In her groundbreaking monograph on black feminist thought, Collins elaborates on intersectionality; defines it as "particular forms of intersecting oppressions, for example, intersections of race and gender, or sexuality and nation"; and claims that the intersectional paradigm "reminds us that oppression cannot be reduced to one fundamental type, and that oppressions work together in producing injustice" (2008, 21). Collins thus brings to the fore the intersection of the different axes of oppression.

Recent analyses of the notion of intersectionality by Lugones and Hames-García call for "intermeshedness" and "blending" rather than intersectionality. They are critical of the notion of intersectionality because they believe that it is being applied beyond the original context in which it was introduced, that of antidiscrimination law (Hames-García 2011, xi; Lugones 2007, 2014). More important, they also explain that appeals to intersectionality assume the separation of the different axes of oppression (Lugones 2014, 75). Consequently, they opt for the intermeshedness and blending of social identities to emphasize that the axes of oppression are to be understood as mutually constituted (Hames-García 2011, 10). As Hames-García puts it,

> Indeed, any adequate theory of social identity must be able to account for multiplicity, understood as the mutual constitution and overlapping of simultaneously experienced and politically significant categories such as ability, citizenship, class, ethnic-

ity, gender, race, religion, and sexuality. Rather than existing as essentially separate axes that sometimes intersect, social identities blend, constantly and differently, expanding one another and mutually constituting one another's meanings. (13)

Hames-García rightly warns us against committing the usual mistake of providing additive analyses of identity. Such additive analyses of identity suffer from what feminists regard as the "ampersand problem," the view that social identities are separable (Spelman 1988, 114–132). In my view, however, not all those appealing to intersectionality assume that the axes of oppression are separable. As Collins states, "As a heuristic device, inter-sectionality references the ability of social phenomena such as race, class, and gender to *mutually construct* one another" (1998, 205; my emphasis). An appeal to intersectionality is not necessarily tied to the assumption of the separability of race, class, gender, sexuality, ability, and other identities and axes of oppression.

Yet it is important to recognize that there have been various other criticisms of intersectionality, including the claim that the concept is too vague and that it lacks a defined methodology (Nash 2008). As Gines points out, however, there are still important reasons to continue appealing to the notion of intersectionality within philosophy, especially when considering the way in which intersectionality can expand our thinking regarding ques-tions concerning existence, freedom, facticity, situation, and oppression and can take us beyond the traditional philosophical resources that are generally derived from the standpoint of white male thinkers (2011, 281). It is my view that it is not necessary to have a closed description of the notion of intersectionality or of the way in which it is to be applied methodologically for it to continue to be helpful in our understanding of the interactions between various social identities. I thus continue to appeal to the notion of intersectionality and, as do Collins and others, I see it as a heuristic device. While Collins also recognizes that there might be problems with the appeal to intersectionality and that we thus need to be careful with its use, she notes that "intersectionality provides an interpretive framework for thinking through how intersections of race and class, or race and gender, or sexuality and class, for example, shape any group's experiences across specific social contexts" (1998, 208). Intersecting axes of oppression shape both individu-als and groups and need to be analyzed if we are to attain a richer, more complex vision of experience. I appeal to the notion of intersectionality while being mindful that different axes of oppression cannot be assumed to be separable and that social identities are intermeshed.[19]

The experience of the multiplicitous self as being-between-worlds and being-in-worlds is informed by intersecting social identities. Consequently, the multiplicitous self needs to be understood as decentered That is, none of this self's identities is a priori central or most important—there is not one primary identity that negates, undermines, or makes irrelevant other identities. Many Latina feminist phenomenologists, including Anzaldúa, Lugones, and Barvosa, appeal to the self's decenteredness given that they recognize the importance of the self's multiplicity. When considering this issue in an interview, Anzaldúa asks, "Can I be both the academic intellectual person and also the streetwise person?" (Anzaldúa 2000, 141). She answers,

> Now people are integrating that desire not to compartmentalize into their lives, into everyday activities. But compartmentalization has been a way of life for so long—to be different people and even aware of it: life forcing us to be one person at the job, another at school, and yet another with our lesbian friends—that it feels really ambiguous to bring all those other identities with you and to activate them all. (141)

While recognizing the difficulty of honoring all of the self's identities, Anzaldúa also warns of the problem of making one identity the most prevalent, even if in different contexts. Nevertheless, despite understanding Anzaldúa's desire for an awareness of all of the self's various identities, my claim that not any one identity is a priori central does not mean that certain identities may not become more prominent in particular experiences.[20]

The multiplicitous self has multiple social identities in terms of race, gender, sexuality, class, ability, nationality, ethnicity, religion, and other social markers, and this self must negotiate such identities while being between-worlds and being-in-worlds. As a self in process or in the making, the multiplicitous self is continually engaged in these negotiations, which include sometimes having to strategically deploy certain identities in certain worlds. This ability to negotiate different identities in different contexts grants the self a flexibility that opposes the fixity of traditional conceptions of selfhood. Anzaldúa explains it best when she states,

> Only by remaining flexible is [the new *mestiza*] able to stretch the psyche horizontally and vertically. *La mestiza* constantly has to shift out of habitual formations; from convergent thinking, analytical reasoning that tends to use rationality to move

towards a single goal (a Western mode), to divergent thinking characterized by movement away from set patterns and goals and toward a more whole perspectives, one that includes rather than excludes. (1987, 79)

Various Latina feminist phenomenologists have interpreted this flexibility in different ways. While theorists like Paula Moya see it as a dangerous fluidity that negates the stability of the self and precludes the possibility of effective political action, others such as Alarcón, Sandoval, Lugones, and Barvosa understand it as part and parcel of the self and as a positive characteristic of the self's consciousness (Moya 2002, 82; Alarcón 1991; Sandoval 2000; Lugones 2003; Barvosa 2008).[21] Sandoval consequently describes new *mestiza* consciousness as a *differential* consciousness that enables shifts between ideological positions and serves like a clutch in a car, "the mechanism that permits the driver to select, engage, and disengage gears in a system for the transmission of power" (Sandoval 1995, 217–218; Sandoval 2000, parts 2 and 4). Lugones understands the shifts as world-traveling, and, as we shall see in the next chapter, as *self*-traveling. She also understands the self as a "plurality of selves" (Lugones 2003, 93). Barvosa understands this mobile subjectivity as important for political action (2008, 65).

Moreover, Latina feminist phenomenologists understand the multiplicity and the flexibility of the self differently when it comes to questions regarding fragmentation and integration. While some are quite comfortable in endorsing a "split subject," a self that is fragmented and that does not need to look for integration (Alarcón 1991; Schutte 1998; Sandoval 2000), others are less accepting of the idea that the self is fragmented for different reasons. For example, Lugones rejects the idea that the self is fragmented and sees the claim of fragmentation as deriving from the logic of purity (2003, 127). She also rejects the need to reduce heterogeneity to homogeneity and multiplicity to unity as part of this logic, which ultimately seeks to create a pure, modern subject with a vantage point that does not consider social location, affectivity, or embodiment (130). On the other hand, as we shall see in later chapters, Moya and Barvosa assign different values to the multiplicity of the self. Moya emphasizes its negative consequences and thus calls nonfragmentation a victory for women of color (2002, 95). Barvosa is more keenly aware of the positive aspects of multiplicity in political life and suggests the option of self-integration through a project of self-craft (2008, 175).[22] My own position is that the multiplicitous self experiences an existential continuity of experience despite its multiplicity. However, this does not mean that the multiplicitous self has necessarily to become fully

integrated. I leave open the possibility that this integration of the multiplicitous aspects of the self might not or cannot be possible or that the self
will not wish to integrate them.

The multiplicitous self as a self in process is flexible and decentered and
does not *necessarily* need to be fully integrated. In terms of social identities,
the multiplicitous self can shift or, as I prefer to see it, *highlight* different identities in different contexts. Of course, this highlighting of different
identities in different contexts is not merely a willful action that does not
have a connection to particular material circumstances. As embodied and
situated in specific locations with specific histories and relations of power,
the multiplicitous self tactically highlights different identities insofar as those
identities are real possibilities. That is to say, the multiplicitous self cannot
change identities indiscriminately. Even articles of clothing are restricted, as
certain garments would not fit our bodies and some would not be appropriate depending on weather conditions. As noted, this decenteredness and
flexibility of the self, however, does not mean that there cannot be an
identity that becomes more salient for the multiplicitous self at a particular
time in her life or in the context of some worlds.

Most important, this decenteredness and flexibility does not mean
that the multiplicitous self always has the opportunity willfully and tactically to deploy certain identities over others. Because the experience being
underscored here is that of marginalized members of society, in many cases
the multiplicitous self will not have the opportunity to highlight certain
identities, especially under conditions of extreme marginalization or when
such identities attempt to resist dominant norms. In various worlds the
marginalized are treated as invisible, "pliable, foldable," "file-awayable, classifiable," or disposable (Lugones 2008, 97). However, for Latina theorists
such as Anzaldúa, Lugones, Sandoval, and Barvosa, it is precisely in the state
of inhabiting the borderlands, in the state of liminality, of being-between-
worlds, that possibilities of resistance arise, precisely because it is while being
in-between that the multiplicitous self can recognize alternative visions of
identity and of worlds.

In sum, the multiplicitous self should not be understood by way of
additive analysis. Rather, this self has experiences shaped by the intersection/
intermeshedness of various social identities. I am not the sum of my social
identities—member of the middle-class + woman + Latina + professor +
other identities. The intersection and intermeshedness of these identities
continually informs my experiences as I am being-in-worlds and being-
between-worlds. Moreover, understanding the multiplicitous self as flexible
or "mobile" means recognizing this self's decenteredness, or not having an

a priori central identity. As multiplicitous, I have the ability to highlight different identities in a tactical way in different contexts, with the under-standing that in some cases, as Anzaldúa notes, that compartmentalizing is not always the best approach. As a Latina academic, I highlight my Latina identity more when I visit my parents and sister in Miami and less so in other contexts. Yet there are times when I need to embrace my complexity and multiplicity and highlight the multiple, sometimes conflicting, identi-ties and characteristics.[23] Like Anzaldúa, I am deeply aware that activating one main identity in particular contexts, the intellectual in the context of academia, the creative person in artistic contexts, and so on, is what is expected of those at the margins. And in some cases, it might be necessary as a matter of survival. However, doing so promotes not only blindness to our complexity as multiplicitous selves but also a dangerous fragmentation of our selves.

Let us then understand the multiplicitous self as an embodied, situ-ated self in process that is being-in-worlds and being-between-worlds and that is characterized by intersectionality and flexibility. These characteristics of the multiplicitous self capture the insights learned from Latina feminist phenomenological accounts of self provided by Anzaldúa, Lugones, and others, accounts that highlight the multiplicity and complexity of selves in the borderlands. As we have seen, although the Heideggerian account of self as *Dasein* indeed shares many characteristics with Latina feminist phe-nomenological views and can be useful to further develop these positions, it still falls short due to its lack of attention to those living in-between worlds. It is my hope that my account of multiplicitous selfhood as being-in-worlds and being-between-worlds captures Latina voices that disclose the complexity and multiplicity of the self and that urge us to pay attention to a lived experience that paradoxically points to multiplicity and oneness.

Oneness as Existential Continuity

Having focused on multiplicity, I now turn to the question of oneness. When considering the oneness of the multiplicitous self, I immediately think of the obvious fact that this self is embodied and consider this embodi-ment in terms of what Merleau-Ponty calls a *synthesis*, a "nexus of living meanings," rather than an assemblage of body parts that are mechanically coordinated (2003, 175). Anzaldúa's discussion of the new *mestiza* is a compelling reminder of the bodily dimension of the self as she describes experiencing the psychic unrest as well as bodily pain from her life in the borderlands. She even states that writing is a "blood sacrifice" (Anzaldúa

1987, 73, 75). "You must plunge your fingers into your navel, with your two hands," she says, calling attention to the fact that we experience through the body (1987, 164). For her, the body does not merely represent a collection of organs; it is a link to the world. The oneness of the multiplicitous self, then, can be thought in terms of embodiment. Yet Anzaldúa herself makes the comment that "One's own body is not one entity" given that one's body is also all the different organisms living in it (Anzaldúa 2000, 158). Here I would like to think of oneness in a different way, in terms of the sense in which I can consider myself an "I" and in which I am aware of my own being, not only by way of my embodiment but also by way of the temporal dimension of my existence, what I regard as *existential continuity.*

What accounts for the oneness or continuity of the multiplicitous self is a key and complicated issue, especially when one is committed to a view that is mindful of multiplicity but rejects traditional accounts of subjectivity, which may appeal to notions such as a transcendental ego to explain the unity of experience. From the outset, I would like to be clear that an appeal to the oneness of the self is not an attempt to resuscitate a traditional type of subjectivity or to long for the unity of a Kantian tran-scendental ego that is outside experience and that makes experience possible. Instead of appealing to a perfectly unified self, I appeal to the continuity of experience that the multiplicitous self has, as multiplicitous and complex as this self is. This continuity of experience provides the multiplicitous self with a sense of being an "I" and an awareness of the self's own being. As such, it is an *existential* continuity. It allows for a sense of "oneness" and "ownness," despite the fact that the multiplicitous self occupies multiple locations and may thus identify with various social identities. While shifting from a discussion of social identity to a consideration of what it means for the multiplicitous self to experience the sense of being an "I," I would like to make a further connection between Latina feminist phenomenology and Heideggerian existential phenomenology. I appeal to Heideggerian notions to explain the oneness of the multiplicitous self, to show how the multi-plicitous self has a continuity of experience and a sense of being an "I."

Heideggerian notions of temporality and "mineness" are helpful onto-logical elements that allow us to understand the multiplicitous self's continu-ity of experience and thus to be concerned with her own being. Having a sense of a continuity of experience is key for the multiplicitous self, since not having such a sense of continuity would render this self's experiences as merely unrelated atomistic moments. The question of how to show the continuity of experience, of how to connect individual moments of experi-ence as a whole, so as to understand them as happening to one self, is a famous and difficult issue. As William Wilkerson notes, there have been two major common trends to explain such continuity: synthesis (Kant) and association (Hume) (Wilkerson, unpublished manuscript). However, given the problems with these two accounts, Wilkerson appeals to a different approach and is inspired by Henri Bergson's view that the whole precedes the parts. That is, rather than asking the question of how discrete parts can be experienced as a whole, we need to recognize that the whole is given first. A notable example of another philosopher who holds this view is Heidegger.

One way to understand this approach is by considering Heidegger's explanation of hearing the sound of a motorcycle. According to Heidegger, we first hear the motorcycle, not all the individual sounds that together make the overall sound (Heidegger 1962, 207 [163]). Although this example is used by Heidegger to show that humans are already in a world in which they have numerous practical connections to things that are part of an equipmental whole, it can provide a sense in which we first have a flow of experience rather than adding particular, discrete moments of this experience after the fact. The self has the experience and understands it as her own; discreet moments can be analyzed in a more theoretical way later. That there is this sense of continuity does not mean that particular experiences comprising this sense are perfectly unified, consistent, or fully integrated. As we will see, the self still experiences moments of ambiguity and contradiction.

In my view, the principal ontological element that accounts for the multiplicitous self's continuity of experience is temporality. Described by Heidegger as "the unity of a future which makes present in the process of having been," temporality is the key ontological element of the self (1962, 374 [326]). In Heidegger's discussion of this fundamental ontological characteristic, the past, present, and future—the three dimensions of time—are intertwined rather than understood in the traditional linear Aristotelian view as a sequence of "nows." Temporality makes it possible for the self to project toward the future while being in a particular present situation and being informed by a particular past, and it thus grounds the continuity of the present, past, and future. This phenomenon is not to be understood as being prior to experience but as coextensive with it. As Heidegger notes, "We therefore call the phenomena of the future, the character of the having-been, and the Present, the '*ectases*' of temporality. Temporality is not, prior to this, an entity which first emerges from itself; its essence is a process of temporalizing the unity of the ectases" (1962, 377 [329]).

Applying this Heideggerian sense of temporality to the multiplicitous self, we can understand this self as a temporal being that projects itself toward the future while at the same time being concerned with its present and being informed by its past, thus having a continuity of experience that makes it possible for it to be an "I." As noted, this temporality is not a feature over and above the self. It is part of the multiplicitous self's experience. Moreover, even though there is a prioritizing of the future as the self always projects herself toward the future, this notion of temporality is not a linear one in which the self is always understood as forward moving. Rather, there is an intertwining of the past, present, and future that is important for understanding the multiplicity of social identities informing the life of the multiplicitous self.

In virtue of this phenomenon of temporality, the multiplicitous self experiences a flow of experience that she can recognize as her own. This recognition that a stream of experience is understood as one's own, a way of being in which I experience events as happening to me or as mine, what Heidegger calls "mineness" (*Jemeinigkeit*), is yet another ontological feature that is key in understanding the oneness of the multiplicitous self. While I previously held that this ontological feature accounted for the self's "togetherness" (Ortega 2001), I now understand it as a way of being of the self that arises from the type of temporality described above.

The notion of mineness needs to be understood within the context of an ontological account that rejects overly materialistic and epistemic accounts of selves. Mineness has to do with the individual character of the self in the sense that it registers the self's awareness of its own being, or how the self is faring. Mineness thus captures the existential dimension of being an "I" that is always situated in particular contexts. According to Lawrence Hatab, mineness points to "the existential meaningfulness of Dasein's endeavors" (2000, 172). As he states, "Mineness is a contextual specificity of existential mattering that is not equivalent to an ego or egoism, or a metaphysical self, but simply those meanings indicated in first-person pronoun usages. The upshot of mineness is that being matters to each Dasein in its mode of existence" (2000, 17). Appealing to this ontological characteristic is not a call to the type of individuality that may be attributed to a Cartesian epistemic subject that has the possibility of finding itself as a *solus ipse*.[24] It does not preclude the way in which the self is relational and always connected to a social milieu. What mineness entails is one's experience of being aware of one's being in any particular circumstance, and thus it captures an existential dimension of the self. For example, as I sit here typing, I am aware of *my* own being and that it is me who is writing these words. In other words, as existing, making choices, and carrying out numerous activities, I am aware of myself and am also aware of how I am faring in the particular worlds I am in. It has to do with what Heidegger describes as *Befindlichkeit*, an immediate attunement rather than reflective sense of how we fare in the world.

The multiplicitous self that inhabits multiple social locations always has mineness or the awareness of how she is faring in particular worlds. Given that this self is being-between-worlds and being-in-worlds, like the new *mestiza*, she might have a sense of how she fares in multiple worlds, say the Latino world and the US white world. This self might experience a sense of ambiguity or contradiction considering her multiple social locations. Following Lugones's famous example, this self might feel playful in the Latino world but not in the Anglo world (2003, 86). There are numerous other examples connected to bi- or multicultural experiences that show ambiguity and contradiction, but this kind of ambiguity does not necessarily result from the fact that the multiplicitous self may be bi- or multicultural. It might have to do with daily facets of the multiplicitous self's experience, for example, seeing oneself as an assertive woman in some contexts but seeing oneself as not assertive in a male-dominated work environment. How does mineness play a role in these moments of ambiguity or contradiction?

Mineness is part of the self's experiences. The multiplicitous self has mineness as she is experiencing the sense of being playful in the Latino world; she also has mineness as she experiences the sense of not being playful in the US white world. The sense that it is my own being that is an issue remains in both cases. While, as we shall see in the next chapter, Lugones interprets this experience differently as pointing to what she calls an ontological pluralism or a plurality of selves, I take the experience as still pointing to a multiplicitous self, a self that can interpret itself differently in different worlds but that is still an "I" that experiences her own being as an issue. The complicated aspect of the experience is that in one context I am playful, and in another I am not playful, and thus there may arise a sense of confusion, ambiguity, or even contradiction about the type of person that I am. This is especially the case when the attribute or characteristic in question is considered central in one's character.

However, the sense of mineness remains despite the complexity of this situation. I am still aware of my own being both at times when I see myself as playful in one world and when I see myself as not playful in another world. It is when I entertain both interpretations at the same time, or when I am in one world understanding myself as playful but remembering myself as not playful in another world, that the confusion and contradiction arises. Yet mineness is still informing my experiences. The way to understand this latter case is that one attribute or aspect of my multiplicitous self is highlighted or enacted in one world but not in the other. This might be due to various reasons, including the manifold power relations that are at place in the different worlds. The point here is that while I am a multiplicitous self that is dealing with norms and practices of different worlds, I am still ontologically directed toward or concerned with *my* being, even while in the midst of ambiguities and contradictions that might arise from being-between-worlds and being-in-worlds and the traveling between various worlds.

But let's go back to the multiplicitous self and her contradictory experience of finding herself as having different attributes in different worlds (i.e., playful in one world, not playful in another). This experience complicates the idea that the self experiences a continuity of experience rather than having to actively connect experiences via some transcendental ego or another mechanism of association. The difficulty arises because the experience of the self as playful in one world but not in another may be seen as a break in the continuity of experience. This point might even lead to the view that there are different flows of experience and thus a plurality of selves, a playful self and an unplayful self. While, as we will see in the next chapter, theorists like Lugones seem to hold a view similar to this, this reading does not accurately assess the experience.

Rather than interpreting this experience as a break in continuity, it should be understood as an unsettling part of a complex flow of experience that includes disparate and contradictory elements. Thus I may be in the Latino world, in which the attribute of feeling playful is highlighted, and, at the same time, I am aware of my being seriously unplayful in the US white world. Yet these are all part of the same flow of experience in which the sense of mineness persists. Rather than a complete break in the continuity of my experience, we can understand the uneasiness, confusion, and feeling of contradiction that arise in this situation as a deeper instance of not being-at-ease in that world or a *thick* sense of not being-at-ease. The possibility of a radical break remains, however, depending on whether an experience or set of events is disruptive to one's sense of mineness and one's sense of having a continuous flow of experience.

In this case of having a thick sense of not-being-at-ease, which can be rather painful and confusing, the uneasiness has to do not only with not knowing the norms and not having a sense of shared history in this particular world (a thin sense of not being-at-ease) but with the additional experience of being confused as to the kind of person that I am—am I playful or am I not playful? This confusion arises from the fact that I hold memories of myself connected to the attribute in question while I have traveled to other worlds. Having these memories creates a deep sense of contradiction and confusion in the present experience of understanding myself as playful in the Latino world but not in the US white world. As described earlier, different attributes or aspects of the multiplicitous self, say playfulness, are highlighted more in some worlds than in others. While the experience is confusing and might even lead one to wonder about who one is—the playful person or the unplayful person—or to question ourselves, we are both. Yet these different attributes are highlighted or negotiated differently in different worlds.

This thick sense of not being-at-ease arises particularly in connection with attributes or characteristics that are considered important for the multiplicitous self. Even though, as pointed out previously, the multiplicitous self is mobile, flexible, tactical, and decentered, there are identities or characteristics of the self that may be regarded as more salient in one's life or as being indicative of one's self. Consequently, when those identities or traits are undermined in different worlds, there arises a sense of contradiction and confusion, even an existential crisis or, to use Anzaldúa's words, "intimate terrorism." As opposed to a thin sense of not being-at-ease, which involves ruptures in everyday norms and practices that complicate the multiplicitous self's experiences and lead to a more reflective being-in-worlds, not being-at-ease in a thick sense leads to existential dilemmas regarding one's sense of self or identity. While here I am differentiating between both thin and thick senses of not being-at-ease, I understand that these two senses might be intertwined in different contexts such that there is the possibility that continuous ruptures of everyday norms and practices might also lead to existential crises regarding one's identity.

It is important to point out, however, that the contradiction that arises in these situations involving the thick sense of not being-at-ease is not necessarily negative. If we think back to Anzaldúa's description of the new *mestiza*, we may recall that encountering contradictions may lead to productive or transformative moments. It may also lead to the realization that we can embody contradictory attributes without necessarily having to choose one or the other as being the defining feature of our self. We can be both playful and unplayful; encountering the contradiction does not have to lead to the view that we are multiple selves, a playful one and an unplayful one. Rather, various identities and characteristics of our self are highlighted in some worlds due to the different ways in which structures of power are organized or to the way in which we actively and tactically negotiate them given our circumstances. One of the features of *mestiza* consciousness, as Anzaldúa calls it, and differential consciousness, as Sandoval understands it, is precisely the ability to hold disparate, contradictory aspects of oneself at the same time, without having to reconcile, unify, or integrate them. Here we must remember the often-quoted words of Anzaldúa,

> The new *mestiza* copes by developing a tolerance for contradictions, a tolerance for ambiguity. She learns to be an Indian in Mexican culture, to be Mexican from an Anglo point of view. She learns to juggle cultures. She has a plural personality, she operates in a pluralistic mode—nothing is thrust out, the good the bad and the ugly, nothing rejected, nothing abandoned. Not only does she sustain contradictions, she turns the ambivalence into something else. (1987, 79)

Anzaldúa does not ignore or avoid the new *mestiza*'s complexity and multiplicity. We need to learn from her as we explore the experience of the multiplicitous self in all her facets, in her moments of uneasiness or in her moments of creativity and transformation. Despite this self's multiplicity, temporality and mineness allow for an existential continuity of experience that captures a sense of oneness despite the confusing, ambiguous, or contradictory moments of a life in-between—yet another instance of a *mestizaje* of multiplicity and oneness.

Through traveling to other people's "worlds" we discover that there are "worlds" in which those who are the victims of arrogant perception are really subjects, lively beings, resistors, constructors of visions, even though in the mainstream construction they are animated only by the arrogant perceiver and are pliable, foldable, file-awayable, classifiable.

—María Lugones

In the World through which I travel, I am endlessly recreating myself.

—Frantz Fanon

3

The Phenomenology of World-Traveling

From world to world I go. In some worlds I matter—I blossom. In others I am drenched with anxiety—I hide. As I cross, can I carry a bag of bones disclosing who I am? This one tells a story of a long time ago, of a time when "Hi" and "Where are you from?" made no sense. This other is from my ribcage—it was touched by my heart. Perhaps they will find me there; I will find me there. There are teeth in the bag, too—they speak "philosophy" and "I am well, thank you." I am those too.

As being-between-worlds and being-in-worlds, the multiplicitous self continually travels worlds. My account of world-traveling is deeply influenced by María Lugones's groundbreaking work, "Playfulness, 'World'-Traveling and Loving Perception," although it ultimately differs from Lugones's influential account (1987 and 2003, ch. 4).[1] World-traveling is not the travel done by those who go to distant lands to enjoy and consume the "exotic" and the "authentic" or to "eat some nice lobster, some nice local food . . . and become a tourist, an ugly, empty thing, a stupid thing" (Kincaid 1988, 12–17). This kind of travel is what Lugones calls a "middle-class leisurely individualized journey" (2003, 19). She states,

> I think that it is precisely the case that tourists and colonial explorers, missionaries, settlers, and conquerors do not travel in the sense I have in mind. That is, there is no epistemic shift to other worlds of sense, precisely because they perceive/ imagine only the "exotic," the "Other," the "primitive," and the "savage," and there is no world of sense of the exotic, the Other, the savage, and the "one in need of salvation" separate from the logic of domination. Those conceptions of others are inextricably connected to epistemic imperialism and aggressive ignorance. (2003, 18)

In the sense discussed in this chapter, however, world-traveling is a practice of both survival and resistance for multiplicitous selves in the margins. When practiced by members of dominant groups, it might also constitute an act of solidarity with struggles against oppression and injustice. Since marginalized, multiplicitous selves constantly have to world-travel, they might develop feelings of ambiguity, confusion, "schizophrenia" (Lugones 2003, 86), or as Anzaldúa vividly reminds us, feelings of "*loquería*, the crazies" (Anzaldúa 1987, 20).

Lugones defines world-traveling as "the experience of being different in different 'worlds,'" an "epistemic shift from being one person to being a different person," an "epistemic shift to other worlds of sense" (2003, 89, 18)—that is, world-travelers experience and understand themselves as different persons in different worlds.[2] For example, I experience myself as being a serious person when I am in the world of US whites and as playful when I am in Latino worlds, very much the experience that Lugones discusses. In her view, world-traveling suggests an ontologically problematic position that is nevertheless true to experience: a person is multiple selves and does not "*experience* an underlying 'I'" (Lugones 2003, 90). In her later writing, Lugones characterizes her position as "ontological pluralism," a view that she thinks is suggested by theories of oppression and the ways in which marginalized individuals can understand themselves differently in different realities (55). I understand Lugones's ontological pluralism as positing a multiplicity of selves as well as a multiplicity of worlds anchored in multiple realities.[3] In the introduction to *Pilgrimages*, she describes space as "multiple, intersecting, co-temporaneous realities" (2003, 16) and states, "I think that there are many worlds, not autonomous, but intertwined semantically and materially, with a logic that is sufficiently self-coherent and sufficiently in contradiction with others to constitute an alternative construction of the social" (2003, 20).

Even though the notion of world-traveling has been influential in feminism, there are no in-depth discussions of it in the literature. Following Lugones, interpreters appeal to world-traveling as a means to "cross-cultural, cross-racial loving" (2003, 78), but they fail to engage with the concept in a sustained manner. In this chapter I engage more fully with her important account of world-traveling and present a critical reading of this notion in the spirit of honoring many of the insights captured by Lugones's discussion. In the first section I analyze Lugones's view of world-traveling and her characterization of the world-traveler self in light of questions concerning her understanding of worlds and her appeal to a multiplicity of selves. In order to avoid the ontologically problematic assumptions that arise in her discussion, I propose an alternative understanding of world-traveling. Rather than constituting a shift from being one person to being a different person in different worlds, or what I understand as *self*-traveling, world-traveling is a practice in which the multiplicitous self has access to an opening or aperture to different worlds. This practice has an epistemic component in that the multiplicitous self can understand herself and different worlds in relation to the particular aspects of self and world that are highlighted or animated while traveling. Instead of being a multiplicity of selves, as Lugones claims, the world-traveler is better understood as a multiplicitous self, as described in chapter 2. I thus agree with Lugones's claim that the experience of world-traveling includes an epistemic shift to other worlds of sense, but I disagree that this shift entails a shift of self or the positing of a multiplicity of selves. My view captures the importance of the multiplicity that Latina phenomenologists like Anzaldúa and Lugones so powerfully theorize, but it does not posit ontological pluralism. My position is better described as an *existential pluralism* that recognizes both the individual and multiplicitous character of the self in terms of the way in which the self fares or *is* in different worlds.

In the chapter's second section I discuss the views on self and subjectivity proposed by Lugones after the original 1987 article on world-traveling, in particular, the notions of the curdled, mestizo self and active subjectivity so as to trace the movement of her visions of selfhood that culminates in her account of an active self that is "I → we" and can be considered "long and wide"—a resistant self that inhabits concrete spaces and is always "touching" or connected to others.[4] Like Anzaldúa, Lugones has a rich, complex understanding of the self that is attuned to both multiplicity and oneness. In her later thinking, however, she moves farther away from what she considers a logic of purity and domination that privileges individual choice and that takes intentionality as happening *within* the subject rather than *between* subjects. She consequently replaces "agents" with active subjects communally engaged in "tactical strategic intending" (2003, 219). We will see that while this latter explanation of active subjectivity engaged in "streetwalking theorizing" provides important layers to Lugones's vision of selfhood, questions regarding the nature of multiplicity, resistance, and world-traveling remain.

World-Traveling and the World-Traveler Self

Following insights from her own experience as an immigrant to the United States who finds herself traveling to what she calls "Anglo" worlds, Lugones offers a compelling Latina feminist phenomenology that discloses important insights about the lived experience of those in the margins. As she notes, her work constitutes a "pilgrimage" that presents "life history in the flesh" (2003, 4).[5] An important part of life history in the flesh is the practice of world-traveling. World-traveling stands as one of the most important contributions not only in her work but also in women of color feminism and feminism in general. Lugones notes that after writing "Playfulness, World-Traveling, and Loving Perception," she became aware of Janet Wolff's (1992) and Caren Kaplan's (1994) work on traveling. While Wolff concentrates on the exclusion of women in traveling, Lugones understands world-traveling as not restricted to women but to "all people who have been subordinated, exploited, and enslaved" (2003, 17). Lugones agrees with Kaplan's critique of discourses that hide the connection between domination and traveling, but she nevertheless continues to appeal to the notion, with the understanding that her vision of traveling involves epistemic shifts to other worlds of sense rather than tourism and colonialism, which lead to consumption, exotization, and oppression (2003, 16–20). Ultimately, Lugones is concerned with proposing world-traveling as a resistant practice that moves "against the grain" of oppression and allows for the play of multiple visions, since it requires "resistant, oppositional thoughts, movements, gestures among variegated heterogeneous aggregates of subjects negotiating a life in the tensions of various oppressing ⇔ resisting relations" (2003, 7).[6] World-traveling, along with other resistant practices that she proposes such as curdling (ch. 6) and streetwalker theorizing (ch. 10), is intended to resist what Lugones considers a "logic of purity" and oppression that calls for univocity, homogeneity, and an abstract understanding of space. As she states,

> Categorial understandings of oppressions; unilinear, univocal, unilogical understandings of history; and abstract understandings of space are all mechanisms that produce atomic understandings of social groups and block interworld and intraworld communication. I use worlds against the grain of atomic, homogeneous, and monistic understandings of the social in any of its dimensions. (2003, 26)

At the heart of Lugones's project is an account of self as multiple but not fragmented and a disclosure of the social as heterogeneous. As she says "*¡Qué bonita la coincidencia que no es azarosa! La relación íntima entre el abortar los mitos de un solo sentido y el romper espejos que nos muestran rotas, despedazadas*" (2003, 42).[7] In her view, it is only through this understanding of a multiple but nonfragmented subject and a view of the social as heterogeneous that it is possible to provide an account of resistance to dominant practices that is not merely reactive. Lugones calls for resistance as a transformative practice capable of disrupting structures of domination and for "taking up the nonscripted possibilities in the cracks in domination" (2003, 30).

World-traveling stands as one of the key practices introduced by Lugones that acknowledges the multiplicity of the self and the heterogeneity of the social. However, Lugones explains that while being true to the experience of outsiders, her account of world-traveling is also philosophically problematic. She states,

> In describing my sense of a "world," I mean to be offering a description of experience, something that is true to experience even if it is ontologically problematic. Though I would think that any account of identity that could not be true to this experience of outsiders to the mainstream would be faulty even if ontologically unproblematic. Its ease would constrain, erase, or deem aberrant experience that has within it significant insights into nonimperialistic understanding between people. (2003, 89)

One of the most powerful aspects of Lugones's discussion of world-traveling is precisely the way in which it accurately captures the experience of so many who find themselves traveling worlds and thus experience a confusion that women of color refer to "half-jokingly as 'schizophrenia'" (2003, 86).[8] I deeply appreciate Lugones's interest in providing a theory that captures this sense of confusion. Here Lugones indeed moves against the grain of a great number of Western philosophical treatments of the self that fail to capture the self's ambiguity, confusion, and even contradiction.[9] She offers a Latina feminist phenomenology that points to a lived experience that does not accord with standard philosophical understandings regarding the self or the world.

In order to better understand Lugones's account of world-traveling, I discuss two main reasons as to why her account of world-traveling may be "ontologically problematic." First, in traditional philosophical accounts, human beings are understood as being in one world and sharing that world rather than constantly traveling to different worlds or having different realities. Second, in such accounts, the self is understood as a unitary subject rather than the plurality of selves that Lugones claims. As she states, "The self is not unified but plural," and "I am a plurality of selves" (2003, 57, 93).

When considering the first reason why Lugones's view of world-traveling might be ontologically problematic or the view that questions a plurality of worlds, we need to keep in mind that her position is one that deviates from traditional philosophical understandings of the world as the sum of all things and from a monistic understanding of reality. Her view includes a conception of space as "multiple, intersecting, co-temporaneous realities" (2003, 16). As noted in the previous chapter, a world in Lugones's sense is not equivalent to a worldview, a culture, a utopia, or a possible world. Lugones states that a world can be a society given dominant or nondominant descriptions of the relationships of production, gender, race, sexuality, class, politics, and so forth; a construction of a small portion of society; an incomplete, visionary, non-utopian construction of life; a traditional construction of life; or at the very least "a community of meaning" (2003, 87, 144). In this view, meanings are a result of an "ongoing transculturation, interworld influencing and interworld relations of control and resistance to control" rather than determined by ossified cultural codes (2003, 26). Worlds in Lugones's sense are not monistic, homogeneous, or autonomous, and they are incomplete (2003, 26). Importantly, they are also intertwined and stand in a relation of power with each other (2003, 21). Lugones's account does not appeal to the view of the world as the sum of all things and does not take reality as one. Instead, she appeals to multiple worlds, and she rejects an "atomistic understanding of heterogeneous reality" or the position that these worlds are isolated units (2003, 16).

In giving up traditional understandings of world and of reality, Lugones places "outsider" selves in a position in which they can travel from world to world. This practice is vital in Lugones's account as it is intimately connected to the self's possibility of resistance against ossified codes, norms, and constructions that appeal to homogeneity and univocity. It is the key to the development of a resistant praxis. As she states in the introduction to *Pilgrimages*:

> The tension of being oppressed ⇔ resisting oppression "places" one *inside* the *processes* of production of multiple realities. It is from within these processes that the practice of shifting to different constructions, different spatialities, is created. One inhabits the realities as spatially, historically, and thus materially different: different in possibilities, in the connections among people, and in the relation to power. (2003, 17)

The self that is constructed as alien, as unwanted, as disposable in one world can travel to another world and find herself as resistant and as a constructor of new visions. According to Lugones, despite the multiplicity of worlds or worlds of sense, communication across and between worlds is possible, although very difficult and complex due to patterns of domination and power. It is precisely these possibilities of inter- and intraworld communication that Lugones wishes to highlight. The role of the multiplicity of worlds here is crucial as Lugones notes that the point of multiple worlds is to resist interlocking oppressions that build walls by way of ideological constructs (2003, 26). Instead, Lugones's project stresses that oppressions are intermeshed, selves are nonfragmented, and "no slice of reality can have univocal meaning" (2003, 28).

While Lugones's account calls for a multiplicity of co-temporaneous realities and thus an ontological pluralism of not only selves but realities, my account introduces an ontological element that makes it possible to see how the multiplicitous self can share specific spatial regions with others and also be in various worlds. As noted in the previous chapter, multiplicitous selves can occupy the same spatial location and yet have different senses of how they fare there. That is, we can occupy the same space, but given our different social identities, we will *be* in that space in many different ways depending on the dominant norms, practices, and relations of power at work. We can thus be in different worlds while occupying the same physical space (Ortega 2001, 11). My account, then, retains Lugones's understanding of worlds insofar as they provide multiple perspectives through which I can understand my experiences and my sense of self. I do not, however, see the multiplicitous self as being in multiple crisscrossing realities. While I do not endorse multiple realities, I attempt to capture the multiplicity of ways in which the self *is* being-in-worlds. I do not consider worlds as atomistic and thus not intersecting or crisscrossing. I take Lugones seriously in her attempt to avoid a position that leads to univocity and fragmentation. Being-in-worlds is meant to capture the phenomenological way in which the multiplicitous self *is* or fares in various overlapping worlds, and thus it has an important existential component.

The second reason as to why Lugones's view may be seen as ontologically problematic is that it posits a plurality of selves. Lugones states,

> Those of us who are "world"-travelers have the distinct experience of being different in different "worlds" and of having the capacity to remember other "worlds" and ourselves in them. We can say "That is me there, and I am happy in that "world." So, the experience is of being a different person in different "worlds" and yet of having memory of oneself as different without quite

having the sense of there being any underlying "I." When I can
say "that is me there and I am so playful in that 'world,'" I
am saying "that is *me* in that 'world'" not because I recognize
myself in that person; rather, the first-person statement is noninferential. (2003, 89)

For Lugones, the world-traveler self is different persons in different worlds;
there is no underlying "I"—that is, when seeing myself as playful and, at
the same time, remembering myself as not playful in a different world, I
do not infer that the "I" who is making the observation, remembering or
making the claim, is the same as the "I" about whom the claim is being
made. From the point of view of both traditional conceptions of selfhood
that privilege the "I" and agency as well as more contemporary phenomenological views of selfhood that reject the unified subject, Lugones's claim
is perplexing.

Lugones explains that the experience of world-traveling becomes more
difficult and confusing when an attribute that the self has in one world is
incompatible with an attribute that the self has in another world: "Sometimes the 'world'-traveler has a double image of herself and each self includes
as important ingredients of itself one or more attributes that are *incompatible* with one or more of the attributes of the other self: for example being
playful and being unplayful" (92). For Lugones, there is even more difficulty
when the attribute being discussed, in this case playfulness, is what she calls
"character central" (2003, 92).[10] Given that in her own example playfulness
is character central, it is not enough for her to feel at ease in that world so
as to start practicing being playful in that world in which she is an unplayful person. In fact, according to Lugones, becoming playful in that world
would be for her to become a contradictory being:

To the extent that there is a particularly good fit between that
"world" and her having that attribute in it, and to the extent
that the attribute is personality or character central, that "world"
would have to be changed if she is to be playful in it. It is not
the case that if she could come to be at ease in it, she would
be her own playful self. Because the attribute is personality
or character central and there is such a good fit between that
"world" and her being constructed with that attribute as central,
she cannot become playful, she is unplayful. To become playful
would be for her a contradictory being. (2003, 92)

To avoid this problem, Lugones makes the following suggestion: "I suggest that I can understand my confusion about whether I am or am not playful by saying that I am both and that I am different persons in different 'worlds' and can remember myself in both as I am in the other. I am a plurality of selves" (2003, 93). She thus states that world-traveling constitutes an "epistemic shift" from being a playful person in one world and an unplayful person in another world: "The shift from being one person to being a different person is what I call travel" (2003, 89). This shift may or may not be conscious and, as Lugones says, we might not even be aware that we are being different persons in different worlds.

In a previous critique of Lugones's view, I question her appeal to a plurality of selves, but this critique is based on Lugones's original 1987 essay on world-traveling (Ortega 2001). A reading of *Pilgrimages* (2003) as a whole, however, leads me to reflect further on her account of world-traveling. In the 2003 text, Lugones provides an introduction that is crucial to understanding the development of her view on selfhood from what we may call an early account of the world-traveler self to her later depiction of the self as an active subjectivity that is better understood as "I → we" and that can be thought as having a "highly attenuated" sense of agency (2003, 6). A consideration of the entire book shows not only the way in which Lugones develops her account of self but also the way in which she introduces explicit discussions of multiple realities and spatiality in her account of resistance. In other words, considering *Pilgrimages* as a whole allows us to see how her account of multiple realities or ontological pluralism is connected to her explanation of world-traveling selves.

In the essay "Structure/Antistructure and Agency under Oppression," first published in 1990, Lugones states,

> I give up the claim that the subject is unified. Instead, I understand each person as many. In giving up the unified self, I am guided by the experiences of bicultural people who are also victims of ethnocentric racism in a society that has one of those cultures as subordinate and the other as dominant. These cases provide me with examples of people who are very familiar with experiencing themselves as more than one: having desires, character, and personality traits that are different in one reality than in the other, and acting, enacting, animating their bodies, having thoughts, feeling the emotions, in ways that are different in one reality than in the other. The practical syllogisms that

they go through in one reality are not possible for them in the
other, given that they are such different people in one reality
than in the other. (Lugones 2003, 57)

While in the 1987 text on world-traveling Lugones describes the practice
as crucial, given that it is a praxis that allows for the shift from being different persons in different worlds, in this 1990 text, Lugones connects her
account of self to a more explicit vision of multiple realities, which she
will later develop further to a metaphysics of "multiple, intersecting, co-
temporaneous realities" (16). Thus the account of multiple worlds becomes
explicitly connected to an account of multiple realities, thus reinforcing a
vision of ontological pluralism in which there is a plurality of selves and
multiple realities.

     As noted previously, Lugones's appeal to a plurality of selves is deeply
connected to her political project of resistance. In this view, ontological
pluralism is necessary so that oppressed people can have the open-endedness
or the ability to know themselves in different realities in which they can be
and act differently than the alternatives offered in those worlds in which they
are oppressed and marginalized. It is necessary if the oppressed, marginalized
people are to envision different possibilities and are to become resistant—if
they are being-oppressed ⇔ resistant. Here the task of remembering one's
many selves becomes a "liberatory task" (2003, 59). Lugones consequently
prompts us to remember our experiences in other worlds so as to remind
ourselves that we are not crazy and can move beyond survival to resistance
(2003, 59).

     It is interesting to note that Lugones's account of world-traveling is
reminiscent of Anzaldúa's treatment of the self in that at one point Lugones
claims that the "I" is identified in "some sense as one and in some sense
as a plurality" (2003, 91), which is "truest to the experience of 'outsiders'"
(2003, 89). However, unlike Anzaldúa—who, as we have seen, sometimes
appeals to an inner self, a center, a nucleus, or a total self (even though
she does not mean by this a unified self in the traditional sense)—Lugones
does not make such appeals and does not explicitly explain why the self
can be identified as "in some sense one," except to say that there is an
"I" that is noninferential. Moreover, while in her later essays she strongly
appeals to spatiality and embodied experience, especially in the last three
chapters of *Pilgrimages*, she does not appeal to embodiment as a marker of
singularity. While Lugones does state that the self is one and many, thus
prompting interpreters such as Jen McWeeny to claim that her view is
somewhere between a strong and a weak pluralism, Lugones does not fully

engage this particular understanding of the self as being one and many (McWeeny 2010, 298).[11] Instead, she moves farther and farther from a consideration of the singular, individual aspect of the self and states, "The use of 'I' in much of this text and my own self-presentation as a streetwalker theorist have an arrogant cast to them that I am wary of" (2003, 226), and, as we shall see later, she develops the account of active subjectivity that has an attenuated sense of agency and a collective self, or "I → we," in which the "I" is always in company and looking for company (2003, 5, 227).[12]

Lugones recognizes the deep problems arising out of traditional accounts. Her important work points to the need for reconstructions of self-hood that take into consideration the experience of those who continually have to travel worlds and constantly experience ambiguity and contradiction. World-traveling as well as other resistant practices that Lugones introduces serve both as theoretical tools and promising practices for liberation. Yet, in my view, the key question that remains is why in Lugones's view *world*-traveling means *self*-traveling (Ortega 2001, 14)? That is, it is not clear why the experience of world-traveling that opens up possibilities of resistance requires an ontological pluralism of selves. Another way to think of this issue is whether in fact Lugones's account of world-traveling is more than an *epistemic* shift to different selves. In the 1987 text, Lugones is explicit about the epistemic aspect of the shift, but she also uses language that conveys that the self not only understands herself as different in different worlds, but that this self is multiple persons, for instance, when she states that traveling is being different persons in different worlds (2003, 89).

In my previous analysis of Lugones's account of world-traveling, I interpret her as already positing a multiplicity of selves and critique this stance, given that an appeal to a multiplicity of selves is problematic when dealing with issues concerning identity, self-identification, recognition of difference, and agency (Ortega 2001, 15–19). Some of my previous points include that even though Lugones's account relies heavily on memory, it does not say enough about memory. Various questions arise. Does the self have multiple sets of memories? Does the self contain all my memories of *all* of my experiences while traveling different worlds? Since the self is different persons in different worlds, from what perspective does the self identify this difference? Since Lugones describes her experience in the first-person perspective, what constitutes such a first-person experience? What does it mean to say that the "I" in this first-person perspective is noninferential and at the same time hold these first-person claims as being significant in remembering and self-understanding?

In my view, an account of world-traveling can avoid some of the difficulties raised by these questions. According to Lugones, for me to understand the confusion that arises when I recognize myself as playful in one world but as unplayful in another world is to understand that I am different persons in different worlds. Yet I can feel this confusion and understand that I am a multiplicitous self being pulled in different directions by norms, practices, beliefs, and so on, in different worlds, for instance, in the white world of the United States or the Nicaraguan world. Traveling to different worlds might highlight different aspects of my multiplicitous self. Even though different attributes might be highlighted or animated in different worlds, I still have a continuity of experience through my temporality and mineness or a sense of how I am being or faring in the particular world that I am in—a continuity that helps explain how I am able to have a first-person experience in the first place. Thus appealing to *self*-traveling is not necessary.[13]

As we have seen, the issue that concerns Lugones is the confusion and feeling of "schizophrenia" that arises when marginal selves travel worlds and have an attribute that is "character central" in one world but not in others (Lugones 2003, 93). In my view, even when the attributes in question are "character central" and incompatible, there is no necessity to appeal to a plurality of selves. In Lugones's account, the appeal to a plurality of selves helps to avoid the view that I am a contradictory being (recall her analysis of playfulness being a central character trait and the problem that arises when one is trying to figure out who one is given that there are two incompatible, contradictory alternatives—I am playful and I am not playful). Yet, following Anzaldúa, my account of multiplicitous selfhood accepts that there are various aspects of ourselves that are contradictory. An important aspect of the multiplicitous self is having a *mestiza* or differential consciousness that is open to and capable of dealing with ambiguities and contradictions. Put differently, the contradiction has to do with the fact that different incompatible aspects of our selves become highlighted or are animated in different worlds. Different aspects of the multiplicitous self come to the fore or become intelligible due to specific circumstances, power dynamics, and patterns of domination found in the worlds to which the self travels. Depending on the specific circumstances of world-traveling, the multiplicitous self might also actively animate different aspects of itself. The experience of finding that I am playful in this world and I am unplayful in another world need not be resolved by an appeal to a plurality of selves, as Lugones suggests.

There will be instances when I will be able to accept my contradictory attributes and not choose one attribute over the other. There will be other times when this option is just not possible. The nature of the contradiction might rest in the fact that certain worlds construct me in ways that I do not even see myself when I am in other worlds. The contradiction arises from power relations that I cannot control, from ways in which worlds are organized so as to undermine my very existence.[14] For Lugones, the world in which I become unplayful (when in fact I am a very playful person in the Latino world) needs to be changed, as there will not be an opportunity for me to become playful or to be-at-ease in that world. In her view, in that world I will just remain a contradictory being with a possibility of resistance that is merely reactive and not transformative.

The fact that world-traveling is so intimately connected to opening up different visions of oneself that can lead to resistant practices is crucial for Lugones. She is thinking beyond the possibility of being-at-ease and being reactive and calling for a more radical politics in which resistance leads to transformation of established norms, institutions, and logics. She states,

> When resistance is reduced to reaction, it is understood in the physical model and thus as contained in action. But resistance is not reaction but response—thoughtful, often complex, devious, insightful response, insightful into the very intricacies of the structure of what is being resisted. Thus, it is not sufficient to say that what there is to resistance is what is already contained in oppression plus an excess. That keeps too much of the logic of reaction. The responses do not have that character a great deal of the time. Indeed, there are reactive resistances, but to interpret all resistances as reactive is to go at the investigation with too crude a logical imagination that keeps too much the logic of reaction. (2003, 29)

For Lugones, the solution to dealing with contradiction is thus not a matter of becoming at-ease. Resistance involves having access to other worlds in which the self is constructed differently and thus can see resistant possibilities that lead to resistant practices. This happens at the limen in specific, concrete spaces in which the self can attain resistant and resisting visions (2003, 59). The limen is a social state in which one is fully aware of one's multiplicity; it is an "anti-structure" in which selves encounter possibilities of "standing aside from one's social position" (2003, 60).

It is relevant to note here that Lugones wishes to provide a more robust account of resistance by calling for responses rather than reactions. She considers responses to be more complex and attuned to the ways in which power structures operate and to the intermeshed nature of oppression (2003, 29), what, according to Kelli Zaytoun, Lugones later develops into a "logic of fusion" (Zaytoun, forthcoming). Her proposed resistant practices, such as world-traveling, curdling, and streetwalking theorizing, which will be discussed in more detail later, are meant to constitute responses in this sense. Lugones considers them as different but related ways of noticing oppression and of fighting it (2003, 12). They involve an epistemic component or shift as well as a spatial attunement, and they are supposed to embody both the theoretical and practical components of resistance.[15] Reactions, on the other hand, are quick, enacted physically, and thus contained in action; they are "what is already contained in oppression plus an excess," a view of resistance that, according to her, points to a logical imagination that is "too crude" (2003, 29).

I agree with Lugones that it is necessary to avoid a simple vision of resistance as reactive. While many practices of resistance are indeed reactive, others might be more fruitful and involve responses in Lugones's sense. I also agree that resistance might be connected to world-traveling and is thus connected to new possibilities of understanding oneself as having different attributes, of seeing oneself as capable of overcoming fear and domination, and as being creative and skillful *in spite* of the perception from the dominant group that considers that self as unworthy, inferior, and expendable. It is also a matter of envisioning different worlds in which these selves have possibilities of not merely surviving or resisting but of flourishing. Yet it seems to me that explaining the possibility of reactions and responses does not require an appeal to ontological pluralism.

By being-between-worlds and traveling worlds, the multiplicitous self can have access to alternative visions of self that are suppressed or erased in oppressive worlds. While I might not always be able to animate those characteristics in worlds that oppress me, I can become aware of them. That is, I do not have to be a different person in another world to encounter different possibilities that might lead to resistant responses. By having access to different worlds and by being being-between-worlds, the multiplicitous self is situated at the limen, where there is more likelihood for seeing differently and thus finding alternative visions of oneself and of worlds. The resistance that arises here is not necessarily always going to be, as Lugones would say, "what is already contained in oppression plus an excess" (2003, 29). It might be complex and insightful to structures of power and thus not merely reactive. Moreover, it might be connected to other practices, including coalition with others with whom the self shares a commitment to work for justice. Yet my point here is that developing or enacting a resistant practice does not necessarily require a multiplicity of selves or a multiplicity of realities.

Rather than presupposing an ontological pluralism of selves and realities, and rather than constituting an epistemic shift in which the self is different from world to world, world-traveling constitutes experiencing an opening, an aperture, from which the multiplicitous self can attain an understanding of herself and the different worlds it travels given its multiple social identities. While traveling, the self highlights different aspects of itself, or different aspects of the self are highlighted or covered over depending on dominant norms as well as structures and relations of power at work in different worlds. For example, when I as a Nicaraguan Latina travel to different worlds, such as the white, male-dominated American academic world, different aspects of my multiplicity are highlighted or undermined. It is possible to see how in that particular world my playfulness, a characteristic that comes to the fore when I am in a Latina world, is undermined. Sometimes my playfulness is completely covered over, making me feel that I am not playful. As a multiplicitous self, I am both playful and unplayful. There are both passive and active components here. I might animate certain aspects of my multiplicity differently in differently worlds, or these aspects might be highlighted given specific power dynamics. At the same time, I may undermine a characteristic or aspect of myself, or it might become covered up in worlds that are oppressive and marginalizing.

There is certainly, as Lugones explains, an epistemic shift in the experience of world-traveling insofar as the multiplicitous self acquires an understanding of herself and the worlds in which she travels. Yet traveling does not entail self-shifting. There is continuity in myself even when different aspects of myself are highlighted or covered over. Like Lugones, I understand myself as a playful person in the Latino world but not in the US world. If the attribute of playfulness is character central for me, and if I travel to a world in which my unplayfulness becomes highlighted (or I animate this attribute), this does not mean that I am two selves, a playful self and an unplayful self, but that I am a multiplicitous self that can be playful and/or unplayful in different worlds. Whether I can highlight or cover over a particular characteristic of myself remains tied to normative structures. Consequently, world-traveling might result in the experience of feeling confused about one's self that both Anzaldúa and Lugones so powerfully describe and that I have previously described as a *thick* sense of not being-an-ease. However, through world-traveling, I might still have access to alternative visions and interpretations that are crucial for resistance.

Importantly, besides having an epistemic component, in my view, world-traveling has a crucial existential, ontological dimension, since the multiplicitous self experiences different senses of being or faring in different worlds. I thus consider my position an *existential pluralism* that captures the lived experience of the self, including the existential sense of understanding myself as an "I," a sense of how I am faring in worlds, and the multiplicity of my experience in terms of the ways I understand myself and in terms of my traveling to and between various worlds.

Impurity, Curdling, *Mestizaje*, and Active Subjectivity

As we have seen, Lugones's account of world-traveling and the world-traveler self presents us with a rich phenomenological description of those whom she calls "outsider selves." Yet her appeal to ontological pluralism leads to difficult questions. As she enhances her understanding of resistance, Lugones enriches her account by explicitly adding various layers to her analysis, most significantly, a discussion of spatiality as connected to resistance and to possibilities of coalition that yield other practices that Lugones describes as "against the grain," such as curdling, streetwalker theorizing, and practices of "trespassing" (8).[16] In the process, Lugones also further develops her account of selfhood and introduces us to the curdled self, or the *mestizo* self, and to an account of active subjectivity. In the next section, I discuss these characterizations of the self with attention to the meaning of multiplicity, the role of memory in resistance, and the practice of world-traveling.

The Curdled *Mestizo* Self

In "Purity, Impurity, Separation," an essay written after the 1987 essay on world-traveling and aimed at analyzing possibilities of resistance against interlocking oppressions, Lugones elaborates on the notions of multiplicity and impurity (1994 and 2003, ch. 6). She also explains in more detail her criticism against the idea that there needs to be unity behind the multiplicity of the self. She differentiates between the logic of purity, the logic in service of domination and the modern unified subject, and curdled logic, the logic of impurity or *mestizaje*, the logic in service of resistance. She associates each of these two logics with two different types of separation. Separation as splitting, associated with the logic of purity, is one in which two elements, say egg white and yolk, are separated completely, yielding two fragmented parts; separation as curdling, associated with the logic of impurity, is one that produces "yolky oil and oily yolk," as when mayonnaise curdles.

Lugones rejects the first type of separation, split separation, as a product of the logic of purity that paradoxically leaves us with beings that can be fragmented but that can also be thought as unified. Instead, she defends the second type of separation, curdled separation, and uses it to describe a self that is not dominant, what here, following Anzaldúa, she calls the *mestizo* self. As Lugones states, `

> According to the logic of curdling, the social world is complex and heterogeneous and each person is multiple, nonfragmented, embodied. . . . When I think of my own people, the only people I can think of as my own are transitionals, liminals, border-dwellers, world-travelers, beings in the middle of either/ or. They are all people whose acts and thoughts curdle-separate. (2003, 127, 134)

One of Lugones's important points in this discussion is to explain how the logic of purity is connected to the logic of domination and to the account of the unified modern subject. This subject is paradoxically both unified and fragmented and is supposed to have a vantage point from which to look at the world. Rightly, Lugones rejects this unified modern subject and discloses it as a fiction trying to maintain itself by way of the logic of purity and as an exercise in domination (2003, 126–133). She also provides an engaging explanation of how these logics work together and make it more difficult to understand the workings of oppression and practices of resistance. In her view, it is necessary to pay attention to the way in which the logic of curdling allows for possibilities of resistance.[17]

An important question that arises in this discussion of curdling is whether Lugones's critique of the logic of purity, which appeals to unity within multiplicity, applies to phenomenological accounts that also criticize unitary modern subjectivity, for example, explanations of selfhood provided by thinkers such as de Beauvoir, Sartre, Merleau-Ponty, and Heidegger. Rather than relying on the unity of the subject or the primacy of the subject's epistemic connection to the world, these views posit accounts of self that challenge traditional understandings of subjectivity and selfhood by appealing to the multifacetedness and richness of lived experience. Lugones's critique thus applies to the more traditional accounts of subjectivity of a disembodied, impartial epistemic subject. The issue here is whether or not phenomenological and existential theories of selfhood have also arisen out of a logic of purity that ultimately fragments the self. While an extensive analysis of the way in which Lugones's understanding of the logic of purity informs various phenomenological theories of self is beyond the scope of this work, I would like to note that the type of ambiguity of the self described in many of these theories is not one necessarily conducive to self-fragmentation. Moreover, these theories also reject the supposed primacy of the epistemic and give up the view that the subject has a godlike vantage point, or what is commonly referred to as a view from nowhere. Existential and phenomenological theories are committed to providing contextual, historically situated theories of self that attempt to do justice to our lived experience. As we have already seen, these theories might not always take into consideration the lived experience of those in the margins, and thus they need to be revised. Yet they are alternatives to the subject of modernity that, according to Lugones, arises out of a dominating logic of purity, and, as such, they represent a movement away from this fragmenting logic.[18]

The critique of fragmentation is crucial in Lugones's vision of self, given her interest in the possibilities of political work not based on homogeneous communities but, in a more expansive and inclusive model of coalition, what she ultimately describes as "impure communities" or complex collectivities not based on sameness (2003, 188). Curdling is necessary so as to rule out a vision of a subject whose various identities could be neatly separated, thus leading to a fragmented self and narrow identity politics that privileges homogeneity and exclusion. Instead, as curdled, the multiple *mestizo* self is "in the middle of either/or, something impure. . . . She has no pure parts to be 'had,' controlled" (2003, 123). According to Lugones, this self cannot be fragmented because her various social identities are intermeshed. Given this understanding of curdling and intermeshedness, what, according to Zaytoun, develops into a "logic of fusion" in Lugones's later work (Zaytoun, forthcoming), it becomes possible to have a complex identity politics rather than a movement against identity politics, as suggested by postmodern positions (2003, 142).[19] Lugones thus urges us to cultivate the "art of curdling," which can lead to a "festive resistance" that includes "bi- and multilingual experimentation, code-switching, categorial blurring and confusion, drag, multiple naming, and other practices" (2003, 145).

As with her previous account of world-traveling, it is important to examine the sense of multiplicity at work here. Is the *mestizo* self multiple in the same sense as the world-traveler self described earlier? Is the curdled *mestizo* self a plurality of selves? If so, is Lugones offering an account that calls for a plurality of intermeshed selves? Or is the curdled *mestizo* self a multiple self in the sense that it has multiple, intermeshed aspects, a view comparable to multiplicitous selfhood? These questions arise because in this text Lugones explains the multiplicity of the self in two different ways, one that points to a plurality or multiplicity of selves and another that points to the self as a singular but multiplicitous being. For example, Lugones writes that "according to the logic of curdling, the social world is complex and heterogeneous and *each person is multiple*" (2003, 127; my emphasis), while she also describes the curdled, *mestizo* self as "the impure/multiplicitous" and complex, nonfragmented person (2003, 133, 141). Is Lugones working with different senses of multiplicity? In an even later writing, "Enticements and Dangers" (Lugones 2003, ch. 9), Lugones also appeals to "multiple," impure selves:

> I start within the midst of subjects, many of them subjected, but understood in our complexity and possibility. The sense of subject from which I start is well described by Inderpal Grewal as not an individual, not "unitary and centered and created out of the binaries of Self-Other, Subject-Object" (Grewal 1994, 234). Rather, subjects are multiple, impure, and thus able to dwell in the intersections between worlds of sense, and negotiate resistances to subjugating reductions at those intersections. (2003, 197)

Similar to the Anzaldúan account of selfhood, Lugones's discussion of selfhood is complex, and it is sometimes difficult to pinpoint the meaning of multiplicity.[20] Is this multiple, impure self to be understood as a multiplicity of selves, a self with multiple aspects (a multiplicitous self), or as a number of multiplicitous selves?

In her explanation of the curdled self, Lugones seems to stress multiplicity as confined to the various aspects of a singular self rather than to multiple selves, although, as we have seen, she also appeals to a multiplicity of selves. An important question that arises, then, is the nature of world-traveling for this curdled and impure self. Does world-traveling entail the epistemic shift of being different persons in different worlds, perhaps being different curdled persons in different worlds? As Lugones does not explicitly discuss the world-traveling of curdled selves, it is hard to know how world-traveling affects the multiplicity of the *mestizo* self. While Lugones's main concern is the possibility of resistance for outsider selves, rather than a metaphysical account of selfhood, a discussion of this issue would clarify her stance on multiplicity and on questions about the relationship between multiple aspects of curdled selves or between multiple curdled selves. A consideration of Lugones's most recent account of active subjectivity adds more layers to her theory of selfhood, but it also raises further interesting questions about multiplicity and the practice of world-traveling.

Active Subjectivity

Similar to Anzaldúa's border-travel, Lugones's *peregrinaje* involves a sustained theoretical, spatial, and thus embodied exploration of the meaning of self-hood for *los atravesados,* or outsider selves. Having explained the curdled self as the alternative to the fragmented subject of modernity, Lugones continues her pilgrimage by becoming more and more attuned to spatial considerations as well as to the complexity of coalitional resistance. She consequently proposes the notion of active subjectivity "for the activity of those who disturb the abstract spatiality of social fragmentation" (2003, 215). She also strengthens her discussion of resistance by recognizing and writing "from within" the oppressing ⇔ resistance tension that leads to a more complex understanding of resistant praxis (2003, 31). That is, Lugones takes into consideration that selves are not in just one side of the oppression/resistance dichotomy. Rather, given their various social locations, their experiences point to a tension between these two modes. While the self can be in a position in which she oppresses or is being oppressed in terms of a particular social location, she might also be resisting in terms of another one. For example, as a Latina academic, I might be oppressed, given the racist norms that structure the academic world. Yet I might also be oppressive in terms of my association with institutions that undermine working-class Latinas. In addition I can be resisting various aggressions in my daily experience as I navigate the academic world. Lugones characterizes this tension as being-oppressed/oppressing ⇔ resisting. In my view, Lugones's recognition and inclusion of this tension theorizing about resistance and possibilities of coalition across differences is one of her most important contributions. Given this view, we can no longer hold on to the simple dichotomy between oppressor and oppressed that informs various theoretical analyses of oppression.[21]

For Lugones, the active subject is always within the being-oppressed/oppressing ⇔ resisting tension. She explains that this subject engages in "street-walking theorizing," yet another mode of resistance against the grain developed by Lugones in her later writing. This mode is not merely reactive but calls for a sociality based on complex communication attuned to the differences between members that share a social location (Lugones 2006).

That is, Lugones is interested in bringing to light the way in which even outsider selves that share social identities come to be in marginalized locations in multiple ways. There is a recognition here that there is not complete transparency between members of specific communities, hence her call for "impure communities." In this later characterization of selfhood as active subjectivity, the "I" is described as dispersed and more relational, thus becoming an "I → we" (2003, 227).

I read this development of the notion of active subjectivity as Lugones's response to what she considers is missing in Anzaldúa's discussion of the new *mestiza*, an account of collective transformation and resistance.[22] The active subject is and performs "I → we," what Lugones describes as "the looking-for-company-but-the enduring not-yet-fulfilled quality of the subject." Here Lugones offers a vision of collective transformation and resistance (227). For her, "I → we" is an iconic index in which the "I" refers to Lugones herself. "I → we" points to her intention to move toward the "we" in the chapter, a movement representing Lugones's offering her text to us; it also points to her call for a more relational understanding of selfhood in which the "I" is no longer the principal character in the story. The arrow thus represents the "dispersed intentionality of the subject" (227).

It is in this later explanation of intentionality that Lugones once again moves against the grain of traditional philosophical explanations. Like Heidegger, who rethinks and ultimately gives up on the notion of intentionality,[23] Lugones finds it necessary to give up the traditional understanding of intentionality as taking place inside a subject's mind. Rather than conceiving of intentionality as a directedness of consciousness to an object that takes place *within* the subject, she rethinks the idea of intentionality by dispersing it *between* subjects. She proposes "tactical strategic intending" or an intersubjective project "without a mastermind" (217).[24] While in this view subjects are still understood as intending, intentions themselves "acquire life to the extent that they exist between subjects" (217). Active subjectivity thus replaces the traditional conceptions of intentionality and agency that Lugones deems problematic because they trick subjects into believing that they are making individual choices. The active subject is the "streetwalker theorist," the self that knows and cultivates "tactical strategies" while "hanging out" in concrete spaces and disrupting and subverting their logic. As Lugones notes,

> A crucial aspect of streetwalker theorizing is to uncover, consider, learn, pass on knowledge of the multiple tools of tactical strategists in having deep spatio-temporal insight into the social. As

> strategists have devised maps, chronometers, and other tools of administration and control, tactical strategists multiply messages deep into the social fabric by writing on money, using cab radios, speaking in the style of vendors on means of transportation, writing on walls, paging, and using electronic mail. (225)

Active subjects are concretely positioned in everyday spaces, locations at the street level that blur the line between the public and the private.[25] They stand within and between worlds as being-oppressed/oppressing ⇔ resisting. They experience both the strategist's abstract spaces as well as the tactical strategist's concrete lived spaces, thus making it possible to see beyond the strategist's sphere of domination. These impure subjects dwell both within and between worlds, but it is in the limen that they are able to develop a resistant practice that responds to oppression. Unlike the unified subject that, according to Lugones, cannot express both a liberating and oppressed consciousness (54), this curdled, impure, active subject, the streetwalker theorist, "cultivates an ear and a tongue for multiple lines of meaning" (224).

In this discussion of active subjectivity, Lugones provides a spatial philosophy of resistance that is meant to enhance her critique against the fragmentation caused by the subjectivity arising from the logic of purity. For example, "Latina/lesbians," construed as fragmented beings under the logic of oppression and purity, become "Latina-lesbians" under Lugones's impure logic, and they no longer have to speak with bifid tongues and fragmented voices—they no longer have to live in the *penumbra*.[26] They can live as impure beings that enact resistant visions through the use of tactical strategies that disrupt the individualism that reigns under traditional theoretical and political modern systems of thought. In this view, hanging out is a practice of the utmost importance in order "to learn, to listen, to transmit information, to participate in communicative creations, to gauge possibilities, to have a sense of the directions of intentionality, to gain social depth" (209). It is a transformative practice, both for the streetwalker theorizer as well as for the collective with which she hangs out.

We can see, then, how Lugones's understanding of selfhood and subjectivity changes as her vision of resistance and oppression becomes more complex by taking into consideration the tension between resistance and oppression that is always at work in the self's experiences. It is also clear that her attunement to embodiment and spatiality also provides important new layers to her vision(s) of subjectivity. That is, a constructive way of reading her work is by seeing how her account of active subjectivity couched on a metaphysical account of ontological pluralism supports her early account of the world-traveler self. Despite the fact that, as we have seen in the previous section, the meaning of multiplicity is not always clear in her writing, we have also seen that an account of multiple realities that becomes more explicit in the last chapters of *Pilgrimages* allows for a fuller understanding of the way in which world-traveling is a resistant practice. In this account, there must be multiple realities in which outsider selves can see themselves as resistors. An interesting question, however, is whether elements from what I have been calling Lugones's early account of selfhood, or the discussion that underscores world-traveling, are also further developed or enhanced in the later account of active subjectivity.

Memory and Resistance Revisited

As noted in the first section of this chapter, one of the important elements in the description of world-traveling is memory. From early discussions on selfhood, Lugones has given memory a key role. As she states in "Structure/Antistructure and Agency under Oppression," "It is very important whether one remembers or not being another person in another reality. In that case, of course, one has first-person memories of that person in the other reality" (Lugones 2003, 58). She illustrates her point by describing how dominant people cannot see themselves as they are viewed by those in the margins or those who are dominated by them. The employer does not remember, does not want to remember, or deceives himself about the ways in which he is seen by the maid. At the same time, those who are "invisible" in certain realities cannot animate themselves in ways that are not subservient to the dominator's world (2003, 56). For Lugones, liberatory experience "lies" in the memory of one's multiple selves, claiming that "one understands oneself in every world in which one remembers oneself to the extent that one understands that world," and that "this is a *strong sense of personal identity*, politically and morally strong" (2003, 59; my emphasis).

The importance of the role of memory remains in her later discussions of active subjectivity and the streetwalker theorist. In the introduction to *Pilgrimages*, she even notes that "by the end of *Pilgrimages*, the importance of memory in multiplicity is unveiled in its more fully social, if dispersed and uncertain dimension" (2003, 32). The liberatory potential of memory is connected precisely to the cultivation of "an ear and a tongue for multiple lines of meaning" and of memory "in its poli-logical, poli-vocal complexity" (2003, 224). As we have seen, in this later account of subjectivity, Lugones renounces a standard account of intentionality with a dispersed intending. Her previous appeal to a "strong sense of personal identity" is undermined by the call for an intentionality that is *between* rather than *within* the subject. I wonder, however, whether Lugones's later account of a self that is more "dispersed" makes it even more difficult to explain the role of memory in that vision of selfhood.

While Lugones's latest explanation of intentionality is indeed more social, given the fact that the "I" is always in relation to or looking for relations with others and becomes an "I → we," it is not clear how memories are formed in the first place. We can think of memories as having an individual component. That is to say, they are owned; a memory is genuine insofar as one has gone through the experience. This does not mean that memories are always accurate or that they do not have a social component as well, but that remembering is connected to a self's own directedness toward something in the world. It is thus necessary to acquire an understanding of the way in which a dispersed intentionality such as the one Lugones describes in the last chapters of *Pilgrimages* is formed. How does the active subject at the limen negotiate her memory of an event or an experience with others' memories of the same event? How does the I → we develop memories, and in what sense do these memories represent the experience of the "I"? If the self intends and intentions do not take place *within* a subject, how are memories to be understood as "my" memories, as memories of me in other worlds? Here I am not suggesting that we might need to hold on to a view of selfhood that posits an account of consciousness as a container of mental representations or memories—consider Descartes's understanding of the mind here. I am pointing to some very difficult questions regarding memory that arise with the appeal to dispersed intentionality.

One of the most difficult questions that arises is, what prompts memories of oneself as resistant in other worlds? If we recall Lugones's explanation of resistance, we can see that the possibility of resistance rests on the active subject's ability to remember herself in other world(s) in which she is not interpreted through the logic of domination (in an oppressive world, the self cannot animate a resistant self). She can see other possibilities when she is at the limen, in which, according to Lugones, she is fully aware of her multiplicity because of world-traveling. So, the practice is one of being able to know oneself in realities in which one can form intentions that are not available or possible in oppressive worlds (2003, 59). Given that multiple worlds and realities intersect, there is the possibility of seeing oneself differently in other worlds and of comparing and critically assessing worlds. Yet it is still not clear what leads to the recalling of memories of oneself as resistant and of seeing alternative possibilities than those at work in oppressive worlds. Another way of posing the problem is through thinking about the practice of world-traveling for a self that has a dispersed intentionality. What is world-traveling in this instance?

If we adhere to Lugones's original explanation, even in this context of active subjectivity, world-traveling would mean a shift in which the self is different in different worlds. Yet this latter characterization of active subjectivity aims at decentering the self. Not only that; it aims at providing an altogether different explanation of intentionality, one that moves us farther away from traditional conceptions of subjectivity that emphasize the epistemic relation to the world and that portrays the subject with a container-like consciousness—hence Lugones's comments about dispersing intentionality and renouncing the traditional understanding of agency. Nonetheless, the crucial role that memory plays in the active subject's ability to resist leaves this account too closely connected to the very vision of the self that Lugones criticizes. Lugones's description continues to return to the "I," even though there is an attempt to decenter it or disperse it. Perhaps at issue here are the limits and constraints of the available philosophical language and concepts, an issue that various philosophers, including Heidegger, have faced. The sense that memories remain encapsulated within one's consciousness is hard to avoid when appealing to an "I." Is Lugones's account still too tied to the conceptual apparatus of the modern account of subjectivity? If not, what is the role of memory for the "I" that is an "I → we."

Another difficulty that arises when considering Lugones's explanation of the relationship between resistance, memory, and world-traveling is how to understand her appeal to resistant possibilities that are derived from various worlds. She states, "Other worlds provide one with syllogisms that one can attempt to make actual in the worlds in which one is oppressed, given one's critical understanding of each world" (2003, 59). As Lugones explains in her introduction to *Pilgrimages*, one of the most important issues that her journey or pilgrimage tackles is to move away from abstraction and overconceptualization in order to provide an analysis rooted in concrete spaces, hangouts, and spatial practices. When explaining her definition of worlds, she criticizes Danto's understanding of the notion, because in his view worlds turn out to be *possible* worlds, logical entities rather than historical ones (Lugones 2003, 24). A rootedness on concreteness and thus an attunement to contextuality and historical intersections of the social motivates Lugones's journey.

Nevertheless, what is the status of the resistant possibilities that the active self acquires through remembering itself in other worlds? Remembering or seeing oneself as different in another world amounts to seeing otherwise. While Lugones explains this seeing otherwise—as not coming from a utopian blueprint, as having an anti-utopian direction to the future (2003, 224), as being connected to multiple actual worlds—there is a strong appeal to a visionary world. For her, a world can be an "incomplete vision-ary non-utopian construction of life" (2003, 88). It remains tied to pos-sibility, even if not a utopian vision. While Lugones's explanation of active subjectivity is intimately connected to actual lived experience, to the lived practices of streetwalkers that navigate through many hangouts, it is also a highly theoretical account that appeals to a complex metaphysics that remains connected to visionary constructions. Can visionary constructions become too closely connected to the strategist's vision? That is, is there a point in which the tactical strategist becomes more of a strategist than a tactician, even if the plan is being developed from the ground rather than from the top or from the strategist looking down at the city? Given the multiplicity of worlds available to tactical strategists, what guides or aids them in having a vision from a particular world that is to help in resistance and transformation?

I see the tactical strategist going from hangout to hangout, connect-ing to others, recognizing the multiple ways in which she creatively engag-es with her environments in order not only to survive but also to resist and ultimately transform oppressive structures and ideologies that leave us fragmented and in the midst of interlocked oppressions. Lugones calls for an "art" of curdling in which "festive resistance" can be practiced by "bi-and multilingual experimentation; code-switching; categorical blurring and confusion; caricaturing the selves we are in the worlds of our oppressors; infusing them with ambiguity; practicing trickstery and foolery" (2003, 144–145). According to Lugones, this art of resistance includes "auto-reflec-tion, looking at oneself in someone else's mirror and back in one's own, of self-aware experimentation . . . an act of social creative defiance" (2003, 145). Yet how does the tactical strategist navigate the various hangouts and relate to those hanging out?

I think of many kinds of hangouts, understood in the general sense of people just spending time together. Lugones's sense of "hangout," however, is specifically connected to fluid spaces in which people defy structures of domination. Yet there are hangouts in which structures of domination are challenged, and the very challenges do not overcome the public/private split or defy dominant logic. Lugones herself considers this issue when she points to the fact that even though gangs might have emancipatory poten-tial, some of their practices clearly reinforce the logic of social fragmenta-tion and thus their spaces cannot be regarded as hangouts (234).[27] She is also quite aware of the way in which certain institutions set up to correct injustices themselves reify fragmentation. The task of the streetwalker theorist, then, is to be attuned to this fact, to be aware of what Lugones calls poli-logical, poli-vocal complexity; that is, unlike the view of the strategist that is perched above and cannot understand practices from below, the streetwalker can see from above and below. Yet the question remains as to how the streetwalker theorist both navigates the various hangouts and avoids the traps of interlocking oppression and fragmentations that lurk even in supposedly liberatory practices and institutions. Not only does the streetwalker theorist need to avoid these traps, she also needs to be careful not to idealize or romanticize hangouts and those hanging out, something that is quite difficult, especially when the streetwalker theorist enters hangouts that are unfamiliar to her. While I don't mean to suggest that Lugones's account should provide a normative account as to detail how the curdled self, active subject, or streetwalker theorist are to navigate hangouts—it is clear that Lugones's logic of impurity allows for complexity, chaos, disruption, nonlinearity—I still wonder how these various active subjects are to avoid these traps, recognizing and passing tools of resistance in order to go beyond survival. What is the role of world-traveling in this endeavor? Given that hangouts already provide concrete visions of resistance, there might not be a need to appeal to memory in order to see oneself differently in other worlds. How much world-traveling does the streetwalker theorist need to practice?[28]

Despite the various questions and complications that arise when considering the practice of streetwalker theorizing that the active subject performs as she goes from hangout to hangout, Lugones's notion of active subjectivity leaves us with an important explanation of the necessity to understand the complexity and multiplicity of the social. It also leaves us with an understanding of a metaphysics that illustrates the intricate connection between space and time, given that the self's own walking and doing make space concrete. Put in Merleau-Ponty's terms, spatiality has to do primarily with situation, not position (Merleau-Ponty, 2003, part 1, ch. 3). Strict dichotomies of subject/object and spatiality/temporality are rejected, thus allowing us to move farther away from the fragmentation that is so dominant in traditional philosophical accounts. However, questions regarding the status of resistant possibilities; complications seeing the fragmenting, oppressive practices of even liberatory institutions; and falling into the danger of romanticizing hangouts and those hanging out remain. This is not surprising since many of these problematic issues can be understood as arising due to the being-oppressed ⇔ resisting tension and to the very complexity and multiplicity of the social that Lugones emphasizes; that is, both resistance to intermeshed oppressions as well as interlocked oppressions are at work. Even the active subject or pedestrian theorist is thus likely to misstep. As Lugones puts it, "Resisting ⇔ oppressing is understood as inter-active, social, body to body, ongoing. In this understanding, resisting can be short lived or it can be long and wide in its sociality" (2003, 223). Yet, I am curious to learn more about those moments in which active subjectivity practices this resistance long and wide and the role that world-traveling has in maintaining this width and length.

Multiplicitous Selves and Decoloniality

To conclude, I return to the question of resistance and address a possible response to my critique of Lugones's view of resistance in light of her writings after *Pilgrimages*. Zaytoun makes the important point that Lugones's work in *Pilgrimages* is connected to her recent work on decolonial feminism (Lugones 2007, 2010, 2011) and is already involved in a decolonial project that aims at providing epistemologies and visions of resistance outside the modern/colonial project (Zaytoun, forthcoming). Although an analysis of the specific manner in which Lugones's various practices against the grain such as world-traveling, curdling, trespassing, or streetwalker theorizing can be seen as decolonial is beyond the scope of this discussion, I agree with Zaytoun that Lugones's explanation of curdling can be seen as consistent with or as part of the project of decoloniality that constitutes her major recent endeavor.

It might, then, be argued that my vision of selfhood as being-between-worlds, including my understanding of how possibilities of resistance become available, could be seen as tied to modern subjectivity and thus to "the coloniality of power" (Quijano 2000).[29] Recall that my view appeals to an existential pluralism rather than an ontological pluralism. That is, I do not think that it is necessary to appeal a plurality of selves in order to explain the multiplicity of the self. Instead, my view is an existential pluralism in that I take into consideration the existential sense of being an "I," as well as the multiplicity of the self in terms of her various social locations and the ways in which she fares in different worlds. Consequently, my view of resistance is not dependent on an account of world-traveling as the shifting of selves and having the ability to remember oneself differently in other worlds. As we have seen, Lugones finds it necessary to appeal to memories of oneself as being different and having different resistant possibilities in another world in order to envision resistance in an oppressive world. As we have seen, for Lugones, this practice is key for a type of resistance that is not merely reactive. However, in my view I do not need to be a different person in another world in order to access resistant possibilities. By having access to multiple worlds and being-between-worlds, the multiplicitous self can encounter or develop possibilities of resistance. The question, then, becomes whether this position remains within an oppressive colonial modern paradigm and thus *is*, as Lugones would say, "what is contained in oppression plus an excess."

Even within the dominant Western philosophical perspective, there are visions of selfhood that attempt to dethrone the unified, allegedly neutral epistemic modern subject. Phenomenological accounts stand out in this endeavor, particularly Heidegger's existential phenomenology as well as his critiques of technology and metaphysics (Heidegger 1969, 1977, 1995, 2000). However, while Heidegger's critiques of metaphysics, the epistemic subject, and technology are important and constitute a critical stance within modernity, his view remains relentlessly Eurocentric and thus still tied to what decolonialists call the modern/colonial matrix of power. Given that my own my view is linked to Heideggerian thought, it remains linked to certain aspects of modernity. However, an important question remains as to whether the logic that goes hand in hand with modernity and is thus tied to domination is the only logic available to us, such that any meaningful resistance has to arise from "outside," as Lugones's view suggests. Even though she is aware of the importance of the limen as a concrete and theoretical space in which the self finds possibilities of resistance, we have seen that she considers resistant reactions as problematic, as they are still within the hegemonic, oppressive system.[30] Her recent concerns about the coloniality of power reinforce her vision of moving beyond or outside the dominant, hegemonic system—that is, beyond the modern/colonial matrix of power.

In my view, "delinking" from coloniality and modernity is indeed important if we are to turn to epistemologies that arise from different geopolitical positions—that is, if we are going to effect a "decolonial turn" and move toward "transmodernity" or a stage in which Europe is not positioned at the center of all epistemic and cultural projects. There is an urgent need to bring to light discourses, epistemologies, *and* phenomenologies that have been made invisible or considered inferior under the vicious and oppressive modern/colonial paradigm (Mignolo 2000, 2007; Dussel 1995).[31] I am aware that my appeal to European thought may be problematic from a decolonial point of view. Yet I am offering a type of "border thinking," a *mestizaje*—a production from the limen that aims at reconfiguring the way we think about selfhood and subjectivity.[32] Even though my vision of multiplicitous selfhood remains tied to a European tradition that values

the notion of subjectivity and selfhood, it nevertheless attempts to provide
an alternative to the notion of modern subjectivity that is undeniably tied
to individuality, domination, and mastery. It is also an account that considers the possibility of meaningful resistance even when such resistance
includes elements from "within" dominant structures.[33] Moreover, it is a
view that remains open to critical assessment of its own origin, of the origin
of "modernity," and to the inclusion and importance of "other" epistemologies.[34] As such, it rejects the universalist impulse of modern subjectivity and
its pretentions to neutrality and objectivity. The multiplicitous self is not
the master, conqueror ego, or the standard notion of self to which all other
conceptions of selfhood must measure up.

My account of multiplicitous selfhood as being-in and being-between-
worlds attempts to avoid the issues that turn out to be ontologically problematic in Lugones's account, such as a vision of worlds that includes multiple
realities as well as an appeal to a multiplicity of selves that shift when
world-traveling. At the same time, it captures Lugones's significant aspects
of her Latina phenomenological description of outsider selves, including the
recognition of the importance of multiplicity in an account of selfhood as
well as her important intuition that world-traveling is a key practice for
resistance. Giving up an ontological pluralism associated with the self does
not necessarily rule out the ability of finding possibilities of resistance that
go beyond mere reaction. Through world-traveling, the multiplicitous self
is able to envision multiple perspectives and interpretations that might disclose new possibilities of understanding the self and those worlds in which
this self is misconstrued, misrepresented, and marginalized. At the same
time, my vision of multiplicitous subjectivity, which appeals to an existential
pluralism rather than an ontological pluralism, attempts to make sense of
the multiplicity and oneness of lived experience as described by Anzaldúa
and in part by Lugones. While understanding the meaning of multiplicity and world-traveling in Lugones's various characterizations of selfhood
and subjectivity is a difficult task, Lugones's recognition of the importance
of multiplicity in a theory of selfhood as well as her understanding of
world-traveling as a key practice of outsider selves remain two of the most
important contributions in Latina feminist phenomenology.

"World"-traveling is one of those ways of keeping oneself focused on resistance.

—María Lugones

To fly we have to have resistance.

—Maya Lin

4

World-Traveling, Double-Consciousness, and Resistance

I continue traveling from world to world to world. I am all ears: "Refugee." "Illegal." "Affirmative Action Mexican." "Where is your green card?" "Why still the accent?" "Boat baby." Confusing, frustrating, demoralizing, even splitting. Yet, illuminating, transformative, transgressive—I can see with many eyes.

In addition to important metaphysical questions regarding world-traveling, there are political issues connected to the practice. Through world-traveling, multiplicitous selves that are perceived arrogantly in some worlds can become "lively beings, resisters, constructors of visions" (Lugones 2003, 97). World-traveling opens possibilities of resistance against oppression and domination. Such political implications are connected to a world-traveling that is loving and playful, that is not connected to competition, imperialism, and conquest but rather to an openness to being a fool, being surprised, not worrying about competence, not being self-important, not taking norms as sacred, and not being afraid of ambiguity (2003, 94–95). In Lugones's view, playful, loving world-travel allows for an openness to construction and reconstruction of one's self and of the different worlds to which one travels, leading to an "openness to risk the ground that construct us as oppressors or as oppressed or as collaborating or colluding with oppression" (2003, 96). In this view, playfulness is at the "crux of liberation" and should be seen as both a process and a goal (Lugones 2003, 33).

In this chapter I examine the notion of world-traveling in light of its connection to possibilities of resistance. Since in its resistant modality, world-traveling is described by Lugones as providing a double-image of oneself, in the first section I briefly examine world-traveling in connection to W.E.B. Dubois's idea of "double-consciousness." Even though Lugones's view of double imaging shares some similarities with Dubois's famous notion, her view is significantly different. My own view is that, given that the multi-plicitous self is between-worlds and in-worlds, this self has a multiplicitous consciousness or imaging that helps to create survival practices as well as of resistance. In the second section, I consider world-traveling as a practice that has the possibility of losing its liberatory and resistant potential. I examine world-traveling in light of the Heideggerian notions of the "they" (*das Man*) and publicness (*die Offentlichkeit*), which, according to Heidegger, are level-ing practices of everyday life. I show that despite its role in resistance, even the notion of world-traveling might be subject to the leveling practices of publicness and thus might lose its liberatory force. I therefore introduce the notion of critical world-traveling. Finally, I consider world-traveling as a strategy that members of the mainstream or of dominant groups may use to combat oppression and point to some possible complications that arise in such an attempt.

World-Traveling and Double-Consciousness

Despite my disagreement with Lugones regarding some metaphysical issues about world-traveling, I am interested in the epistemic implications of world-traveling in her account.[1] I agree with her point that world-travel leads to the self having a double imaging or, as we shall see later, what I regard as a multiplicitous imaging or consciousness that is crucial when look-ing at the potential that world-traveling has for resistance to and liberation from dominant practices. When describing world-traveling, Lugones writes,

> Sometimes, the "world"-traveler has a double image of herself and each self includes as important ingredients of itself one or more attributes that are *incompatible* with one or more attributes of the other self: for example being playful and being unplayful. (2003, 92; see also the introduction, where she discusses "double consciousness," 2003, 9)

This description of the world-traveler having a double image of herself is reminiscent of Du Bois's influential notion of double-consciousness in his classic explanation of the experience of African Americans in a racist US society.

Lugones's description of the experience of seeing oneself in two very different and sometimes conflicting ways is reminiscent of the experience that Du Bois, following some Romantics and Transcendentalists as well as James and other psychologists of the time, calls "double-consciousness."[2] In his often-quoted passage from *The Souls of Black Folk*, Du Bois explains double-consciousness:

> After the Egyptian and Indian, the Greek and Roman, the Teuton and Mongolian, the Negro is a sort of seventh son born with a veil, and gifted with a second-sight in this American world,—a world which yields him no true self-consciousness, but only lets him see himself through the revelation of the other world. It is a peculiar sensation, this double-consciousness, this sense of always looking at one's self through the eyes of others, of measuring one's soul by the tape of a world that looks on in amused contempt and pity. One ever feels his twoness—an American, a Negro; two souls, two thoughts, two unreconciled strivings; two warring ideals in one dark body, whose dogged strength alone keeps it from being torn asunder. (1999, 11)

Rather than providing an exhaustive analysis of Du Bois's notion of double-consciousness in the context of his influential writings, here I would like to discuss the notion in terms of the connections with world-traveling. While there are similarities between the experience of world-traveling and double-consciousness—both Du Bois and Lugones share an understanding of a life marked by multiplicity—there are also important differences. These differences are illuminating both for a proper understanding of world-traveling and for a general understanding of multiplicitous selves.

Like Hegel's master/slave dialectic, Du Bois's account of the experience of African Americans takes self-consciousness to be dependent on recognition or mediation by another being. Du Bois's view has in fact been understood as a recontextualization of the Hegelian master/slave dialectic.[3] Du Bois, then, can be understood as interested in the question of recognition in the context of African American experience within a deeply racist U.S. society. The others that constitute the measuring tape here are the dominant white others. Du Bois brings to light the experience of African Americans as they interpret themselves by way of the negative, racist views whites have about them ("measuring one's soul by the tape of a world that looks on in amused contempt and pity"). As in Hegel's famous master/slave dialectic, the process of recognition does not run smoothly. It includes strife at the physical, intellectual, and emotional levels as Du Bois portrays the difficult lived experience of African Americans in a racist society. He explains double-consciousness as involving "unreconciled strivings," thus pointing to a painful experience that will not necessarily be resolved, to a strife that is part and parcel of the African American experience.

While Lugones's account of world-traveling recognizes the various experiences of alienation, oppression, and violence that are a result of structures of power that work through a logic of domination, she underscores playful world-traveling that can lead both to an understanding of the other and to an understanding of what it means to be ourselves in others' eyes (Lugones 2003, 97). Playful world-traveling is seen as one of the resistant practices capable of alleviating the pain and strife connected to the lives of selves that are in the margins. For Lugones, there is a need to be open about different practices of resistance. She not only recommends playful world-traveling but also prompts us to consider "*tantear* for meaning, for the limits of possibility; putting our hands to our ears to hear better, to hear the meaning in the enclosures and openings of our praxis" (1).[4] Playfulness and *tantear* remain key in Lugones's analysis. Both Du Bois and Lugones disclose marginalized lived experience; yet Du Bois concentrates on the strivings of those caught in the midst of a world that looks at them with contempt due to their race, and Lugones emphasizes the intermeshed nature of oppressions and the need to be open to playfulness and *tantear*.[5]

Although it is clear that, for Du Bois, self-consciousness is relational, the exact meaning of double-consciousness and the status of the experience of having double-consciousness are not as clear. While some commentators see double-consciousness as both a "mythic blessing and a social burden" (Bell 1996, 95), others see it as "a lack of racial identity" (Lott 1995, 100), a "false consciousness" (Gooding-Williams, 2009, 21),[6] and even a "double sleight of hand" on Du Bois's part.[7] Yet, the element that it shares with Lugones's view is the recognition of the self's confusing and contradictory experiences. As we have seen, in the case of Lugones's account, the conflict arises because one sees oneself as different in different worlds, for example, as playful in the Latino world and unplayful in the Anglo world, or, in my view, different, perhaps contradictory, aspects of the self are highlighted when world-traveling. In the case of Du Bois's view, the conflict arises because African Americans see themselves as both "American" and "Negro," and this is problematic as the dominant social discourse in the United States for decades did not include African Americans as rightful citizens of the United States.

For Lugones, the conflicting and contradictory sense of self leads to an appeal to ontological pluralism. For Du Bois, it discloses the force of double-consciousness, a feeling that he is a "twoness." Similar to William James's solution to the problem of the divided self or divided will in *The Varieties of Religious Experience*,[8] Du Bois's solution to the problem he encounters as an African American living in racist US Society is an appeal to unity and a desire to "melt and weld conflicting ideals" (1999, 15). Lugones, however, takes the experience of world-traveling as an experience that opens up the possibility of resistance. She does not call for the unification or integration of the self. Du Bois sees the possibility of freedom in the training of the talents of African Americans in "conformity to the greater ideals of the American Republic" (16); Lugones sees the possibility of freedom and the possibility of structural critique in the very in-betweenness, in the liminality of the world-traveler (2003, 61). Furthermore, Lugones would take these possibilities of freedom and structural critique further by questioning the very idea of "unity" and undermining the desire for a national identity, thus moving farther away from the Du Boisian ideal (Lugones and Price 2009).

Although Lugones and Du Bois write from different historical periods and with different aims, both are deeply aware of the complex nature of consciousness as it relates to selves in the margins.[9] Both provide rich phenomenological explanations of the lived experience of those who have to travel worlds continually and who are deeply aware of the conflicting, sometimes contradictory, aspects of their selves. While Du Bois's description relates to a sense of twoness felt specifically by African Americans in the context of the United States, we can extend the discussion to multiplicitous selves described by Latina feminist phenomenologists. While considering the differences as well as similarities between world-traveling and the notion of double-consciousness, I propose that we think of multiplicitous selves as capable of having not a double image but a multiplicitous imaging or consciousness, given the fact that they are being-between-worlds and being-in-worlds and are constantly world-traveling. This multiplicitous consciousness or having multiple perspectives provides them with possibilities of understanding multiple dominant paradigms differently and of understanding multiple contexts and perspectives that allow for the possibility of liberation.[10] In other words, the multiplicitous self has multiple perspectives attained from various worlds, multiple visions of how this self is seen in those worlds, as well as numerous self-understandings. Such perspectives might overlap, allowing for the possibility of looking and interpreting worlds differently. For example, as a Latina residing on the East Side of Cleveland, who was born in Managua, Nicaragua, and lived in Los Angeles, California, when I travel to the world of Latinos on the west side of Cleveland, an area that has a large Puerto Rican community, I can see this world through the perspective of not only a Nicaraguan but also of a Latina who previously resided in Los Angeles, a city with a Latino population that is largely Mexican, as well as from the perspective of being a lesbian, an academic, and so on. Interestingly, traveling to this world of Latinos on the west side of Cleveland highlights different attributes of myself—for example, I find myself feeling a bit isolated as I am more familiar with the norms and practices of Mexican culture. A sense of sadness in terms of future possibilities is also highlighted, because this community suffers from various economic problems. I also feel alienated due to my sexual orientation, which is not always accepted by Latinas/os. Since I have worked in a primarily white environment, I can also get a glimpse of how Latinos, whether Puerto Ricans or Mexicans, are understood by the white majority and how I would be understood by this majority. This multiple imaging allows me to have different senses of this world of Latinos of the West Side of Cleveland, of how I may be seen by various groups involved, as well as how I see myself, given the various perspectives involved. While some of these perspectives might include negative characterizations of me and my community (not just from the point of view of whites but also from the point of view of other Latinos, given my sexual orientation), some of these perspectives might also allow for a critical perspective.

Of course, having a multiplicitous imaging or consciousness does not guarantee that one may find resistance or liberation. Lugones herself reminds us that logic of oppression pushes members of minorities to see themselves differently within groups due to the alleged dichotomy between "real" and "imaginary" groups. This logic claims that there are those who are "real" Latinos because they speak Spanish fluently and keep their customs alive, while there are also the ones who are supposedly "whitewashed," who have sold out—or the ones who are simply too gringo to be able to count as Latino in this country. It is a logic that further divides, a logic of fragmentation: there are the "real" Puerto Ricans from the island and those who have never stepped on its shores, the "real" Mexicans who have crossed the border and the Chicanos who have not been in Mexico and are not at ease when speaking Spanish. This logic of domination builds dominant negative constructions of being Latino within and outside Latino communities. In what follows I discuss the manner in which world-traveling functions in the context of this dominant logic that, while fragmenting us, also calls for homogeneity.

World-Traveling, Publicness, and Authenticity

While Lugones critiques a pervasive logic of domination and fragmentation that both fractures and calls for a unified subject, Heidegger critiques *Das man* or the "they," the everyday mode of being of *Dasein* that, according to him, ultimately robs individuals of their choices and responsibility for those choices. In this section I would like to explore the way in which even a practice such as world-traveling that has tremendous potential for liberation and resistance might become ineffectual, given dominant constructions of the social. Dominant negative constructions of being Latino, for example, that Latinos are all lazy, "illegals," or "Mexicans who like to eat salsa and dance," can be seen as upheld by "publicness," what according to Heidegger is a way of being characteristic of the "they."

Publicness is characterized by a leveling down of all differences, a push toward averageness, and a tendency to distance oneself from others by being aware of how one compares or differs from others.[11] In other words, publicness leads us to maintain the status quo, a status quo that helps us distinguish ourselves from others who are not in our group. We do this, according to Heidegger, as a matter of fact; it is part and parcel of being human. All of us, regardless of our race, class, sexuality, and so on, regardless of what Heidegger sees as ontic characteristics of human beings, are immersed in publicness to such a degree that we fail to take our own stances and simply follow the crowd, avoiding responsibility for our decisions, all of this happening for the most part without our being conscious of it. Publicness solidifies intragroup as well as intergroup differences, leaving us with less likely possibilities to form coalitions against dominant paradigms, all while striving for averageness.

Imagine, then, one of the many new *mestizas, mulatas,* multiplicitous beings who make up the largest minority in the United States, and try to understand what it means for them to travel across different worlds. To what extent can they become immersed in publicness? World-travelers are not exempt from the negative repercussions of living a life dominated by publicness. World-traveling itself is part of our public engagement in the world. According to Lugones, the experience of world-traveling might not even be conscious. As she says, "This shift [world-traveling] may not be willful or even conscious, and one may be completely unaware of being different in a different world" (Lugones 2003, 89).

At this point it might do us well to look more in depth at the experience of world-traveling. If we recognize it as part of the multiplicitous self's everyday experience, it may be connected to the mode of being of the "they." It would be hard to see it, then, as the experience that many theorists are appealing to in their attempt to resist racism. It would be hard to see it as a way to move against the logic of oppression, as Lugones sees it (2003, 12). Consequently, it is necessary that we further unwrap and dissect the concept of world-traveling in order to get a better look at how it is to help us resist dominant, oppressive practices.

First, let's recall my previous explanation of world-traveling. It is a practice in which the multiplicitous self has access to an opening or aperture from which she is able to understand herself and the conditions of the numerous worlds to which she travels. That opening or aperture gives access to a nexus of relations in the various worlds traveled as well as to specific self-understandings connected to the self's various identities. That is, while world-traveling, some characteristics of the self connected to her multiple identities are highlighted or covered over, thus accounting for specific self-understandings and interpretations of worlds.

Moreover, it is important to recognize that multiplicitous selves might world-travel for various reasons. It is thus not possible to provide an exhaustive explanation of the practice. We can, however, distinguish between (1) the world-traveling performed by multiplicitous selves that are members of nondominant groups who might be facing conditions of alienation and oppression and (2) the world-traveling practiced by members of dominant groups who stand in a position of privilege in society but also are in solidarity with those who are marginalized. Here, I concentrate on the first practice because this type of world-traveling is done constantly and is a means of survival. It is a necessary practice for *los atravesados*. Having to travel worlds constantly as a matter of necessity is quite different from doing it occasionally or when we are our most "pc" selves. At the end of this chapter, I briefly discuss world-traveling as practiced by members of dominant groups in their attempt to resist oppression.

World-traveling as practiced by marginal selves can be further analyzed in terms of two ways in which we can interpret the practice in light of the Heideggerian notion of publicness or the manner of being dominant in everyday, inauthentic life prescribed by the they. The first way to understand world-traveling is as an experience that is part and parcel of our everyday life and that is consequently intimately tied to the averaging tendencies of publicness. The second way is that world-traveling constitutes a deviation from the average, dominant norms and practices and thus constitutes a possibility of resistance. If world-traveling is a constant practice of the everyday life of the multiplicitous self, then it is connected to publicness and runs the risk of losing its liberatory potential. This possible loss of its liberatory potential is connected to the fact that, according to Heidegger, publicness aims at averageness, at keeping the status quo and thus maintaining the dominant paradigm. As Heidegger says,

> In this averageness with which it prescribes what can and may be ventured, it [the they] keeps watch over everything exceptional that thrusts itself to the fore. Every kind of priority gets noiselessly suppressed. Overnight, everything that is primordial gets glossed over as something that has long been well known. Everything gained by a struggle becomes just something to be manipulated. (1962, 165 [127]).

That publicness maintains averageness is not in itself necessarily a problem. Averageness can be associated with everydayness; it does not necessarily have a negative connotation. There might be a positive aspect to the "they," given that averageness maintains the background against which our norms and practices make sense. That is, it constitutes a background of intelligibility without which communication or group identity would not be possible. Heidegger's analysis suggests this reading to an extent.

Nevertheless, the problem lies in the fact that averageness is also the reason why, according to Heidegger, we no longer take responsibility for our actions and thus "take pleasure and enjoy ourselves as *they*; we read, see, and judge about literature and art as *they* see and judge. . . . because the they presents every judgment and decision as its own, it deprives the particular Dasein of its answerability" (1962, 164 [127], 165 [127]). If we understand world-traveling as becoming one of our everyday practices, to what extent can it be seen as an opening that allows for possibilities of resistance? When does the experience of world-traveling cease or lose its force as a resistant practice? In this reading, the multiplicitous self that continually world-travels would be left with the double movement involved in publicness of both seeing her differences or multiplicity and trying to preserve the status quo, all as part of an everyday attempt to survive within unwelcoming worlds. The relevant question here is whether part of surviving involves eventually giving in, settling in, accepting the norms, practices, and even the definitions of the multiplicitous self assigned by members of dominant groups.

Perhaps by surviving, multiplicitous selves are already performing an act of resistance. But it is hard to see how this is the case. I think of the new *mestiza* traveling to various worlds dominated by the framework of whites that are racist or who continually undermine, do violence, or make invisible marginalized selves. I see this new *mestiza* in the midst of an unwelcoming world, who sees herself not as a strong, smart agent worthy of respect but as someone who does not matter, who is sometimes invisible, whose existence is looked down by dominant others. I see her constantly thinking about what whites think of her, and I see her thinking it of herself, believing the lie. And Du Bois's question comes to mind: "How does it feel to be a problem?" For him, it is more painful because he is a stranger, an outcast, a "problem," in his own land. For her, it is also painful, for she might be a stranger in a land that belonged to her ancestors but that was taken, or because she is no longer at "home" and now she has to start a new life. How does she transform this experience into one of resistance? How is one to pick up the pieces and drag them along to a more welcoming world or pick them up and use them to fight what puts us down and demeans us?[12] We need more than survival or even more than adeptness in convenient world-traveling—when we act out, play the role that we are supposed to play—eat salsa and dance—so that we are left alone or so that we are compensated for being the Latina that we are supposed to be.

We can also look at world-traveling in light of the second alternative in which world-traveling is itself a deviation from dominant norms and practices, and, as such, an opening for possibilities of resistance or an act of resistance as such. This reading would mean that to have an opening through which I understand myself differently in a particular Latino world (the world of Nicaraguans who have lived in the United States for a while) and where I understand myself differently in a dominant world (the world of primarily white academics or philosophers) is to perform a disruption of publicness. It is to shatter the so-called background of intelligibility on which the world is to make sense; it is to understand that the background itself can be looked at differently and, thus, that I can have alternative meanings. In other words, when I travel to the dominant white world and my seriousness is highlighted but I can also see myself in the Latina world as being a fun-loving person, I am led to question that interpretation of myself as a serious person. I am led to question those aspects of the white world that point to my seriousness. When I travel the world of primarily white, male academic philosophers from the point of view of being an immigrant who has also lived in the United States for most of her life, of being a Latina, of being a lesbian, I can see this academic world from various perspectives that point to lacks, deficiencies, problems, oppressions, and erasures happening in this world that are not always seen by those fully immersed in it.

Examined in Heideggerian terms, this practice would amount to disrupting the readiness-to-hand with which I primarily deal with the world.

As mentioned in chapter 2, while world-traveling, the multiplicitous self constantly encounters ruptures of everyday habits. This feature of the lived experience of multiplicitous selves in the margins has led me to question the standard view upheld by classical phenomenologists such as Heidegger, Sartre, and Merleau-Ponty that human beings are in the world in a primarily nonreflective way. This is not to say that world-travelers are always reflecting on their actions, living the world in a purely reflective way—in a present-at-hand way, as Heidegger would say, or always involved in thetic consciousness, as Sartre would say. Yet the various times in which there are disruptions of sedimented norms and practices lead not only to experiences of not-being-at-ease but also to critical appraisal of those norms. World-traveling understood as an experience in which there are openings for possibilities of resistance due to disruptions of everydayness is key to the experience of multiplicitous selves. However, the complication that arises is that, as previously discussed, world-travelers experience psychic restlessness, the feeling of being a problem, the feelings of thin and thick not being-at-ease, the "intimate terrorism" that accompanies the life of the those in the margins as described Du Bois, Lugones, Anzaldúa, and others—they might experience these feelings so much that they are completely undermined. In many cases, as Paulo Freire reminds us, the oppressed internalize the paradigm of the oppressor to such an extent that they are erased as autonomous agents capable of liberating themselves (2000, chs.1–2).

Moreover, there are cases in which the characterization given to marginalized multiplicitous selves by the dominant group becomes part of everyday existence to the point that it is not questioned, that world-traveling loses the possibility of providing a critical edge, or to the point in which the only traveling is to the Latino world organized and prescribed by whites. The issue, then, is that world-traveling can lead to possibilities of resistance, but it can also succumb to influences that make life average and familiar and that ultimately threaten the possibility of resistance. What to do, then? How do we world-travel and maintain the liberatory aspect of the experience while avoiding its becoming more and more dominated by publicness?

Authenticity and World-Traveling

Heidegger's solution to the general problem posed by the self's everyday immersion in a life prescribed by publicness and dominated by the "they" or the anonymity and generality implicit in everyday interaction is an appeal to "resoluteness" or "properness" (*Eigentlichkeit*; also translated as "authenticity") (Heidegger 1962, Division 2, §§1–3). The notion of a resolute or authentic world-traveler, however, does not seem viable, especially if one understands the complexity of the multiplicitous self and if one considers the connotations behind the idea of authenticity, for example, the view that authenticity has to do with the "real" self. Even though Heidegger's account of authentic selfhood is actually an attempt to move away from the idea that there is a more real or essential subjectivity that needs to come to the fore and leave behind everydayness, I prefer not to endorse the notion of authentic self-travelers. Instead, I want to use a Heideggerian insight about resoluteness or authenticity in order to show the need for a richer phenomenological account of human beings that takes into consideration the experience of multiplicitous selves.

When explaining resolute or authentic existence, Heidegger appeals to the shared history that the self has with others. Because of that history, we inherit certain values, norms, and practices that will aid us in making choices. As opposed to a life of everydayness or immersion under the "they" in which the self becomes one of the others, in resolute existence the self learns to choose with the understanding that she creates her own ground through her very choices. No longer does the self simply follow the standard norms and practices that make life familiar and preserve the status quo. The authentic self chooses while taking responsibility for those choices. While this self might still choose to follow some standard norms and practices, under the authentic mode, the self is able to follow them not as a matter of habit but as attuned to her own wishes and desires. Moreover, these choices are not made without regard to others, but, according to Heidegger, they constitute a retrieval of the inherited past that we share with others (1962, §§74–75).

This sounds well and good until we take into consideration the experience of multiplicitous selves that are multicultural or that are in the margins. Just what exactly is the shared history that the new *mestiza* is going to inherit, the one in which she is the conquered, the colonized, the bastard, the impure, the problem? Or is it the one in which her ancestors fight and resist until they no longer can? Or is it the newly formed history of the good *mestizos*, "Hispanics," the ones who assimilate and become part of the great large family that is "America"? Heideggerian existential phenomenology cannot answer this question. It is stuck in a model that, despite being revisionary in terms of its attack against the unified, epistemic subject, fails to capture the experience of multiplicitous selves. Heidegger wishes the resolute, authentic being to find that one history that she shares with others and to repeat it, enhance it, or modify it, all while being part of the one destiny and fate of her people.

The multiplicitous self, however, is caught between histories and traditions and is forging new histories as well. She cannot be the resolute, authentic *Dasein* that Heidegger has in mind. She shares multiple histories with others. In Lugones's words, there needs to be a collective struggle:

> But, of course, merely remembering ourselves in other worlds and coming to understand ourselves as multiplicitous is not enough for liberation: collective struggle in the reconstruction and transformation of structures is fundamental. But this collective practice is born of dialogue among multiplicitous persons who are faithful witnesses of themselves and also testify to, and uncover the multiplicity of, their oppressors and the techniques of oppression afforded by ignoring that multiplicity. (2003, 62)

In my view, this collective practice requires that multiplicitous selves be vigilant to the multiple histories that they have inherited and to the very experience of world-traveling. As discussed earlier, a daily life of world-traveling might lead to becoming accustomed to world-traveling to the point where it loses its possibility of resistance. The new *mestiza* that I have in mind is the one that keeps the multiple histories alive and does not try to reconcile them so as to assimilate. She needs to examine her experience of world-traveling, dissect it, and never let it lose its force; she needs to practice *critical* world-traveling. Critical world-traveling requires that the world-traveler be engaged in an ongoing process of evaluation and interpretation of not only what is learned through traveling but also of the very practices of traveling across worlds. This requires even more awareness. Constantly traveling worlds is already a departure from the nonreflective understanding of life that Heideggerian being-in-the-world is supposed to be, but multiplicitous selves have to be even more vigilant so that the very experience of world-traveling does not lose its possibility for transformation. Consequently, critical world-traveling entails both a personal and a broader political component. As a critical project, it entails a commitment to effect change by way of reinterpreting, reconfiguring, restructuring dominant practices and paradigms. Multiplicitous selves need to embrace world-traveling, fully understanding its complexities both in its possibility of relegating them to the dominant world and in liberating them from dominant, oppressive practices. While world-traveling, multiplicitous selves have a multiplicitous imaging or consciousness of themselves, and they have the possibility of being able not only to survive dominant worlds but to effectively resist and transform them.

World-Traveling as a Strategy of Resistance

In Lugones's account, the key to world-traveling's possibility of effective resistance is playfulness rather than agonistic play or play that is ultimately connected to competition, battling, and winning. According to Lugones, playful world-traveling allows for the possibility of construction and reconstruction of oneself and of the worlds to which one travels. Lugones describes the positive and negative playful attitude, both of which allow for possibilities of change and resistance in the following way:

> So positively, the playful attitude involves openness to surprise, openness to being a fool, openness to self-construction or reconstruction of the "worlds" we inhabit playfully, and thus openness to risk the ground that constructs us as oppressors or as oppressed or as collaborating, or colluding with oppression. Negatively, playfulness is characterized by uncertainty, lack of self-importance, absence of rules or not taking rules as sacred, not worrying about competence, and lack of abandonment to a particular construction of oneself, others, and one's relation to them. (2003, 96)

Playful world-traveling on the part of members of marginalized groups, then, opens possibilities of alternative understandings and of change. Through playful world-traveling, Lugones is able to better understand both herself and her mother; she is able to appreciate her mother as more than the Argentinean patriarchal system's construction of her. She is able to understand her own arrogant perception toward her mother. Playfulness when world-traveling is key to Lugones, because it allows for critical self-understandings in connection to the ways in which we all might fall prey to perceiving others arrogantly.

In my view, marginalized multiplicitous selves can use the strategy of critical world-traveling in order to create alternative possibilities for understanding themselves and their oppressors. The multiplicitous imaging or consciousness that they have, given their constant world-traveling, might serve as perspectives from which to analyze societal norms and practices as well as personal practices. It might lead them to understand themselves as capable of being not just oppressed but also of being oppressors and as also being capable of resistance. As previously noted, this is one of Lugones's most important contributions in her discussion. Understanding how members of marginalized groups themselves are capable of being arrogant perceivers and oppressors rather than upholding a simplistic dichotomy between oppressor and oppressed is crucial for carrying out a critical project and not romanticizing the status of marginalized selves (Lugones 2006). Even when I as a Latina can be oppressed or marginalized in different worlds that I travel to due to my race or my sexual orientation, my status as a university professor places me in a class that is not always attuned to the oppression of other Latinas or other marginalized groups.

I wonder, however, whether the experience of world-traveling capable of opening possibilities of resistance needs to involve playfulness, as Lugones suggests. The value of playfulness in her account stems from the fact that it allows us not to take ourselves so seriously that we cannot construct and reconstruct ourselves, others, and societal norms. In other words, nothing is sacred, and it is okay for me to be a fool. Yet I suspect there are moments when those who are marginalized experience world-traveling that is deadly serious. For example, I as a political refugee can land in a completely different country, find myself traveling to a completely different world, and I must try to get things as right as I can in order to survive—and to have the possibility of later doing more than surviving. In this particular kind of world-travel, I have to make it, not in the sense that I will win or dominate, not in the sense of agonistic play, but in the sense that my well-being and, to some extent, my life depends on my not failing, whatever this failing means in the particular construction of the world to which I have to travel.

It might be the case that this particular example is one in which there is no possibility of resistance but only of survival. Yet world-traveling does not need to be understood so dichotomously as either pertaining to survival or to resistance, although a great number world-travels might clearly fall into these categories. World-traveling can go beyond survival and can open up possibilities for resistance. Is playfulness the only attitude that could yield an opening for possibilities of construction and reconstruction in this case? Would serious world-traveling make us lose that openness to being surprised, to being a fool, and thus to thwart possibilities for change? More important, when engaging in world-traveling explicitly as a strategy of resistance, must the experience always require playfulness, as Lugones describes? I am deeply aware of the importance of play for Lugones and other feminists, and I don't want to minimize this notion here, but I do not consider play as central as it is in Lugones's view. For her, play is at the "crux" of liberation.[13]

As noted earlier, for Lugones, playfulness is a crucial attitude for world-traveling because it allows for more creativity, willingness to explore, to change, to revise, to be wrong. I certainly agree with her that playful world-traveling would indeed to allow for more creative space for critique, change, and reconstruction. We should all be more willing to be fools! Yet her account contains elements that allow for a critical edge even when playfulness is not necessarily involved. As we have seen, one of these elements is liminality, an element that both Anzaldúa and Lugones regard as key for multiplicitous selves that are not part of the dominant groups. As Anzaldúa says, "This is her home this thin edge of barbwire" (1987, 13). It is from this thin edge of barbwire, from the borderlands, that Anzaldúa tells us her moving story of inner struggle, survival, creativity, and resistance. Lugones, inspired by Anzaldúa as well as by Victor Turner, develops the notion of liminality further. She states, "But one may also inhabit the limen, the place in between realities, a gap 'between and betwixt' universes of sense that construe social life and persons differently, an interstice from where one can most clearly stand critically toward different structures" (2003, 59). While the condition of liminality, of being-between-worlds, is clearly associated with the notion of playfulness in Lugones's work, it does not need to be. What one experiences while being-between-worlds is one's multiplicity and thus one's ability to see beyond the dominant paradigm, given the various perspectives one has while crossing borders or traveling worlds. Lugones says,

> The experience of victims of ethnocentric racism of moving across realities, of being different in each, and of reasoning practically differently in each, can be understood as liminal. To do so is to understand its liberatory potential because, when the limen is understood as a social state, it contains both the multiplicity of the self and the possibility of structural critique. (2003, 61)

It is the ability to see from different perspectives that Lugones and others see as key to the possibility of carrying out critiques against dominant paradigms. Yet, as noted, Lugones warns against the view that liminality is a sufficient condition for resistance. She also warns that liminality as such does not provide members of oppressed groups with a transparent understanding of each other for the purposes of coalitional work, since there is not one given limen in which we can all meet to fight oppression. Even liminality has to be understood as being permeated by specific power relations and having specific spatialities and histories (2006, 83).

In my view, the key to understanding how the state of liminality or in-betweenness can open up possibilities for resistance for members of nondominant groups is Anzaldúa's idea that while being in the borderlands there are openings, "some kind of fissure, gate, rajadura—a crack between worlds" (Anzaldúa 2000, 266). It is during these openings that the multi-plicitous self is most aware of her multiplicitous imaging or consciousness. As noted, Edwina Barvosa, inspired by Anzaldúa's account of borderlands, uses the idea that being in a state of in-betweenness can be a source for critical thought, because it is in a state of in-betweenness that the multiple identities or aspects of the self overlap. Such overlapping, according to Barvosa, opens up the possibility of critical thought. As she states,

> As I interpret Anzaldúa, being in a nepantilist state produces two different but related modes of thought; 1) learning and practicing "how to access different kinds of knowledges" including feelings, different moral outlooks, and images, and 2) the generative mode of "creating your own meaning and conocimientos" from the experience of accessing those different knowledges. . . . It is possible that such intersections may be the basis for inner tension and/or critical vantage points that are derived from—not independent of—multiple identities. (Barvosa 2008, 90, 91)

I agree with Barvosa's claim that the fissures and cracks Anzaldúa discusses may be understood as intersections or overlappings between worlds. While this overlapping takes place, the multiplicitous self is located at a point from which she is able to see the various worlds she inhabits through her multiple imaging, and she might be able to evaluate one world by way of her understanding of other worlds. It is here where the possibility of seeing things anew arises. It is here where fixed, sedimented views can be looked at through a new light and questioned, revised, and even negated. Thus the multiplicitous self as being-between-worlds has the possibility of developing a critical attitude precisely at the points where her different worlds overlap and intersect.

Consequently, it is necessary that we engage in what I previously described as *critical* world-traveling. In this instance, critical world-traveling recognizes the possibilities of a critical attitude by virtue of liminality, and it does not necessarily have to be playful. While it might be playful, playfulness does not need to be a key attitude when practicing it. Moreover, the critical aspect of this world-traveling refers to both the critical attitude that might arise from the experience of world-traveling so as to change, revise, reinterpret the world to which one travels, as well as a reflective stance of one's own world-traveling, including an understanding of one's own social location as one travels. Given the problems noted previously in connection to the possibility of world-traveling losing its liberatory potential due to its becoming an everyday practice dominated by publicness, multiplicitous selves *must* practice critical world-traveling. We need to be mindful not only of the possibility that world-traveling can lose its liberatory potential but also of its tremendous possibilities for disclosing resisting dominant practices. As I discuss in the next section, it is of the utmost importance that members of dominant groups that choose to world-travel in order to combat oppression also practice critical world-traveling. Critical world-traveling does not necessarily guarantee a critical stance or resistance to oppression, but it creates more openings for such a stance and for the possibility of both resistance and transformation.

World-Traveling by Members of Dominant Groups

While world-traveling is an experience that many members of nondominant groups have to engage in as a matter of course and survival, as well for purposes of resistance, it is also an experience that members of dominant groups may choose in order to understand marginalized experience. In fact, many feminists appeal to world-traveling in their attempt to provide ways in which oppression can be resisted. World-traveling is thus understood as a way to combat arrogant perception or a failure to identify and to love others whom we deem inferior to us (Frye 1983, 66–72). Since world-traveling allows for openings so that we can understand different worlds and understand ourselves and others differently, it can provide insights into how someone lives in another world. It can be seen as a powerful tool that members of dominant groups can use for the purposes of undermining oppression and injustice. However, some feminist theorists warn of possible problems with endorsing world-traveling as a strategy for resistance and opposition to oppression at the hands of members of dominant or mainstream groups. It is necessary to point to criticisms of world-traveling in order to prevent this important concept from becoming romanticized, misunderstood, and even misused at the hands of theorists from dominant groups, even when they are well meaning.

In discussing Linda LeMoncheck's call for an emphatic understanding of "the Other" by way of world-traveling, Sandra Bartky points out some of the problems with the notion of world-traveling understood as a retrieval from my world, a provisional suspension of certain conceptual and normative dimensions of my world, and a traveling to the other's world (Bartky 1998). First, Bartky asks, "To whose world ought we to travel?" According to Bartky, answering this question already involves a political decision in which our choice of destination informs some of our agenda. Bartky asks,

How can one travel without luggage? Differently put, the choice
of what to take along already colors somewhat—even before we
arrive—aspects of the world to which we are traveling. . . . "what
if she (the Other) doesn't want me in her world? Or what if
my efforts to enter it are met with abuse?" (1998, 388–389)

Bartky wishes to emphasize the difficulty that white women have in traveling the world of African American women and suggests that sometimes
the alternative is reading texts that may or may not be world-disclosing.
Moreover, Bartky asks, "The oppressed: have they no reason to travel to my
world, i.e., the world of the white middle-class feminist?" (1998, 390), suggesting that African American women need to have a better understanding
of their potential coalition partners.

   This last question that Bartky asks is puzzling, and, at the same time,
revealing. While I am sympathetic to some of Bartky's claims about the
difficulty of white women traveling to the worlds of women of color—it
might be uncomfortable, unsettling, confusing—her analysis, specifically
this question, suggests a misunderstanding or a choice to ignore the power
at play in relations between African American and white women. Bartky
seems to be forgetting her privileged position as a white academic woman.
It is most likely that women of color already have traveled to her white,
middle-class feminist world! While Bartky recognizes possible problems with
world-traveling, the fact that the travel might not be welcomed or that it
might be met with abuse, she misses the importance of her own social location and the privilege that it entails—in other words, she does not analyze
the very baggage that she is carrying while reminding us that one always
travels with baggage.

   That one always travels with baggage is precisely the point in Bartky's
analysis of world-traveling. Thus we need to remember that world-traveling
is not a neutral activity, that the world-traveler already carries a certain baggage about the world to which she is traveling or baggage due to her own
social position. Yet does this mean that a member of a dominant group
should not world-travel, that she should give up using this experience as
a tool against domination? I think not. What it means is that she cannot
overlook the fact that she has to be engaged in *critical* world-traveling or
the type of travel in which one is aware of the baggage that one is bringing
along, of one's presuppositions about the world to which one is traveling,
and of the ways in which what is learned in world-traveling can be used
to change worlds. That is, a critical world-traveler needs to be aware of
the possibilities of criticism that arise through the practice. It is precisely

through world-traveling that a different viewpoint or perspective can be attained. So, the world-traveler has to be willing to toss out some of the baggage that closes the possibility of understanding the worlds traveled and the people in those worlds.

While I support critical world-traveling on the part of members of dominant groups, since world-traveling might help both the world-traveler and might open possibilities for fighting oppression, in some cases whites or members of dominant groups have to decline world-traveling, as doing so may be more harmful than beneficial. This might be a view that many whites might not be willing to accept, especially if they suffer from what Shannon Sullivan calls "ontological expansiveness," the view that a great number of whites have that they have the right to occupy geographical, linguistic, moral, and other spaces, even if these spaces are for people of color or for groups other than privileged whites. In other words, those suffering from what is indeed a terrible condition of ontological expansiveness believe that they belong in any space they choose to occupy and that they should be welcomed there, a condition that, like various other forms of racism, Sullivan describes in terms of unconscious operations (Sullivan 2001, 2003a, 2003b, 2006). Shannon Sullivan points out that even well-intentioned world-traveling might not only reinforce white privilege but also erase an advantage that groups of color have by having their own spaces, languages, codes, and so on (Sullivan 2004). In fact, she warns that both choosing to world-travel and opting out of world-traveling give rise to various problems. Consequently, there is no general recipe as to what members of dominant groups must do in regard to world-traveling. Instead, she suggests that

> . . . just as Black philosophers must be knowledgeable and responsible when issuing invitations to white people, white people also must strive to be knowledgeable and responsible when accepting them: knowledgeable of the racist harm they can inflict with their acceptance. (303–304)

Although Sullivan is here discussing specific invitations from people of color to travel to their world, her suggestion can be seen as applying even when there is no specific invitation from marginalized groups of color to members of dominant groups. Again, a critical world-traveling, critical about the worlds to which one travels and about one's own practice of world-traveling, is necessary.

Perhaps the problem with Bartky's discussion is the one-sidedness of world-traveling. Gail Weiss criticizes Lugones for having an account of world-traveling that is too one-sided in the sense that only one person seems to be engaging in world-traveling—thus, only Lugones herself attempts to world-travel in order to understand her mother, but her mother makes no such attempt—in fact, her mother might see Lugones's attempt as patronizing (Weiss 2008, 110–112). There are plenty of cases in which the world-traveling might be one-sided. In the end, there is not one a priori rule as to the extent of reciprocity required in world-traveling. Attunement to the spatiality, sociality, and historicity of each circumstance will be needed, as well as special awareness of how the knowledge acquired in world-traveling is used.

Sue Campbell is more sympathetic to the possibilities that world-traveling has for members of the mainstream to fight oppression. Campbell notes that, according to Lugones, world-traveling is characteristic of outsiders from the mainstream Anglo world, but it can be available to those who are at ease in the mainstream (Campbell & Babbit 1999). Campbell takes into consideration the asymmetry between the outsider's and the insider or dominant person's world-traveling and analyzes how world-traveling applies to members of the dominant group who are interested in antiracist responses. She agrees with Lugones that a metaphysical attitude that is positive toward uncertainty is necessary for a shift in the self toward nonracism. Yet she rightly notes that playfulness is not what happens when this shift takes place. Rather than playfulness, according to Campbell, what takes place is an unsettling of expectations.

In addition, Campbell makes the important point that one cannot leave the rules of one's world or stand at the limen if one carries those rules unconsciously. I share Campbell's concern about our inability to leave the rules our world if we carry those rules unconsciously. There might be an unconscious aspect to the norms that we all hold as well as to norms particularly connected to racism and other forms of oppression.[14] Such an unconscious aspect will indeed make it very difficult for members of dominant or privileged groups to stand at the limen and to engage in world-traveling. Yet it seems to me that those members of dominant groups interested in fighting oppression will be more likely to question themselves and their attitudes and norms. The unconscious motivations that they have, if any, will jeopardize their practices of world-traveling but will not necessarily stop them.

Sonia Kruks adds the worry that world-traveling demands full identification with others in the world to which one travels. She reads Lugones's view of world-traveling as requiring not just a perceptual or cognitive shift but an ontological shift from being one person to being another person. (Here Kruks is picking up on the already discussed confusing aspect of

Lugones's account, given her appeal not only to an "epistemic shift" but also to the ontological status of the self as multiple.) Kruks notes that this view is problematic because, no matter how much a white person learns about the Latino world and how much good faith she has in learning about this world, she will never *be* a Latina. She thus says that "our experience of attempting to enter the world of others is both more complex and less complete than Lugones assumes in describing the process of 'identification'" (Kruks 2001, 157). However, Lugones herself does not claim that the world-traveler must fully identify as or be one of the members of the world to which one travels. In my own reading, world-traveling, understood as experiencing an opening through which the multiplicitous self understands herself or the various worlds traveled, does not require full identification with or becoming like the selves encountered in the different worlds traveled.

In other analyses, feminist theorists have seen world-traveling as a methodological tool. Christine Sylvester employs the notion of world-traveling as a practice in her development of a "method of empathic cooperation" that also recognizes feminist differences and does not become "feminist tourism." She is interested in advancing the practice of world-traveling as a methodology that feminists can use so as not to get trapped in static feminism, in which a researcher has to choose one view over another competing view. Interested in research about women in Southern Africa, she is also concerned about outsider, privileged women researchers objectifying African women by exoticizing them, seeing them as victims, denying their agency, as well as turning them into research objects. She reminds us that looming behind world-traveling there is the "shadow of an affluent, educated contemplator of 'the other,'" and that the line between feminist world-traveling and "'the arrogant perceiver [who] sees himself as the center of the universe' can be jagged" (Sylvester 1995 946–947). Yet she still sees the constructive possibilities of a world-traveling that is neither compulsive nor methodologically willful but that produces possibilities beyond this dichotomy.

These possibilities are to arise from not just one journey of world-traveling but from a nonlinear and complicated world-traveling that includes many trips—mental journeys, physical travel, and cultural negotiations. There is not one final trip that alleviates arrogant perception. As Sylvester puts it,

> The world traveler is a subject moving in, through, and around subject statuses of self and other as she goes abroad. Hers is not a journey of isolation that has one wandering around lost in the "strange" streets of exotica. It is a series of journeys of empathic

social recognition, of acknowledgement, which lead the traveler into cooperations to "negotiate respectfully with contentious others" encountered on the journey or with identities that proliferate as newly noticed political possibilities. (954)

I am very sympathetic to Sylvester's understanding of world-traveling as a practice and as a methodological tool that is multipronged and that involves multiple travels, although I wish her account developed more her view of a world-traveling that is neither compulsive nor methodologically willful. She also needs to discuss further the possible problems that arise in using world-traveling as a methodology, for example, the fear that the practice might become used primarily in intellectual work. Yet her request for world-traveling is an important one because it suggests that members of dominant groups need to make world-traveling a praxis. The extent to which members of dominant groups will engage in world-traveling in order to show solidarity or fight oppression varies. I suspect that the motives vary as well, some being true attempts at understanding those at the margins and at fighting oppression, and others being what I would call political excursions, a type of politically correct tourism—fleeting moments of experimenting with being political while not really being committed to effecting change.

In addition to the danger of political tourism, in the hands of members of dominant groups world-traveling might become a sort of play. In part, my wish that world-traveling include all sorts of attitudes, not just playfulness, has to do with the fact that for members of dominant groups, world-traveling might become just that—play, a sort of game in which one learns some interesting things about the "other" but that ultimately has no real consequences for the practitioner. In other words, playfulness does not only mean openness to learning new things, to being a fool, to reframe and rethink paradigms; it also conveys the idea that there is not much at stake. One can world-travel as some sort of entertaining game. In such cases, there is not much resting on the practice, since members of dominant groups can return to their world and continue enjoying their privilege (and also get some points for having world-traveled). Or an academic can mention world-traveling and its importance but never engage with the concept or practice it! I do not mean to imply that all members of dominant groups who take up the practice of world-traveling will have this attitude, but some will. It is thus important to remember the various ways in which world-traveling can go wrong—for members both of dominant and nondominant groups—hence, my appeal to a *critical* world-traveling in which we become vigilant not only of our critical attitudes within worlds but also of the practice of world-traveling itself, what we bring into it, what we derive from it, and what we can reimagine and refashion with it.

Let us, then, not lose the force of the incredibly rich concept and practice of world-traveling that offers not just the opportunity for survival but also openings for self-understandings, understandings of worlds, and the creation of possibilities of resistance against the domination, oppression, and arrogant perception that continues to fold, classify, and file away those whom Lugones so aptly describes as "lively beings, resistors, and constructors of visions."

As women, we have been taught to either ignore our differences or to view them as causes for separation and suspicion rather than as forces for change. Without community, there is no liberation, only the most vulnerable and temporary armistice between an individual and her oppression. But community must not mean a shedding of our difference, nor the pathetic pretense that they do not exist.

—Audre Lorde

Know where you stand, what your privileges are, and who is standing on your toes. And when you holler, "Get off my toes!" look around at the others, some most unlike you, who are also stepped on.

—Mary Matsuda

5

Multiplicitous Becomings

On Identity, Horizons, and Coalitions

Identity. Identities. Wounded and wounding attachments, empowering affirmations; causes for love . . . and fear. Me and the other. Words that teach me to fear the other. Will not give in; cannot give in. I am with the other; I want to become-with you.

Criticisms, defenses, and reconstructions of the notions of identity and identity politics have been numerous in feminist theory.[1] While conceptions of identity and identity politics have been regarded as powerful tools, especially by women of color who call for strong political solidarity, they have also been considered pernicious as they have led to both essentialism and group fragmentation. Various feminist theorists have thus attempted to rethink and reconstruct the meaning of identity and identity politics. In this chapter I wish to elaborate on the sociality and relationality of the multiplicitous self by way of a discussion of these highly contested notions. Identity and identity politics inform both the self-understanding and the experience of being-in and being-between worlds of multiplicitous selves. In the first section of this chapter I discuss Linda Martín Alcoff's analysis of the philosophical critique of the notion of identity that, in her view, is fueled by a "fear of the power of the other." I also introduce Martín Alcoff's reconstruction of identity as "interpretive horizon" to show how the account of the multiplicitous self benefits from a vision of identity as horizon that highlights the inextricable link between self and other. We will see that, while the view of identity as horizon is helpful in understanding the sociality of the multiplicitous self, Martín Alcoff's account needs a stronger consideration of multiplicity. In the second section I call for a rethinking of identity politics that goes beyond the framework of category, oppositional identity, and what has been understood as an epistemology of provenance (Kruks 2001). I first discuss important criticisms of identity politics and engage with Allison Weir's recent reconstruction of the notion. To conclude, I propose a view of coalitional politics that takes into consideration both location and relations with others, being and becoming, the intersectional aspect of the multiplicitous self, and the possibility for what María Lugones calls "complex communication" and "deep coalition." Coalition politics can open the possibility for *becoming-with*, the possibility that my relations with others with whom I fight oppression is an experience that stands to change both who I am and my understanding of the worlds I inhabit. In my view, the notions of identity and identity politics continue to be relevant even for a multiplicitous self that is in process and that occupies multiple social locations. Yet there is a need for rethinking the concept of identity so that it will not mean sameness, essence, or ahistoricity and for reconfiguring identity politics so that it is not conducive to homogenization, essentialism, fragmentation, or separatism.[2]

When considering the question of identity, it is not necessary to posit a dichotomy between a unified, substantial self or an appeal to multiple selves; we do not need to choose between an "I" and a "we." Such dichotomous thinking regarding identity is misguided. While the "I" represents a continuity of experience, it is also quite complex, embodying a multiplicity of social identities. There is an "I" always connected to a "we," the "we" being both representative of the multiple identities of the "I" as well as of other selves. As we have seen, the multiplicitous self is both multiple and one. Moreover, considering the question of identity leads me to capture that aspect of lived experience that provides the sense of being an "I," an existential sense of being me—a sense that, as we have seen, Anzaldúa has even when recognizing the ambiguities and contradictions that arise from her multiplicity. Hekman calls the sense of being an "I" the "experiential dimension of identity" (Hekman 1999, 18). She interprets this experiential dimension of identity as meaning that even though I know that my identity is constructed of different elements in my experience, "I must know myself as a stable self, as the entity that provides continuity to the disparate elements of my life, as the deep self that makes choice possible" (Hekman 1999, 18). According to Hekman, this is the reason why some feminists (e.g., Butler) jettison the notion of identity altogether.[3] While Hekman is correct in appealing to this experiential dimension of identity, this dimension does not necessarily call for a "deep self" that is understood as a perfect unity. Instead, it can be understood as the awareness of myself as having an experience that is *mine* as previously explained. The notion of identity does not need to be jettisoned; nor does it need to be associated with a "deep self" or with the category of sameness. Instead, it needs to be reconceived and critically reconstructed so as to preserve its importance in our lived experience.

Reconceiving Identity

Fear of the Power of the Other

In philosophical debates concerning the viability of the notion of identity, the most common criticism stems from the worry that an appeal to identity constitutes an appeal to essentialism, absolute sameness, and an ahistorical understanding of self that threatens the self's freedom and autonomy. In her recent important study *Visible Identities: Race, Gender, and the Self*, Martín Alcoff points to the interesting fact that both Cartesians and Kantians, as well as their critics (Foucault, Butler, et al.), condemn identity. She concludes that the critique of identity is specially linked to the Hegelian-influenced view that the self is indeterminate, and that freedom resides in the self's ability to resist external influences; that is, identities are seen as artificial, oppressive constraints on the self's natural indeterminacy.[4] Martín Alcoff notes that what follows from these metaphysical assumptions is that "freedom in any sense must be a move away from identity" (80). She takes it as implausible, however, that so many critiques against identity rest on a mistaken equation of identity categories with absolute, reductive, essentialist identity. Rather, she claims that they rest on a fear of the power of the other to impose identities on the self (81). Rather than giving in to that fear, Martín Alcoff proposes an existential, phenomenological, hermeneutic notion of identity as horizon that takes the other as "internal to the self's substantive content, a part of its own horizon, and thus a part of its own identity" (82).

Like Martín Alcoff, Allison Weir assesses critiques of identity and concludes that the numerous critiques against identity are not just a matter of opposing the view of identity as a category representing sameness but a result of "sacrificial logics" and fear of the other (Weir 1996, 2008, 128). In her evaluation, the critiques stem not just from the fear of restrictive categories and thus the fear of closure and exclusion but also from a "fear of the necessity, in any collectivity, of opening up—to deeper relations to others, to self-critique, to inclusion of difference, to the risk of participation, conflict and dissent," all of which Weir regards as essential to identification

(2008, 128). She calls for alternative notions of identity and identity politics that move away from understanding identity as a category and, instead, interpret identity as identification-with. In this manner, the debate moves from focusing on the "objectivity" of the category to the "subjectivity" of the identifications, which, according to her, offers an affective, ethical, existential ground for solidarity (111). In her recent work, Weir expands her vision of identity by developing a conception of identities as connections rather than categories and as sources of freedom (Weir 2013, 4). Rather than considering identities as merely subjugating and thus as negations of our freedom, she sees them as potentially liberatory. Ultimately, Weir appeals to a notion of transformative identification that emphasizes the ethical and political role of identities rather than their metaphysical import.

Both Martín Alcoff and Weir are persuasive in connecting the critique of identity to a certain fear of the other, whether it is the other's power to impose identities on us or the other's power to make us question cherished beliefs and norms that are important parts of our existence and self-definitions. Following Martín Alcoff and Weir, I see the necessity to rethink, reconfigure the notion of identity as well as identity politics. As Martín Alcoff suggests, any such reconceiving of identity needs to grapple with the fear of the other and to offer a conception of identity in which our interaction or relation with others is not rejected as harmful or overlooked as trivial but is constitutive to the self.[5] As Weir notes, discussions of identity need to avoid the paradox of identity or the idea that identities subject individuals to relations of power, but they are also said to be the very means that enable the self's agency (7).[6]

Interestingly, Heidegger's existential phenomenological account of the self proposes a view that takes the relational aspect of the human being to be a key ontological characteristic and thus constitutive of the self. Heidegger criticizes views that need an account of empathy or other means to connect the "I" to others—consider Husserl's famous Fifth Cartesian Meditation and its intricate explanation of intersubjectivity (Husserl 1993). He consequently considers being-with, or *Mitsein*, one of the ontological characteristics of *Dasein*. As I noted earlier, being-with amounts to the self always having the possibility of encountering and understanding others, and it is an integral part of the Heideggerian account of self. Even though it is a key existential characteristic, it might become obscured or disguised. As Heidegger states,

> Not only is Being towards Others an autonomous, irreducible
> relationship of Being: this relationship, as Being-with, is one

which, with Dasein's Being, already is. Of course it is indisputable that a lively mutual acquaintanceship on the basis of Being-with often depends upon how far one's own Dasein has understood itself at the time; but this means that it depends only upon how far one's essential being with Others has made itself transparent and has not disguised itself. And that is possible only in Dasein, as Being-in-the-world already is with Others. 'Empathy' does not first constitute Being-with; only on the basis of Being-with does 'empathy' becomes possible. (Heidegger 1962, 162 [125]).

Moreover, Heidegger distinguishes between positive and deficient modes of being-with. Rather than elaborating on the positive modes of being-with, Heidegger claims that others are disclosed by what he calls a deficient mode of being-with, which includes indifference, passing one another by, and closing oneself (161 [124]) and, even when he includes a short discussion of the positive modes of being-with, he focuses in what he calls leaping-in, a mode in which the other becomes dependent and dominated (158 [122]). While there is the possibility of opening oneself to others in more constructive modes, Heidegger does not engage in this discussion; instead, as mentioned earlier, he concentrates on an account of the "they" that undermines positive social engagements and points to the pitfalls of sociality, especially the lack of responsibility that stems from being in the everyday mode of the "they."[7]

I value Heidegger's inclusion of being-with as constitutive of the self that is being-in-the-world and thus his desire to overcome a philosophical position that starts with an "I" and then has to find a bridge to the other by way of empathy or other means. Nevertheless, had Martín Alcoff included an analysis of the way in which the other appears in Heidegger's philosophical account of self, Heidegger's view would also have been found guilty of showing a fear of the power of the other. This is a tremendous fear, given that in his account the other is translated into an ontological notion, the "they," which, as we have seen, involves a number of negative ways of being, including not wanting to take responsibility for one's actions. Martín Alcoff is correct in pointing out that it is understandable that the acknowledgment of the other might lead to great anxiety and even be experienced as a deep threat, but she reminds us,

We need, however, a material and historical accounting of when the look of the Other poses a threat rather than an existential

> universalizing of this threat to every self/other relationship, and
> we need an account that can take note of the real differences in
> the extent and manner of the threat. (Martín Alcoff 2006, 70)

A recognition of the other's connection to the self does not, as Martín Alcoff
warns, need to turn into a pathological fear of the other that influences all
of the self's interactions with the other. It should also not turn us away from
the notion of identity in a quest for a supposedly indeterminate, autonomous "I." Guided by Martín Alcoff's understanding of identity as horizon,
I hold on to the notion of identity in my account of the multiplicitous
self and go beyond the Heideggerian account that, while acknowledging the
importance of the other, stresses the ontological dimension of self-other relations and provides an overly abstract and negative account of such relations.

Identity as Horizon

In Martín Alcoff's account of self as interpretative horizon, hermeneutics,
which was originally seen as a method to interpret scriptures, becomes a tool
for the disclosure of the self, a self no longer conceived in the traditional
way as the "I" that exceeds all properties, the proud transcendental ego,
or the pedantic epistemic subject. The self that Martín Alcoff theorizes is
historically situated, gendered, raced, and it is linked to others. In this view,
the other is part of the self's horizon. Martín Alcoff states,

> The hermeneutic insight is that the self operates in a situated
> plane, always culturally located with great specificity even as it
> is open onto an indeterminate future and a reinterpretable past
> of its own creation. Given this view, one might hold that when
> I am identified, it is the horizon itself which is identified. No
> "internal" movement, judgement, choice, or act by an individual
> can be made intelligible except within this specific horizon
> which is constituted by Others. Thus, the Other is not here
> the mere prompt for subjectivizing processes that are essentially
> performed by the self; rather, the Other is internal substantive
> content, a part of its own horizon, and thus a part of its own
> identity. (2006, 82)

For Martín Alcoff, the horizon stands for the condition in which the self
occurs. It is "a site from which one is open to the world, a site from which
one must engage in the process of meaning making" (Martín Alcoff 2006,

43). Here experience, identity, and knowledge are intertwined. Each person has what Martín Alcoff calls an individual and particular substantive perspective "that makes up who that person is, consisting of her background assumptions, forms of life, and social location or position within the structure and hierarchy" (96). In other words, a horizon provides a point of view from which to experience and understand the world. For example, Martín Alcoff notes that a servant and a queen have different interpretations, the servant seeing the castle and its objects in terms of the maintenance that she has to provide for it, while the queen views them in terms of their possibilities for entertainment.

Horizons are also to be understood as not simply discursive or ideological but also materially situated, so much so that a horizon serves as a metaphor for the body (102). Martín Alcoff thus turns to Merleau-Ponty's phenomenological account of subjectivity as embodied experience to show how the self is constituted by particular historical and cultural practices but, at the same time, makes those practices her own. Adding this phenomenological approach to the hermeneutic approach allows Martín Alcoff to provide an account of horizon that includes embodied, tacit presuppositions and perceptions of visible identities such as race and gender. Importantly, Martín Alcoff adds that horizons are shared among members of a social identity; for example, I as a Latina share aspects of my horizon with other Latinas. This feature is of utmost importance in this account, as it points to the interrelatedness between self and other and to the fact that self/other relations do not necessarily have to be conflictive or constitute impositions on the self.

It is interesting to note that Martín Alcoff equates the self as well as social identities with the notion of interpretative horizon, thus applying this notion to the self in general and to its various social identities. The notion of horizon is used both in the singular and the plural, and we are faced with the question of the difficult relation between the singularity of the self and the self's multiple social identities. This tension is not resolved in Martín Alcoff's account. Yet Martín Alcoff remains mindful of the importance of multiplicity as she criticizes Western hermeneutic and phenomenological traditions of adhering to a monotopic hermeneutic that assumes coherence and monoculturalism. Instead, she appeals to a "plurotopic" hermeneutic and claims that multiple others are part of our horizon. She states,

> A necessary complication for the account of identity arises when we consider the incoherences, multiplicities, and hybrid aspects of selves, cultures, communities, and horizons. . . . We need to

reformulate the account of the formation of identity as well as the theorizing of self-Other relations in an increasingly hybridized, multicultural frame. (2006, 124)

A question remains, however, as to the role of the "incoherences, multiplicities, and hybrid aspects of selves [and] cultures" in her account. More needs to be said about the way in which these multiplicities inform the constitution of selves as horizons. Unlike writers such as Anzaldúa, Lugones, and Barvosa, Martín Alcoff does not engage with the question of the multiplicity of the self and consequently does not bring to light the constructive possibilities that such multiplicity offers.

Nevertheless, the situational, social, and intersubjective aspect of Martín Alcoff's account of horizon can help us understand the multiplicitous self as always connected to others and as having multiple interpretative horizons shared with others. The multiplicitous self is the process and interactions of all its social identities while being-between and being-in worlds. The multiple interpretative horizons constitute openings to worlds in that they inform the way in which those worlds are experienced and understood. As Martín Alcoff notes, such social identities or interpretive horizons are "profoundly significant in determining the state of the 'world' or worlds a person inhabits" (2006, 91). Some of these social identities, for example, those connected to race and gender that Martín Alcoff highlights, are fundamental to the way in which the multiplicitous self understands her experiences and the worlds she inhabits or travels. The extent to which the self's other identities help or influence meaning-making varies in each case.

As a case in point, let's consider my own experience as a Latina teaching in a predominantly white institution. I am in- and between-worlds, worlds of US white academics, teachers, students, administrators, Latinas, academic Latinas, academic women, philosophers, among others. I am in and between those worlds in very different ways, and I have access to those worlds in particular ways. I share a horizon with Latinas and academic Latinas, a site that allows me to understand my experiences in my primarily white institution in very specific ways. For example, I am deeply bothered by the way the few students and faculty of color are treated, how they are undermined, devalued, classified. This is not to say that others are not interested in these issues, but rather that, in my experience, these issues are crucial, whereas they are not or they don't seem to be for many of my white colleagues: "Why are you so *angry* about this? Why can't you see things are getting better?" they say. My being a Latina deeply informs the way in which I interpret my experiences in a school with a primarily white faculty and student body. Moreover, my gender and sexual orientation help shape my experiences further; through them, I understand and navigate possible unwelcoming spaces. While sometimes I can be at-ease given that I am familiar with norms and practices regarding academic institutions, I also experience what I have previously described as thick not-being-at-ease, especially when dealing with issues connected to race, gender, and sexual orientation or when I am "presumed incompetent," presumed angry, presumed sensitive, or presumed as having an agenda (Gutierrez y Muhs et al. 2012).

While teaching in a predominantly white school in a predominantly white neighborhood, I am *in* the US white world, but I do not *share* a US white identity, and thus I do not share the interpretative horizon that some US whites in my school might have.[8] That is, I do not share this horizon in the same way that US whites might share it. I am in this particular world in a way that is between-worlds. I can interpret my experience and this particular world from the perspective of being a Latina, but I can also partly understand the perspective of US whites in that world. I might have an understanding of the perspective of a white individual given my experience of continuously having to travel to that world. My understanding or my glimpse into the perspective of whites is partly a result of my experience of world-traveling. As we have seen, in my view, world-traveling provides an aperture to different worlds. Viewed from the perspective of horizons, world-traveling provides an opening into these horizons through which the self understands various worlds. These might be horizons of others with whom I might not share an identity.[9] While the experience of world-traveling does not guarantee a glimpse to such horizons or solidarity with those that I encounter in other worlds, it stands as an important possibility for accessing such horizons and hence glimpses or more in-depth understandings of different worlds. It is this ability to see various perspectives from various worlds that is especially important for multiplicitous selves because it allows for the possibility of critical reflection and resistance.

Such critical reflection and resistance is connected to our understanding of the incongruity between what Martín Alcoff calls "exterior" public identity, "our socially perceived self within the systems of perception," and "interior" lived subjectivity or how we understand ourselves to be.[10] As the marginalized, the *atravesados*, those in nondominant positions, continually point out, exterior identities and interior lived subjectivities do not always coincide. An understanding of the complexity and multiplicity of our self and various social identities as they are informed by horizons that share meanings with multiple others, both in their explicit and tacit manifestations, is of the utmost importance for current philosophical discussions on selfhood. Such complex and multiple social identities profoundly influence how we experience the world, whether that world is friendly or unfriendly, whether individuals are seen as simply walking in the neighborhood or plotting to commit a crime, whether we are seen as "lively beings" and "constructors of visions" or as "pliable, foldable, file-awayable," and ultimately disposable (Lugones 2003, 97).[11]

While I am emphasizing my experiences of being a Latina philosophy professor in a primarily white institution, this is but one aspect of my lived experience. There are many more aspects of my life that I could point to, such as my being a Latina living in an area of Cleveland where there are not many Latinos and experiencing various instances of racism.[12] I point to my experience as a Latina professor in a primarily white institution because it encompasses a great deal of my life and illustrates issues connected to being between worlds and traveling worlds. As many women of color are pointing out, our experiences in primarily white institutions, in institutions in which we are not supposed to belong, in which in many cases we are "presumed incompetent," leave us scarred and, at the same time, provide a deeply important perspective in our lives that illustrates not only the intersectional character of our experiences but also the constant world-traveling that we are engaged in (Gutierrez y Muhs et al. 2012).

While the experiences of being a Latina woman academic in a primarily white institution are difficult, I also recognize the tremendous privilege that comes with such a life. My point in using my experience is to illustrate the different ways in which I, as a multiplicitous self, am in various worlds, in-between worlds, and constantly traveling to different worlds. Given my multiplicitous consciousness, I thus have access to multiple horizons that allow for multiple interpretations. I can use such interpretations not only to understand my self and different worlds but also to attain critical, resistant perspectives. Being-in-worlds and being-between-worlds, then, is connected to the notion of horizon, not a surprising connection given that the Gadamerian notion of horizon to which Martín Alcoff appeals is deeply informed by Heidegger's vision of the self and his view of interpretation. Following Martín Alcoff's call for the necessity to rethink identity while taking into consideration the multiplicity of the contemporary self, I connect her notion of horizon to the multiplicitous self that is being-in-worlds and being-between-worlds. Multiplicitous selves have multiple horizons that themselves highlight the relational, intersubjective aspect of this self. That is, incorporating multiple horizons into the view of multiplicitous selfhood allows us to understand more specifically the way in which the multiplicitous self has multiple shared social meanings and is always connected to multiple others. Such a connection to others need not be understood as necessarily threatening to the self, as provoking fear of the way in which others will deny my freedom. By way of Martín Alcoff's Gadamerian, hermeneutic, phenomenological approach to identity, we may see the manner in which multiple others are connected to us, not in a pathological way or as add-ons but as integral to our very selves.

Identity Politics

Given the multiplicitous self's various shared social meanings and thus social identities, an important question that arises is whether this self can appeal to a politics based on social identities. While notions of identity politics have been controversial, indeed, raising the danger of essentialism, homogenization, narrowness, parochialism, and tribalism, they need not be jettisoned even in the present account of multiplicitous selfhood that has multiple social identities and is in-between worlds. It is necessary to move away from what Matsuda calls "a regressive use of identity politics" or an attempt that seeks "merely to reverse conditions of domination and put one's own group on top," what is ultimately a "useless exercise" (Matsuda 1996, 18). The problem is not identity politics but how identity is conceived (Lloyd 2005, 38). The concept of identity politics needs to be reframed in such a way that it allows for political solidarity while recognizing the multiplicity of political identifications that are available to the multiplicitous self. In my view, both location/positionality and relationality are involved in political identification. In this section, I first discuss the critique of identity politics and the need to reconceive this notion. I also introduce a recent mode of transformative identity politics proposed by Allison Weir (2008, 2013). I conclude by appealing to coalitional politics, a politics that is not based on essentialist or categorical identity and that is mindful of both social location and relations with others. Coalitional politics relies on the understanding that we are both being and becoming, that we occupy certain social and material locations, and that we are relational. It is also informed by a recognition of the ways in which race, class, gender, sexuality, ability, nationality, and other categories intersect or are intermeshed. Moreover, coalitional politics requires, in Lugones's words, "complex communication" and "deep coalition," which recognizes others in their resistant possibilities. Ultimately, coalitional politics can lead to *becoming-with* that involves not just understanding others but being transformed by them and with them.

The Critique

The critique of identity politics has been extensive within feminist philosophy. Key moments of this critique include Butler pointing to a paradox of those who claim identities and act from the very subject positions that they must oppose (1997); Brown reminding us of identity as a wounded attachment (1995); Hekman claiming that identity politics entails a harkening back to modernism and liberalism (1999, 2000); and Kruks condemning identity politics as an "epistemology of provenance" or "the claim that knowledge arises from an experiential basis that is fundamentally group-specific and that others who are outside the group and who lack its immediate experiences cannot share that knowledge" (1995, 4). For Kruks, identity politics remain "simple" and are the space from which "unproblematized, or self-identical, selves claim to present their own direct experience as reality" (1995, 7). So strong are these critiques that claims are made about the impossibility of retaining a politics of identity, given that *any* definition of identity will erase differences within the category that is constructed. Thus, Hekman claims that "[t]he political conclusion for feminism must be a nonidentity politics that defines politics in terms of pragmatic political action and accomplishing concrete political goals" (1999, 24).

Despite recognition of the way in which identity politics have been empowering to women of color, especially in a feminism that professed to be capturing women's experience but that in reality was illustrative of the experience of middle-class, white women, and despite the understanding that identity politics has been helpful in critiquing existing power relations, the notion has been widely condemned both in academic and political circles. Kruks claims,

> The unintended end-point of an epistemology of provenance can be an acute and politically debilitating subjectivism, which belies the possibility of communication and common action across difference. . . . a central dynamic of identity politics is to move toward ever-shrinking identity groups, for which the logical terminus would have to be not merely subjectivism but solipsism since no one person's set of experiences is identical to another's. (1995, 4)

Yet, do conceptions of identity politics necessarily lead to solipsism, as Kruks suggests? These extreme claims regarding identity politics miss the fact that identity politics may be redefined so as to avoid the familiar problems associated with it, such as essentialism and homogenization and the possibility of tribalism.

It is interesting to note, however, that most critics of identity politics do not fully engage with the work of women of color, who have been some of its strongest advocates. So, while admitting the success of identity politics in helping some of the most marginalized and disenfranchised members of society, these thinkers generally ignore the work of the very beings who have benefited from appeals to experience as women of color, appeals that have allowed them to forge political connections in order to gain rights and to be recognized. One would think that, given the recognition of the unforgiveable exclusions that took place in early waves of feminism, feminists interested in identity would indeed fully engage with texts by women of color in order to appreciate why so many of them continue to appeal to both identity and identity politics, even after many years have passed since the Combahee River Collective made its famous statement about black lesbian identity, a statement that, as pointed out in chapter 1, is mistakenly associated with narrow, oppositional identity politics (Combahee River Collective 1979).[13]

While many women of color recognize the pitfalls of early identity politics, especially as connected to early political movements such as the black and Chicano empowerment movements, they still recognize the importance of identity and identity politics (Blackwell 2011; García 1997). This is not to say that all women of color appeal to identity politics. Recent studies by women of color point to the difficulties connected to identity and identity politics (Beltrán 2010; Carrillo Rowe 2008; Rodriguez 2003). However, we need to be cognizant of the importance that identity politics has and continues to have in the theorizing and praxis of women of color. As Patricia Hill Collins noted in her presentation at the Intersectionality Symposium held at Michigan State University in April 2013, there is still a need for identity politics, although such politics needs to be nonessentialist and politically effective. In her presentation at this same conference, Kimberlé Crenshaw pointed to the various ways in which identity still matters, especially for women of color, since it is because of their identity that they are treated differently in society.

While a number of academics maintain a circumscribed discussion on issues of identity and identity politics, women of color suffer the consequences of the value that is assigned to some identities versus others. As Crenshaw notes in her now-famous early piece on intersectionality, "Mapping the Margins," there is a "vulgar" position that does not see any possibility of a "meaningful" identity politics due to the claim that given that categories are socially constructed, one cannot appeal to any identity. Crenshaw notes that one must be aware of the ways in which power has clustered around certain categories and how these positions conflate two different manifestations of power: the power exercised through the process of categorization, and the power to make the categorization have social and material circumstances (1995, 375). In her view, it is not necessary to jettison the notion of identity but rather to understand the way in which different values have been given to various categories of identity. Women of color cannot simply jettison their identity as black or as Latina, since their day-to-day experiences are marked by the value that is assigned to those categories. It is thus not surprising to see that a great number of those who call for a jettisoning of the notion of identity and who are the staunchest critics of identity politics are generally white conservative politicians and radical theorists.

As Crenshaw notes in this important discussion, it is ultimately history and context that determine the utility of identity politics (1995, 376). For Crenshaw, the question that arises is whether occupying and defending such a politics, a politics that is tied to location, yields the "most critical resistance strategy" (1995, 375). In 1989, her answer was a definite "yes." Since that time we have been alerted to the various pitfalls of appeals to identity politics. The question is whether, at the present time, there can be what we call a "constructive" conception of identity politics rather than what Matsuda calls a "regressive" use of identity politics. Despite the theoretical critiques of identity politics, despite the warnings and admonitions about the dangers of identity politics in academic and political discussions, the fact still remains that members of marginalized groups, particularly women of color, as Crenshaw's work repeatedly points out, continue to be treated different because of their identity (2006, 2012).[14]

A theoretical position that does not seriously consider the way in which identity affects the lived experience of women of color is problematic. While it is the case that critics of identity politics prompt us to give up our so-called wounded attachments so as not to perpetuate a system that is based on those attachments, it is not necessarily the case that an appeal to identity has to be harmful. We have to remember Crenshaw's point that we need not conflate the power exercised through the process of categorization and the power to make categorizations be socially and materially relevant. As Collins powerfully reminds us as well, members of marginalized groups, particularly women of color, need to play an active role in defining our own identities (Collins 2008). This is not to say that such self-definitions are unproblematic or easily carried out but that attention must be paid to the process through which a category of identity becomes harmful, thus understanding that the process of categorization is itself not necessarily harmful. Such an understanding allows us not to give up the category of identity and opens a possibility for a reconceiving of identity politics that is not necessarily based on wounded attachments and a reification of an oppressive system.

The Reconstruction

In her insightful early commentary on identity, Allison Weir discusses the "paradox of identity"—finding conceptions of identity and identity politics that can affirm individual agency and lead to collective solidarity without affirming domination or exclusion (Weir 1996, ix). Like Martín Alcoff, she is deeply interested in contesting the familiar assumption that a concept of self-identity necessarily undermines the multiplicity of the self and the self's connectedness with others. She traces this assumption in various feminist theories and diagnoses these discussions of identity as the product of "sacrificial logics," a logic of domination in which an appeal to identity necessarily rules out difference, multiplicity, and relationality. Weir is ultimately interested in a theory of identity and identity politics that does not rely on sacrificial logics. In her latest work on "transformative identity politics," she develops such a view (2008, 2013).[15]

Weir distinguishes between an account that takes identity as a category of sameness (an identity that is given) and a view that considers identity as identification-with (an identity that is constructed). Identification-with is a constructed and transformative type of identity that moves away from an objective understanding of identity (identity as category) (Weir 2008, 111). She believes that accounts of identity that appeal to the notion of positionality fall under the umbrella of identity as category. This "positional identity politics," according to her, is the more popular theoretical model for women's identity politics, but, according to her, it is incapable of yielding political solidarity. When discussing this type of identity politics, she points to Ferguson's definition of it as "an identity we find ourselves assigned to by social definition, usually by opposition to another social category, such as 'women' = 'not-man.'" Weir explains that women do not feel solidarity with other women because they belong to a category (2008, 114). In her view, what is necessary for political solidarity is the subjective component of identity or what she calls "identifications-with." Identifications-with are constituted by identifications with others and with values and ideals, as well as by identifications with ourselves as individual and collectives. According to Weir, identifications-with add an affective, ethical, and existential ground for solidarity with others.[16] Thus this notion of identification is key to her account of transformative identity politics.

Weir is interested in transformative identity politics not only in the context of US feminism but also in a global, transnational context. She believes that this transformative politics is already taking place, but we need to become more cognizant of it and the way in which it can be used to promote solidarity. She states,

> Identity politics has always been a complex process involving finding ourselves identified as belonging to a particular category (women, blacks, gays), and identifying with these particular "we's," and constructing our identity through active processes of resistance, of making meaning, through political struggle, through identifications with each other, through creating new narratives, and thereby (re)creating ourselves, and our identities. (Weir 2008, 119)

Her view of transformative identity politics thus rests on various processes of identifications-with as well as practices of recreating or transforming ourselves through our interactions with others. Her point is to show that belonging is not simply a given but a complex, active process in which the self does not simply register others but is transformed by interacting with them.[17]

In this model of identity politics, one can identify with various social justice ideals and values as well as with various particular "we's"—for example, feminists, women, women of color—and recognize these groups as resistant. Importantly, one can identify with those with whom identities are shared or not. These webs of identifications-with are for Weir the ground for feminist solidarity.[18] Like Martín Alcoff, Weir recognizes that an appeal to identity or identity politics does not necessarily undermine relationality or promote exclusivity. While for Martín Alcoff this relational aspect is integrated in the very idea of self as a horizon in which horizons have shared meanings with others, for Weir the relational aspect leads to a process of self-critique and self-transformation through identification-with.

While I am sympathetic to Weir's observation that feminists should not concentrate on the so-called objective component of identity, and I welcome her account of transformative identity politics, I wonder whether she is assuming too strict a dichotomy between objective identity (as a category that is found) and subjective identity (as constructed).[19] While she is right in appealing to the relational aspect of identity, we do not have to understand the notion of positionality as merely a given but also as subject to construction, as connected to intersubjectivity, and as subject to interpretation and reinterpretation. Some of our social locations are indeed connected to material aspects and features of the world that could be considered as merely given, such as my being a Latina who was born in Managua, Nicaragua. Yet my understanding of what it means to be Latina is tied to a number of networks of shared meaning and understanding that are not fixed. A politics of location, then, is not to be associated necessarily with a found category that is devoid of culture, history, and discourse.

As I read Martín Alcoff's view of identity as interpretive horizon, it includes positionality (social location and specific material contexts and conditions), as well as relationality (relations with others within specific historical and discursive contexts). Weir does not engage with Martín Alcoff's view. She does not consider the possibility of going beyond an understanding of positionality as objective and as a given. She misses the way in which Martín Alcoff's account of identity involves a positionality that is already deeply connected to relationality.[20] We do not need to choose between identity as category or as identification-with. Rather, I suggest that we consider identity politics in a more complex way that does not leave us trapped in a dichotomy that does not do justice to the manner in which we experience and build our self-identities as well as our group identities. If I expand the phenomenological stance that we are in fact *thrown* into particular worlds, I accept the manner in which my embodied self has, as it were, landed in particular worlds. Yet, what is "given" to me in those worlds is intricately connected to intersubjective, relational experiences colored by the traditions, histories, and multiple discourses of those worlds and of others. My positionality is not a neatly packed and accepted given; my group membership is not solely determined by relations with others with whom I share social identities or goals. In the midst of a manifold array of voices, some whose languages I may not understand, I do not only become attuned to those whose words I understand—words that satisfy the common thirst for the familiar—I also become attuned to *other* voices, different voices, that I neither silence nor take as incomprehensible.[21]

Coalitional Politics

Various critics, most notably Kruks, claim that identity politics cannot lead to coalition. Both terms are commonly understood and opposed to one another. This view is the result of a characterization of identity as sameness that relegates identity politics to those who share some category or social identity. As we have seen, in Martín Alcoff's and Weir's respective analyses of identity, this view is wrong and misses the complexity of both individual and collective senses of identity. I wish to keep in mind both Martín Alcoff's and Weir's words as I walk the complex terrain of identity politics. I do not wish to be engulfed by sacrificial logics or afraid of the power of the other. My life and the lives of others are always intertwined. Here, I come back to the notion of the multiplicitous self in terms of its possibilities for having a politics that is informed by identity-in-process and by both positionality and relationality. Given my previous discussion about Weir's analysis of identity, I do not take positionality as meaning categorical identity. Rather, it means a location that involves material as well as discursive elements that are shared. I hold a contextualist view of identity.[22] Relationality, moreover, is always connected to multiple identifications-with others. Given that the multiplicitous self is between-worlds and in different worlds, this self is more likely to see the problem of developing strong affinities to particular groups and has more possibilities to create coalitions across differences.[23] I propose that we understand the multiplicitous self as capable of having a coalitional politics that is attuned to multiplicity, difference, and the intersectional or intermeshed aspect between race, class, sexuality, gender, ability, nationality, and other categories. This coalitional politics is about *being/belonging* or about identifications with others with whom I share identity markers, but it is also about *becoming* or the possibility of being transformed through my interactions with others.

In addition to being inspired by Martín Alcoff and Weir, I continue to be influenced by Anzaldúa's view of self and identity. If we recall Anzaldúa's struggle to name herself, discussed in chapter 1, we see that she offers various conceptions of identity, including the new *mestiza*, which is closer to an oppositional identity and external identifications, as well as *la nepantlera*, which describes a self that is not based on external identifications. *La nepantlera* is a conception of self that is trying to move away from oppositional forms of identification. Anzaldúa is deeply aware of the problems with strong forms of identification and thus tries to develop this latter sense of *la nepantlera*. In her attempt to define herself, in her travels from seeing herself as a new *mestiza* and *la nepantlera*, we encounter a *mestizaje* of oneness and multiplicity, an understanding of a lived experience that paradoxically includes an existential sense of being one self and a recognition of the self's multiplicity. This sense of oneness might lead us to try to identify with a specific group of people with whom we share identity markers, whereas our sense of being multiplicitous leads us to understand ourselves as being capable of identifying ourselves with various groups, even when we don't share strong affinities with them. We have to be aware of this tension in our lived experience and provide a politics that does not fall into the trap of translating the sense of oneness into a call for sameness or reading our multiplicity as a rejection of all identifications. Keeping in mind this tension, let us take a closer look at coalitional politics.

There are three elements that are key to coalitional politics, the first being an understanding that coalitional politics is both a matter of being/belonging as well as becoming, which includes location, being-with, and becoming-with that lead to transformation. The second element is an attunement to the intersectional or intermeshed aspect of our identities or an understanding that the experience of multiplicitous selfhood is informed by the intersection of various axes of power. The third element is a recognition not only of shared oppression but resistant agency, which is dependent on what Lugones theorizes as "complex communication" that can lead to "deep coalition."

When thinking about the possibility of a coalitional politics, we need to take into account the fact that we find ourselves being part of or belonging to different groups by virtue of some characteristics, such as race, gender, sexuality, ability, class, and so on, that are part of our material conditions. As Collins notes regarding African American women, "Common location within power relations, not the result of collective decision making of individuals, creates African-American women as a group" (Collins 1998, 205). However, common location and material conditions are understood by way of a complex nexus of meanings that are shared. So there is a certain being/belonging by virtue of our sharing certain characteristics or a standpoint that we get from being in a common location, a location in which we also interact with others and multiple we's. As multiplicitous selves, our politics involve a double movement of being and becoming. Although Angela Davis's famous call for "basing identity on politics rather than politics on identity" is an important response to narrow conceptions of identity politics in which politics necessarily followed from identity, we need to recognize the intertwining of politics and identity (Lowe & David 1997, 318). Coalitional politics recognize the importance of not only common location for members of groups but also of relations-with others.

Interestingly, this being and becoming that is connected to claiming an identity is illustrated by the way in which women of color theorists describe their coming to identify as "women of color." That is, woman of color identity is not just a given name but something one becomes due to one's location as well as one's relations with others; it is a process. As

Alexander and Mohanty note, one "becomes" a woman of color (1997, xiv).[24] The experience of becoming a woman of color is instructive about the active process of identification rather than a passive or a given politics of location. The dichotomy of being/belonging and becoming, which is understood in terms of a politics of location versus a politics of relation, is thus misguided. The complex interplay of what is given and what is transformed given discursive considerations as well as relations with others cannot be overlooked.

The second key element of coalitional politics is an attunement to the intersectional or intermeshed aspect of the multiplicitous self's social identities, to the recognition that the self's experience is a product of the intersection or intermeshedness of identity. As already noted, I appeal to the notion of intersectionality as a heuristic device to help us make sense of our complex lived experience at the crossings of multiple axes of identity and of power. In coalitional politics, both individuals and groups are to be understood through an intersectional framework. The self cannot be interpreted by way of separable categories, but as multiplicitous. Groups are composed of individuals that are better understood intersectionally; groups themselves, moreover, are constructed through different intersecting axes of power. Nevertheless, as Collins warns, individuals and groups are to be seen as different units of analysis, so that we can understand the different ways in which choice plays a role in individual and group experience, and so that we can understand the contributions of group-based experiences in producing standpoints (1998). Since standpoints are produced by shared histories from shared location groups, they are not a result of collective decision making. Rather, they are the result of common location within power relations, collective decision making playing a role insofar as members decide the kind of group that they wish to be.

Collins also warns that intersectionality is not to be understood as being equally efficacious in dealing with individuals as well as groups. The notion is more effective in helping us understand an individual's experience and to compare the lived experience of different individuals. While an individual can see how categories (race, class, gender, etc.) intersect to produce her experience, it is more difficult to see how these factors intersect to produce group identities and to compare groups. Yet understanding individuals and groups as intersectional or intermeshed is necessary if we are to capture the complexity and multiplicity of individuals and groups. Intersectionality remains particularly helpful when considering coalitional politics, which, as Collins reminds us, allows for the recognition of the fluidity of groups. For example, when using race-only or gender-only paradigms, it is easier to delineate boundaries within groups. However, when looking at groups as intersectional and through an intersectional approach, the group's boundaries become more fluid, and members of different groups can align themselves to other groups by virtue of different categories. Following Collins's understanding of a group as a "heterogeneous commonality," Anna Carastathis takes identity categories as potential coalitions that are constituted by both differences and commonalities, an approach that simultaneously reveals both intragroup and intergroup differences and moves us away from starting from a desire to form coalitions across differences to starting from the recognition that groups are already internally heterogeneous (Carastathis 2013, 945). Group members are not necessarily bound by the specific category chosen as the major reason for alliance. It is thus possible to conceive the many ways in which individuals can align themselves or have solidarity with members or other groups with whom they do not share social identities or locations and also those with whom they share relations that open up possibilities of meaningful engagement.

A third element that is important for coalitional politics is the recognition of not only shared oppression but also of other resistant identities, a possibility that arises in what Lugones terms "complex communication" (Lugones 2006). In other words, it is important for individuals as well as for groups to understand themselves as capable of resisting oppression and to align themselves with other resistant groups. I thus appeal to Lugones's sense of "deep coalition," which requires a "recognition of the intersectionality of oppressions as real and important for struggle, as well as a movement outward toward other affiliative groups recognized as resistant" (2006, 76). While Lugones considers her project as a movement "outward" toward other resistant groups and thus seems to start from the position of needing to forge connections across differences, we can be mindful of the manner in which groups are already heterogeneous, as Collins and Carastathis suggest. What this means is that coalitional politics depend on an acknowledgment of the need for us to work with the heterogeneity of members within our groups as well as with other resistant groups. It also depends on the recognition of the need for "complex communication" within and across groups if we are to avoid the unfortunate splintering of groups by way of an alignment with a single particular identity.

Despite her call for an "outward" movement toward other affiliative groups, Lugones already recognizes intragroup differences. This is evident in what I consider one of her most important contributions to the discussion on coalitions, her explanation that not all liminal selves understand each other because of their liminal status. An important point that needs to be understood if deep coalition is to be possible is that it is not accurate to assume that if we meet in a liminal space, away from the constraints and rules of the dominant order, that we will understand each other, that we will, as Lugones describes it, be "transparent" to each other. The fact of the matter is that we all arrive at the limen from different travels, all of us having had different experiences of resistance. There is much about us that remains "opaque." While Lugones explains that in our journey we have a "double perception" that encompasses the visions of both oppressed and resistant reality, I, as described in chapter 4, think of the multiplicitous self as having a multiplicitous imaging or consciousness that holds multiple horizons that are helpful in understanding multiple dominant and resistant paradigms. Having a multiplicitous consciousness does not guarantee success when resisting, but it is necessary for understanding and resisting dominant paradigms—the possibility of deep coalition remains tied to this consciousness.

A multiplicitous consciousness allows for the possibility of understanding the transparency or opaqueness of other members of one's groups or of other groups. According to Lugones, it is only when we acknowledge that we are not just simply transparently together in the same limen that there can be complex communication. As Lugones states,

> If we recognize liminality in others and in ourselves and if we recognize a need for company and for coalition then we can decide to enter a conversation with other liminals that is not a liberal conversation. Liberal conversation thrives on transparency and because of that it is monologized. Complex communication thrives on recognition of opacity and on reading opacity, not through assimilating the text of others to our own. Rather, it is enacted through a change in one's own vocabulary, one's sense of self, one's way of living, in the extension of one's collective memory, through developing forms of communication that signal disruption of the reduction attempted by the oppressor. (2006, 84)

Complex communication does not rest on monolinguistic gestures that are reductive and assimilationist but rather in what Lugones refers to as "intercultural polyglossia" that makes it possible for the oppressed to communicate with intercultural resisters (Lugones 2006 83). Complex communication is creative and requires that we be disposed to understand the different ways in which others communicate and resist without trying to assimilate or reduce them to our language and to ourselves.[25]

Lugones's account of complex communication echoes some of the concerns of Ofelia Schutte's analysis of cross-cultural communication in her call for postcolonial feminism. While coalitional politics needs to develop complex communication and to understand differences and resistant capabilities within and across groups, it also needs to recognize what Schutte has termed cross-cultural incommensurability or a "minus effect" in cross-cultural communication (Schutte 1998, 56). This minus effect has to do with a residue of meaning that cannot be reached, a cultural or linguistic difference that does not come across in cross-cultural communication. The speakers have to recognize this minus effect, an effect that does not allow for complete transparency among speakers and that prompts us to hear the so-called other in her difference rather than assimilating her into our language or the dominant language. As Schutte puts it, "Cultural alterity demands that the other be heard in her difference and that the self give itself the time, the space, and the opportunity to appreciate the stranger without and within" (1998, 61).

The conversation, then, is about that which is and is *not* said; it is also about the different ways in which speakers, especially those speaking from a dominant position, need to be aware of differences instead of simply relegating those who are not easily understood to the category of "other" whose voices do not matter. A conversation that includes complex communication also needs to include the voices of those in nondominant positions and the manner in which there is also heterogeneity among those voices. In other words, even when there are points of convergence among people, there will always be differences that need to be taken into account; these voices cannot be reduced or assimilated. Even our journeys that have led us to the limen, to being-between-worlds, vary, thus locating us in different locations in the intricate map of power relations. That complex or cross-cultural communication is challenging and marked by moments of incommensurability does not mean that it is not possible or that we should not engage in it. Rather, our awareness of its complexity allows for more possibilities for developing practices to engage with it more productively rather than relying on traditional dominant practices that lead to an appeal to monolinguism and a subsequent reduction of all speech to the chosen dominant language. As Schutte points out, "Recognizing how culturally incommensurable clusters of meaning affect basic everyday interactions will bring culturally differentiated speakers one step closer to improved communication and understanding" (1998, 63).

Coalitional politics rests on our ability to engage in complex communication that discloses how we have arrived at our locations and the multiple ways in which those in nondominant locations communicate with each other and with those in dominant positions. Complex communication and critical world-traveling, what I previously described as the resistant practice through which we reflect on our practices of world-traveling and engage world-traveling in a restructuring, reconfiguring of worlds, allow for the possibility of *becoming-with*. In my view, becoming-with is necessary if there is to be deep coalition in the sense suggested by Lugones. That is, deep coalition does not involve only an understanding of one another as oppressed and resistant in our differences (a nonreductive, nonassimilationist attitude). It also includes a change or alteration, a becoming other, through my relations and communication with others. Becoming-with amounts to becoming open to the interests of groups with whom I may not share identity markers; it means understanding these interests as being as important as my own interests.[26] As Weir rightly reminds us, identity politics must be ultimately about transformation, not about sameness. When I meet you, I don't become you by being assimilated by you, and you don't become me by being assimilated by me—the Hegelian move that is to blame for philosophy's fear of the power of the other, or rather a dread of otherness. I become-with you, and we remake each other. Despite our differences, we can struggle against oppression, not necessarily because I identify with your values or your identity markers but because our standpoints intersect in ways that lead us to recognize how we stand within relations of power and how working together with a good sense of our differences (or understanding the zones where contact is uncomfortable, challenging, and even hurtful) might provide avenues to undermine oppression.

Becoming-with is thus a way of being with others that prompts us not only to understand ourselves differently, insofar as I can now join forces with others with whom I do not necessarily share identity markers, but also to connect with others affectively—through the experiences our bodies go through as we engage each other in resistant practices. As with many philosophical interventions on issues of resistance to oppression, it is quite easy to theorize, to offer a set of notions meant to capture what in reality are embodied practices—thus Anzaldúa's emphasis on the flesh, Lugones's call for streetwalker theorizing, Martín Alcoff's self as embodied horizon, and Weir's affective, transformative politics. While becoming-with captures a sense of the way that we are in worlds, it is also always connected to ontic embodiment and to others. The process through which one becomes-with another is multilayered and involves not only affect but also cognition and what has been characterized as "sensuous knowing," a socially situated, embodied knowing that may or may not be propositional and that gives us a sense of freedom or alienation, as well as possibilities for developing new attunements to features of worlds and new possibilities for change (Shotwell 2011, ch. 3). Such knowing can be connected to social movements, and our participation with others in such movements allows for the possibility of feeling otherwise, of experiencing joy and freedom from oppression (Shotwell 2011, ch. 6).

An embodied coalitional politics recognizes the experiential and contextual nature of our resistant practices. Given this recognition, there cannot be an exhaustive account of what such politics looks like or must look like. There is also no guarantee that it will yield constructive relations, actual change, or a becoming-with others. It depends on our being open to go out of our comfort zones as we engage with others, even cultivating such a discomfort so as to shift our habits of perception (Martín Alcoff 2006, 1994).[27] This is not an easy task, but it is a necessary one as we look toward being-in-worlds in a way that opens multiple resistant possibilities rather than relegating us to a life of more cactus needles embedded in our flesh and of more fear of the power of the other. As multiplicitous selves who are being-in-worlds and being-between-worlds, we have multiple intermeshed identities that serve as horizons from which to interpret and experience worlds. Rather than taking our freedom away, such identities sharpen our vision, tune our hearing, enhance our taste, expand our knowledge—and disclose possibilities of me becoming-with you.

We recognize that all knowledge is mediated through the body.

—Audre Lorde

6

Social Location, Knowledge, and Multiplicity

How I know worlds, how I know myself, is informed by my flesh, my blood, my bones, the earth under my feet. They help me know worlds—daringly and lovingly. I see myself and I am seen. Nicaraguan, bicultural, woman of color, exile—also Americanah. They are all me. As I walk in time, I am present, moving forward while carrying the bones of my past with me. A tight bundle of nostalgia, melancholia, fear, and blurry images of what was.

In addition to being concerned with questions about the manner in which an appeal to the notion of identity might promote or preclude coalitional political action, Latina feminists are also concerned with drawing attention to the way in which the notion of identity is connected to epistemic concerns—to the important link between social location and knowledge. Following the work of Satya P. Mohanty, Latina theorist Paula Moya proposes a postpositivist realist theory of identity (PPRI), an account of identity worthy of attention due to its in-depth treatment of the claim that there is a causal connection between identity and social location (i.e., the self's location in terms of race, class, gender, sexuality, ability, and so on.) (Moya & Hames-García 2000; Moya 2002). Like Martín Alcoff, Moya defends the notion of identity and considers it key not only in terms of its political deployment but also in terms of its link to knowledge. According to PPRI, conditions of social location, which are neither completely fixed nor completely constructed, not only influence the way we see ourselves but also the way we think and know the world. In *Learning from Experience*, Moya explains the postpositive realist theory of identity and illustrates the theory with examples from her own experience as a Mexican American. While Moya's theory deserves praise for clearly articulating the important connection between social location and epistemic claims and for acknowledging the multiplicity of the self, it fails to note and engage with the positive values of multiplicity and the liminality and marginality associated with such multiplicity, and thus it misses the constructive potential of multiplicity in the lives of women of color. When analyzing the multiplicitous condition of women of color, Moya opts for integration and synthesis. As she states,

> Moraga and the other women of color whose work I admire and teach understand that instability is not necessarily a comfortable or desirable situation in which to exist; life on the margins or in the interstices, while potentially exhilarating and creative, also can be difficult and exhausting. As a result, they struggle to find a way to bring all of the disparate aspects of their social identities together into integrated or synthesized selves . . .
>
> Certainly, one of the major victories to date of women of color feminism is the ability some women of color now have to conceptualize themselves as non-fragmented beings constituted neither by lack nor by excess. (Moya 2002, 95)

In this chapter, I analyze the postpositive realist view of social identity as proposed by Moya with the aim of showing that this theory of identity undermines multiplicity and thus does not fully capture the lived experience of multiplicitous selves. I wish to make the point that a theory of identity that centers around social location and wishes to do justice to the experience of multiplicitous selves needs to consider the complexity of multiplicity and thus recognize not only its negative, distressing aspects but also its positive or constructive value, as various Latina feminist theorists such as Anzaldúa, Lugones, and Sandoval have done. Given that PPRI emphasizes the connection between identity, social location, and epistemic claims, in the first section in this chapter I briefly discuss PPRI's claims regarding this link. In the second section, I analyze an example provided by Moya regarding a shift in her understanding of herself from "Spanish girl" to "Chicana," a shift toward what Moya considers a truer identity. This move constitutes what I call the "forward-moving, truer identity model," the view that selves are better off as linearly progressing toward a truer identity. An analysis of this move toward a truer identity points to PPRI's misunderstanding of the temporality at work in multiplicitous selves. It also brings to light a preference for synthesis and integration and an undercutting of the positive, constructive value of the difficulties experienced by multiplicitous selves.

Identity, Social Location, and Epistemic Claims

Moya and other theorists endorse the postpositivist realist theory of identity (PPRI) in order to draw attention to the relationship between identity and social location.[1] According to Moya, PPRI occupies a space between essentialist positions that lead to reductionism and the universalizing of experience and postmodernist views that, according to her, lead to self-fragmentation, loss of agency, and loss of one's connection to a real, social, and natural world.[2] At the same time, PPRI constitutes a response to attacks against identity politics by neoconservatives such as Shelby Steele and Richard Rodriguez that undermine the important work of ethnic studies scholars that emphasizes the significance of social location.

PPRI underscores the links among identity, knowledge, and social location understood as the material conditions of race, class, sexuality, culture, and history, and takes these links as having important consequences for how we understand ourselves and interpret our worlds. One of PPRI's major contributions is that it takes seriously the epistemic consequences of identities, consequences that, according to Moya, pertain not merely to theoretical issues but also to how one lives one's life. Another advantage of PPRI is that it allows us to see how these categories function in our lives but does not completely reduce us to them. Moya believes that PPRI's commitment to postpositivism and to realism allows for a better theory of identity that doesn't leave women of color as fragmented, reduced to social categories, and unable to make or revise truth claims or enact strong political activism.

PPRI's appeal to postpositivism and to realism pertains to its commitment to empiricism and to a conception of objectivity inspired by feminists of science in which objectivity is seen not as the product of disinterested theoretical inquiry but as a theory-dependent, socially realizable goal (Moya 2002, 27). As Moya states, following Mohanty,

> I conceive of objectivity as an ideal of inquiry necessarily involving theoretical bias and interest, rather than as a condition of absolute and achieved certainty that is context transcendent, subject independent, and free of theoretical bias. . . .
>
> 'objective knowledge is the product not of disinterested theoretical inquiry so much as of particular kinds of social practice'; it is thus context sensitive and empirically based, while being valid across social and cultural contexts. (2002, 14, 28)

In this view, experience is seen as theoretically mediated. In other words, experience is not interpreted as meaningful only if it is self-evident; it is meaningful because it is causally related to the world. One can evaluate the reliability of one's experience by seeing how it refers to the world. One can also evaluate one's theories by seeing how they refer to the world as well:

> By seeing experience as theory mediated, realists understand that it can be a source of real knowledge as well as of social mystification; by seeing experience as causally related to the (social and natural) world, realists provide a way to evaluate the reliability of the knowledge humans have gained from their experiences. The realist proposal is that the truth of different theories about the world can be evaluated comparatively by seeing how accurately they refer to real features of the world. (28)

Identities are seen as referring outward to the world. This claim is of utmost importance in this view, since one of the problems that Moya sees with postmodern views is that, given their commitment to social construction, they theorize identities as reducible to those constructions and theorize difference as merely a "discursive illusion," which can lead to the claim that "we are all marginal now" (Moya 2002, 24). The importance of the notion of difference, then, goes out the window, and, according to Moya, we are left with a delegitimization of all accounts of experience and the undermining of all forms of identity politics. Even though Moya doesn't want to foster a competition between marginalities, it is clear to her that some individuals' differences lead them to more difficult struggles and to a more marginal existence, that there are significant differences between the experiences of white males or white females and women of color, and that these differences, in turn, lead to different understandings of the world. She believes that "there is a non-arbitrary limit to the range of identities we can plausibly 'construct' or 'choose' for any individual in a given society" (2002, 45). Moya doesn't want the notion of identity to be put to rest or to be used only in a strategic or tactical fashion, as some theorists suggest, especially now when women of color claim it and need it in their fight against racism, sexism, homophobia, and other injustices.

A recognition of the link between identity and social location is important, especially for theorists interested in the manner in which identity informs epistemic claims. As we have seen in Martín Alcoff's explanation of identity as horizon, various social identities serve as lenses through which we interpret the world. Understanding the role of identity in making worlds intelligible as well as understanding the importance of identities insofar as they influence the manner in which we inhabit worlds, whether worlds are safe, welcoming, or hostile and threatening, is key to envisioning resistant possibilities and practices. PPRI's claim regarding the connection between identities and knowledge is thus relevant for those interested in changing various conditions of oppression. Since PPRI recognizes the importance of the connection between social categories and how the self understands the world, it recognizes the epistemic privilege of marginalized individuals. In other words, given their experiences in oppressive environments, marginalized individuals might have a richer, more complex understanding of societal conditions because they have the possibility of understanding the point of view of dominant as well as marginalized groups. As Moya states,

> The key to claiming epistemic privilege for people who have been oppressed in a particular way stems from an acknowledgement that they have experiences—experiences that people who are not oppressed in the same way usually lack—that *can* provide them with information we all need to understand how hierarchies of race, class, gender, and sexuality operate to uphold existing regimes of power in our society. (2002, 38)

This access to understanding different ways in which various structures of power are deployed and maintained is indeed necessary for enacting resistant practices. Theorists and activists can use the insights of those who are marginalized in order to have a more objective understanding of the dynamics of racism, sexism, and other forms of oppression.

It is important to note here that Moya is well aware of the difficulties raised by the notion of epistemic privilege and thus is clear to point out that she is not claiming that people of color always know better or that there is an *a priori* link between social location, identity, and knowledge. As she states,

> The simple fact of having been born a person of color in the United States or of having suffered the effects of heterosexism or of economic deprivation does not, in and of itself, give someone a better understanding or knowledge of the structure of our society. (Moya 2002, 38)

Moreover, Moya is also careful to distinguish between her position and that of standpoint theory, which proposes that nonoppressed people start their inquiries from the standpoint of those marginalized. Moya believes that "the first step in the recovery of the experiences of oppressed peoples will involve a reexamination by oppressed peoples of their own lives" (2002, 132). Thus, those who are marginalized can carry out a project of self-examination that can be shared with those who are not marginalized. For Moya, one's social location as oppressed or marginalized is a necessary but not a sufficient condition for developing the skill of *la facultad* or, as we have seen, Anzaldúa's term for the ability marginalized people have to perceive their particular situation, including possible dangers.

PPRI, then, emphasizes the links among identity, social location, experience, and epistemic privilege. Importantly, this position neither jettisons the concept of identity nor resurrects an essentialist, foundational, traditional notion of identity. Key for PPRI is the claim that social categories do influence identity, but they do not determine it. Rather than determining our identity, "those 'physical realities of our lives' will profoundly *inform* the contours and the context of both our theories and our knowledge" (2002, 37). According to Moya, PPRI constitutes a relational, culturally and historically grounded notion of identity that is also committed to objectivity. She proposes a theory in which the notion of identity remains a key and necessary concept and a powerful tool that can be used by feminist and ethnic studies scholars as well as activists of color in their struggles and opposition to oppression. However, while Moya's account of PPRI is to be commended for pointing to the link between social location, identity, and epistemic claims, thus bringing to the fore the way in which marginalized people might have epistemic privilege that might help in the struggle against various manifestations of oppression, her account is problematic in its treatment of the notion of multiplicity.

From "Spanish Girl" to "Chicana"

Many women of color are attuned to the various self-identifications that they experience as they travel worlds. These shifts in self-identifications are instructive not only about ourselves but also about the dominant norms present in these worlds.[3] Moya brings up her own experience of having a very important shift in self-identification, a shift from seeing herself as a "Spanish girl" to identifying as a "Chicana," a move to what she considers a truer identity. In this section I analyze this important shift in terms of issues regarding both temporality and the positive, constructive aspects of

multiplicity. Given that Moya engages with Chela Sandoval's theory of differential consciousness, I also discuss Moya's critique of this notion.

Moya holds that social identities are not just the result of construction, discursivity, or performativity. They are both real *and* constructed and
have very real effects in our lives and our understanding of our world. As
noted, identities have more or less epistemic validity to the extent that they
refer outward to the world (2002, 41). The truer they are to the outside
world, the more epistemic validity they have, and the greater the possibility
that they are accurate and objective. To illustrate this point, Moya takes us
back to her own experiences as a student at Yale, where she saw herself as
a "Spanish" girl from New Mexico and could not understand why other
students were not friendly to her. After spending some time in Texas, where
there is more prejudice against Mexicans, she realized that she was seen as
a "Mexican," and thus she realized that her claim to Spanish identity was
"both factually and ideologically suspect" (2002, 40). In other words, her
understanding of her experiences was mediated by her interpretation of herself as "Spanish." Once she realized that this interpretation was not accurate,
she could reinterpret her past experiences and understand why she had a
difficult time with some students at Yale. Having understood her identity
as Mexican American and Hispanic as well, Moya ultimately understands
herself as a "Chicana." She states,

> I want to consider now the possibility that my identity as a
> "Chicana" can grant me a knowledge of the world that is truer
> and more "objective" than an alternate identity I might claim
> as a "Mexican American," a "Hispanic" or an "American" (who
> happens to be of Mexican descent). (2002, 41)

She chooses "Chicana" over "Mexican American" because her Chicana
identity better represents who she is, a politically aware woman of Mexican
heritage who is also aware of her disadvantaged position. If she were to see
herself as "Mexican American" or as "Hispanic," she thinks that she would
be forced to ignore some salient aspects of her social location in order to
maintain the present self-conception (2002, 41)—"Mexican American" and
"Hispanic" do not carry the political implications that "Chicana" does.[4]
According to her, since "Chicana" refers more accurately to who she is in
the world, it constitutes what she refers to as a "truer" identity. The interpretations of her experiences will be mediated by her views as a Chicana,
and thus she claims that they will have more objective validity.

While I understand Moya's experience of going through a process of "becoming" Chicana, since multiplicitous selves have to negotiate their various identities and sometimes highlight one identity over others, her discussion of the shift in self-identification from "Spanish girl" to "Chicana" leads to important questions regarding issues connected to temporality and multiplicity.

Temporality

One question that comes to mind when looking at Moya's discussion of her trajectory from seeing herself as a "Spanish girl" to a "Chicana" and her claim that her Chicana identity is truer is whether Moya is working with a traditional, linear account of temporality that ultimately does not do justice to the experience of multiplicitous selves. Moya's example is one in which identity is understood in progressively truer stages. That is, Moya moves from the inaccurate "Spanish" identity to what she sees as the truer "Chicana" identity. She also provides another example of a move to what she considers a truer identity, that of Cherríe Moraga's coming to identify as a "lesbian woman of color."[5] For Moya, Moraga's shift in understanding herself from "white" to "lesbian woman of color" represents a voyage toward a truer identity and a more objective understanding of the world, because "Moraga's new-found identity, "woman of color," is more epistemically and politically salient than her former identity (2002, 93).[6]

Yet, should the identity of a self such as Moraga's or Moya's be thought of as progressing linearly from one aspect of identity to the next or one kind of identity to the next toward a truer identity, what we might call a forward-moving truer identity model? One's identification with a particular identity does not necessarily move linearly in a forward manner toward a truer identity. The experience of multiplicitous selves is complex. If we think back to the accounts of selfhood provided by other Latina phenomenologists such as Anzaldúa and Lugones—and I believe we must—we find that they don't experience themselves as moving from one identity to another that is more accurate or truer. As we have seen, they describe their experience as one in which there is a sense of ambiguity, liminality, multiplicity, and even contradiction. Recall Anzaldúa's description of the new *mestiza*:

> The new mestiza copes by developing a tolerance for contradic-
> tions, a tolerance for ambiguity. She learns to be an Indian in
> Mexican culture, to be a Mexican from an Anglo point of view.
> She learns to juggle cultures. She has a plural personality, she

operates in a pluralistic mode—nothing is thrust out, the good the bad and the ugly, nothing rejected, nothing abandoned. Not only does she sustain contradictions, she turns the ambivalence into something else. (1987, 79)

And Lugones's description of a subject that is plural:

> The sense of subject from which I start is well described by Inderpal Grewal as not an individual, not "unitary and centered and created out of the binaries of Self-Other, Subject-Object." Rather, subjects are multiple, impure, and thus able to dwell in the intersections between worlds of sense, and negotiate resistances to subjugating reductions at those intersections. . . . It is that plurality that enables us to acknowledge, discern, investigate, interpret, remake the connections among crisscrossing oppositional subaltern worlds of sense, oppositional to the very logic of subjection. (2003, 197).

The selves that Latina feminist phenomenologists such as Anzaldúa and Lugones describe, as well as my own view of multiplicitous selfhood, are characterized by multiplicity, plurality, ambiguity, and contradiction. An existential understanding of temporality rather than the traditional, Aristotelian linear sequence of "nows" does more justice to the experience they describe. We can think of these selves as not experiencing themselves moving from one identity to another truer identity but having various experiences ranging from not identifying at all, to identifying with multiple identities, to experiencing glimpses of past identifications while holding on to present identification, identifying with a salient identity in particular worlds, and so on.

As Moya herself believes, not all of these identities would be equally epistemically or politically salient, but they would all be important parts of one's self. Even though Moraga as well as Moya can be seen as having an identity that comes to consciousness of political issues, and thus being "Chicana" or "a woman of color" becomes an important issue, this does not mean that Moya is no longer a Mexican American and Moraga is not part white, or that these other aspects of herself are not important or salient. Our coming to consciousness of our different identities or of the way in which our various social locations inform our experience is part and parcel of being a multiplicitous self. As multiplicitous, the experience of self-identification involves a complex process informed by various material conditions and relations of power present in the worlds to which we travel. Moreover, as multiplicitous beings who are constantly between-worlds, we have a sense of the traps of narrow self-identifications.

From a perspective that takes into consideration the temporality of the multiplicitous self, my main point here is that a traditional linear model of temporality as a sequence of "nows" does not do justice to these selves that occupy multiple social locations and that understand themselves by way of various identity markers. As described in chapter 2, the temporality at work in multiplicitous selves is one in which the past, present, and future are interrelated in the sense that Heideggerian existential phenomenology describes.[7] Thus, rather than thinking of multiplicitous selves as understanding themselves as going from one identity to the other—to the truer, more accurate identity as Moya desires—and thus following the account of a "now" that becomes a past and is taken over by another "now," multiplicitous selves have multiple social locations that inform their self-understanding in various ways. Just as an existential phenomenological account of temporality takes all the moments of time—past, present, future—as intertwined or interrelated in our experiences, the multiplicitous self that inhabits multiple positions might be aware of all or some of her different social identities at any given time. As noted, this self is decentered, and different social identities or characteristics are highlighted at different times. While she might in some instances regard one of those identities or characteristics as more salient, this is not always the case. It is not necessarily the case either that she is better off moving toward what Moya describes as a truer identity.

Importantly, Moya does not claim that our self-identifications must always move through this forward-moving truer identity model. She states that "the realist claim is not that humans are always successful in their efforts to make successive approximations toward the truth—just that they *can* be" (2002, 91). That is, women of color will not necessarily get to their truer identity. I doubt that Moya would want to appeal to a sense of *the* true identity or what some consider one's authentic identity, as this would move her position too close to essentialism. Yet while she is aware of the complexity of multiplicitous selves, she concentrates on underscoring the political salience of some identities as opposed to others and defending the position that it is better to find an identity that is truer and that is salient.

Moya recognizes that there could be other identities that could be important or salient for the self. She also emphasizes that an important aspect of her discussion is that not all identities a self can claim have equal political or epistemic salience. As she says,

This is not to say that there could not be another identity that might also, or more accurately, refer to the complex being she is. The realist claim I am making here is limited: not all identities a given individual can claim to have equal political or epistemic salience. (2002, 93)

Moya's reminder that not all identities have equal salience, whether in political or epistemological contexts, is well taken, as it is the case that multiplicitous selves have various social identities that play different roles in different worlds.[8] As we have seen, given their being-in-worlds and being-between-worlds, multiplicitous selves highlight different social identities in different worlds, or different social identities are highlighted by virtue of the power relations at work in such worlds (or they might be covered over). However, a preference for a "truer identity" undermines the salience and importance that other identities might have as well as the intersectional or intermeshed aspect of our identities as multiplicitous selves.

Even though it is the case that multiplicitous selves might find some identities more salient than others at different times and places, there are cases in which many of their identities are salient, however ambiguous and contradictory this experience may be—recall Anzaldúa's new *mestiza* here as well as Lugones's account of the world traveler. The finding of a truer identity that is most epistemically and politically salient, while beneficial in the lived experience of some women of color, should not be understood as the desired or preferred goal for multiplicitous selves, especially when they consider their social location and that location points to their complexity and multiplicity. The multiplicitous self's temporality is such that it does not move linearly. It includes a intertwining of past, present, and future that allows for a complex interaction between social identities. While it is the case that multiplicitous selves might find "truer identities" as they navigate their various worlds, their other identities continue to matter while they are involved in the many negotiations this self performs as it travels and resides in different worlds and between-worlds.

The Value of Multiplicity

Another question that comes to mind when considering Moya's preference for a forward-moving model is whether PPRI undercuts the positive, constructive aspects of multiplicity and thus undermines multiplicity. As we have seen in previous chapters, while it is certainly the case that the life of the multiplicitous self has many instances of pain, restlessness, contradiction, and psychic restlessness, Latina feminist phenomenological accounts also vividly describe how these moments are also sources of creativity and resistance. PPRI, however, emphasizes how these difficult moments might lead to unrest and to fragmentation, thus calling for synthesis and integration. As we will see next, an analysis of Moya's response to Sandoval's account of differential consciousness shows how her response disregards the ways in which multiplicity can be seen as beneficial for women of color. It also raises some questions about Moya's treatment of so-called postmodern elements in Sandoval's view. Ultimately, Moya's account of PPRI undermines its own claims about the importance of social location for a theory of identity, because recognition of the importance of social location is connected to an acknowledgment of the positive value of multiplicity.

Moya disagrees with Sandoval's view on the grounds that Sandoval's theory of differential consciousness involves shifts in identity and leads to the view that oppositional consciousness is available to all first-world citizens. According to Moya, Sandoval's postmodern tendencies predispose her to view identity as radically unstable and to see shifts in behavior and emphasis as shifts in identity. She understands Sandoval's view of differential consciousness as claiming that women can shift identities, such as "Chicana," "lesbian," "mother," "worker," in different contexts, but she doesn't agree with the successive nature of these shifts (2002, 82). Moya states,

> According to Sandoval's theory of differential consciousness, she undergoes several successive shifts in identity. A realist theory of identity, by contrast, would acknowledge that different aspects of the woman's social identity become more or less visible in different situations, but would see that identity as remaining more or less constant over the course of her movements. Throughout Sandoval's argument, in fact, U.S. third world feminists remain U.S. third world feminists. In the course of enacting differential consciousness, they do not become white men, or white women, or children, or nonfeminists. They may privilege one or more aspects of their identity (gender, sexuality, race, class) over others at various times and in various situations, but they do not actually "shift" their relatively stable social identities. (2002, 82)

Moya's view is that the shifting of identities is not supported in Sandoval's own argument, and that Sandoval mistakenly claims that shifts in identity are taking place (2002, 83). Nevertheless, it is not clear that Sandoval and Moya mean the same thing when they appeal to the notion of identity.

Despite the fact that Moya's discussion emphasizes *social* identity, here Moya seems to be referring to *personal* identity as traditionally understood, or an identity that remains constant over time. In a footnote, Moya agrees that perhaps she and Sandoval mean different things when discussing identity, but even then she thinks Sandoval's view is misleading as it has "the effect of obscuring the unequal salience of different aspects of identity" (2002, 83n24). Sandoval, however, is concerned with the ways in which social identities can be deployed in different situations and does not claim that all social identities are equally salient or that they can be equally deployed. In fact, the very tactical appeal of different social identities in dealing with particular circumstances of oppression points to differences in the salience of such identities. As previously noted, it is understandable why Moya is very concerned that identities be understood as having different political and epistemic salience, but this view is compatible with a tactical or a pragmatic deployment of identity as connected to differential consciousness. Again, Sandoval does not make a claim that all identities are equally politically and epistemically salient.

Another issue that arises is whether, given Moya's commitment to realism and her attunement to material conditions, she misinterprets Sandoval's appeal to tactical subjectivity as meaning that a woman of color constantly shifts identities to the extent that it is not clear what her identity is and, furthermore, to the extent that she might even choose an identity that is not connected with her material conditions. In my view, Sandoval's call for this survival tactic as a commitment to a well-defined view of identity in light of an understanding of power relations within given circumstances is not equivalent to the claim that one can choose any identity whenever or wherever, regardless of concrete material and societal facts. Sandoval's account speaks to the multiplicity and complexity of the multiplicitous self rather than muting it, undermining it, or attempting to synthesize or integrate it, or claiming that there is one social identity that is always most salient as opposed to other identities. Instead, her concern is to provide a method based on, among other things, ways in which we can creatively and tactically deal with oppression. This is an Anzaldúan feature of her view. The survival tactic that she proposes is what she considers a commitment to a well-defined, context-sensitive structure of identity that can be transformed depending on its usefulness to resist oppression. As Sandoval states,

> The differential mode of social movement and consciousness depends on the practitioner's ability to read the current situation of power and self-consciously choosing and adopting the

ideological stand best suited to push against its configurations, a survival skill well known to oppressed peoples. Differential consciousness requires grace, flexibility, and strength: enough strength to confidently commit to a well-defined structure of identity for one hour, day, week, month, year; enough flexibility to self-consciously transform that identity according to the requisites of another oppositional ideological tactic if readings of power's formation require it; enough grace to recognize alliance with others committed to egalitarian social relations and race, gender, sex, class and social justice, when these readings of power call for alternative oppositional stands. (2000, 59)

In her critique of Sandoval's view, Moya is guided by her preference for a view that explains identity as moving toward a truer identity, a movement that is key to Moya's vision of nonfragmented and integrated selves with potential for strong political action. Here Moya misses an important aspect of Sandoval's account—attention to social location leads to recognition of multiplicity and to different strategies for fighting oppression. Moya sees Sandoval's view as based on an unstable identity rather than the desired truer, constant, and most salient identity, and thus she interprets this feature of multiplicity in a primarily negative way. Yet attention to the importance of social location demands attunement to the ways in which such location is experienced and points to multiplicity, precisely what Sandoval's view recognizes.

Moya, however, criticizes Sandoval's view as having postmodern elements that make her view problematic. In fact, when evaluating Sandoval's view, Moya states that in Sandoval's account, "cogent insights are compatible with the kind of realist framework I propose, while her postmodernist presuppositions unnecessarily limit her project of apprehending and representing the experiences of women of color" (2002, 82). She understands Sandoval's postmodernist presuppositions as leading her to weaken the link between social location, experience, and identity. Consequently, she sees Sandoval's view as minimizing the differences between the experiences of multiply oppressed people (2002, 89–90). She criticizes Sandoval of abstracting the consciousness of women of color in order to make it accessible to everyone and presenting an "idealized portrait of mobile subjectivity," thus covering over the pain involved in the development of *la facultad* (88).

However, Sandoval's view pays a great deal of attention to the link between social identity and location and is quite attuned to differences among oppressions and relations of power. Sandoval does not claim, as

Moya believes she does, that the skills and knowledge of women of color "can be arrived at, in any sort of willful way" (Moya 2002, 90). Moya seems so intent to criticize any postmodern element in Sandoval's account that she undermines the latter's position. Even though she recognizes that Sandoval does not fit what Moya regards as the "ideal postmodernist" that she is positing, the theorist that completely denies the connections among identity, experience, and social location (90), Moya nevertheless criticizes Sandoval's tactical subjectivity and even claims,

> It is *only* when we have a realist account of our identities, one that refers outward to the world we live in, will we be able to understand what social and political possibilities are open to us for the purpose of working to build a better society. (2002, 99; my emphasis)

Unfortunately, Moya does not see how any postmodern aspect of Sandoval's account could be constructive. She critiques postmodern views in general and holds on to criticisms of postmodernism based on oversimplified readings of views that advocate social construction—for example, the view that whatever is constructed or produced has no connection to material circumstances. Such readings of postmodernist positions have already been critically assessed by various feminists in the 1980s and 1990s and shown to be inadequate. Even Seyla Benhabib, whose critique of Butler's work included similar criticisms that Moya has against postmodernism, has revised her position (Benhabib et al. 1994).[9]

An incredibly interesting issue here is how Latina feminist theories reproduce some of the early debates among feminists regarding social construction. Rather than continue on this path, it would be best if Latina feminist phenomenologists avoided getting caught up in a battle between postmodern Latina thinkers and postpositivist realist Latina thinkers that reproduces early conversations and mistakes and that limits the field of Latina theorizing. Unfortunately, Moya claims that a postpositivist realist view is the *only* theory that would be beneficial to Latinas when fighting oppression and acquiring knowledge (2002, 99). This view is another instance in which her position undermines multiplicity. Yet there are various theories that might be helpful in the important task of fighting oppressive conditions. Ultimately, Moya's postpositivist realist account of identity undercuts the multiplicity of multiplicitous selves and does not fully capture their temporality and their lived experience as complex beings capable of residing at the borderlands and of inhabiting multiple social locations while still being able to have positive, constructive experiences and political engagements.

However, it is important to note that a postpositive realist view does not need to undercut the value of multiplicity. For example, Michael Hames-García, another proponent of postpositivist realism, introduces a "realist theory of multiplicity" inspired by Lugones's view that social identities are intermingling and coconstitutive (Hames-García 2011; Moya and Hames-García 2000). Such a view recognizes the important and positive value of multiplicity. Moya herself acknowledges Hames-García's view but does not have the same commitment to multiplicity. Ultimately, the two positions differ in terms of their vision of identity—that is, while Moya is interested in a view of identity as "remaining more or less constant" (2002, 82), Hames-García does not share this view. As he states,

> When I use the terms "social identity" and "group member-ship," I do not mean to imply absolute sameness or constancy. According to the Latina feminist philosopher María Lugones, "We have to constantly consider and reconsider the question: Who are our own people?" Realism similarly calls for a constant process of verification and revision with regard to the status of our identities. (2011, 111)

This constant process of verification and revision is actually compatible with the postpositive realist claims that Moya makes. Hames-García himself reminds us that, according to Moya's account of PPRI, identities can be verified and changed given existing material and societal conditions (2011, 111n9). However, as discussed earlier, Moya undercuts multiplicity and shows a preference for the forward-moving, truer identity model, along with synthesis and integration. Presumably, once an individual has found her truer identity, there will not be much need for verification and for change.[10]

An analysis of Moya's understanding of her trajectory from seeing herself as a "Spanish Girl" to a "Chicana" reveals problems with the role of multiplicity in this account of PPRI. It points to a lack of attunement to the temporality informing the experience of multiplicitous selves, a temporality that does not privilege the present but rather recognizes the complex inter-action between present, past, and future. Moreover, by privileging a truer identity, this account misses the salience of other identities, as well as the intersectional, intermeshed nature of the self's various identities. Accounts of the lived experience of multiplicitous selves reveal that not all identities have equal salience, and that the intermeshedness of various relevant identities informs such experience. A preference for a forward-moving, truer identity model undermines multiplicity, since this preference for a truer and most salient identity undercuts the significance of other social identities informing one's life. Ultimately, in this account of PPRI there remains a dichotomy in which finding a truer identity, synthesis, and integration is seen as more constructive, while a recognition of the multiplicity of the self's identities and their tactical deployment is seen as negative and connected to lack and fragmentation. While Moya's account of PPRI should be commended for elucidating important points between identity and knowledge, it does not follow through to the implications connected to acknowledging social location in a theory of identity, especially in connection to the multiplicitous selves that writers such as Anzaldúa and Sandoval describe. We are thus left with a fractured, dichotomous vision of self—as searching and finding our truer identity or as being multiple and fragmented without potential for constructive political action.

Recognition of the importance of social location for a theory of identity demands an understanding of the importance of multiplicity, including its positive, constructive moments. As various Latina feminist phenomenologists have shown, multiplicity is not to be understood as having a primarily negative value. The fact that multiplicity leads to liminality, ambiguity, and contradiction is crucial in terms of its ability to lead us to possibilities not only of creativity but also of resistance to various forms of oppression. Indeed, PPRI's drive to truth and truer identity cuts away at the multiplicity and complexity of multiplicitous selves that is not only the cause of many a tear but also many a creative and resistant moment. Many women of color remain unable to find their truer identity or to synthesize the various aspects of their existences, cultures, or ideologies. While it is the case that their being-between-worlds might be a source of stress and pain, it can also lead to creation and transformation. As Lugones states,

> To understand that you are in a limen is to understand that you are not what you are within a structure. It is to know that you have ways of living in disruption and domination. That is, in my mind, a very good beginning toward understanding your liminal world. So, though it is not true that if we stand together in the limen we will understand each other, we can make the weaker claim that if we recognize each other as occupying liminal sites, then we will have a disposition to reach each other away from structural, dominant meaning, or have good reason to do so as oppressed peoples. What we need then is both to be able to

recognize liminality and to go from recognition to deciphering resistant codes. (2006, 79)

Multiplicitous selves remain complex selves; they have multiple under-standings of themselves and an existential as opposed to a linear temporal-ity. The question of which view of identity is best for political action and resistance is a difficult one. As we have seen, Latina feminists envision vari-ous political practices. My own account of coalitional politics is one of the practices we can engage in as we continue with the arduous task of finding ways both to resist and to reconfigure dominant theories and practices that undermine the lives of those at the margins. PPRI should not be understood as the *only* account that would help women of color to fight oppression effectively. It is my hope that more attention is paid to the variety of posi-tions offered by Latina feminists working on issues of self and identity so as to open up discussion of the various ways in which their views intersect or differ from each other, thus promoting more in-depth scholarship in this area and showing different alternatives for thinking about and deploying resistant praxis. We should keep in mind Ofelia Schutte's view,

> Identity politics is important because if we believe in equality, we need to stop the injustice against groups that have been the target of serious prejudice. I don't think, however, that it is necessary to agree on a theory of identity in order to join together politically to struggle for a worthy political end. While I think it is very important to document how racism, sexism, heterosexism, and so on, hurt individuals and turn them into second- or third-class citizens, appealing to people's ability to care about eliminating injustice does not require that we share the same meanings regarding ontology, hermeneutics, a philosophy of perception, and so on. (2009, 33)

While the account of PPRI as described by Moya remains an important contribution in Latina feminism, it is in need of recognizing the importance of multiplicity by seriously considering its positive, constructive value in the multiplicitous self's personal and political endeavors. An account that recognizes the intricate connections among identity, social location, and knowledge needs to consider multiplicity in all its complexity—to do jus-tice to the experience of multiplicitous selves, theorists of identity need to recognize multiplicity, neither undermining it to make our theories more elegant and our selves more neat and accessible, nor exalting it so as to miss the importance of identity, as complicated or multilayered as it might be.

Home is a name, a word, it is a strong one; stronger than magician ever spoke, or spirit ever answered to, in the strongest conjuration.

—Charles Dickens

A whole history remains to be written of spaces—which would at the same time be the history of Powers—from the great strategies of geopolitics to the little tactics of the habitat.

—Michel Foucault

There is nowhere you can go and only be with people who are like you. It's over. Give it up.

—Bernice Johnson Reagon

7

Hometactics

City ordinances that prohibit red doors and colorful houses. Rows and rows of white, gray, light brown houses—sad looking, needing joy. I need more colors, more plants. I want to feel warmth, when beautiful trees lose their every leaf, when whiteness blankets all there is to see, when I shiver and my skin cracks—a nurturing if fleeting sense—I am here.

To start, I have a confession to make: this writing is an exercise in self-mapping, an attempt to deal with a certain nostalgia, a painful fixation on loss and a desire to return to a place called home, a persistent desire that keeps returning as the snow of February in Cleveland, the city I some-times call home. In self-mapping, one locates oneself in life and space and recognizes locations imbued with histories, power relations, cultural and economic forces, and personal dreams and imagination.[1] Home, says bell hooks, is "the safe place . . . the place where the me of me mattered" (2009, 215). Quoting Michael Seidel, Kaplan says that home is the exile's " 'belated romance' with a past, through memory heightened by distance" (Kaplan 1996, 39). I am that exile that unwittingly falls for this romance yet is perfectly aware of its traps. Perhaps it is exile that brings forth the will to belong in a more insistent and gripping way—I am not sure. I think of Ana Mendieta, the Cuban artist who imprinted her silhouette on so many places—grass, sand, earth—only to see it disappear, until she returns to Cuba and carves figures on rock—so as to mark her return "home," the end of her exile—except, of course, she would always be an exile (Ortega, 2004a). I am writing my way home by leaving it, by stripping it away of its magic and its strong conjuration.

The notion of home calls forth the personal, the affective, such as "home is where the heart is," where I can feel comfortable and safe, where I can scratch my itches, where I can be who I am. "Home" is, as Dickens reminds us, a truly magical word, offering a most-needed relief from the world of the weird, the unsafe, the *unheimlich*. Yet, as personal as this notion is, Chandra Mohanty reminds us that it is also profoundly political. She asks, "What is home? The place I was born? Where I grew up? Where my parents live? Where I live and work as an adult? Where I locate my community, my people? Who are my 'people'?" (Mohanty 2003, 126). Answers to these questions are complex and call forth a nexus of histories and experiences, playful and painful, chosen and inherited. Home is where the personal sometimes unexpectedly, sometimes inextricably, meets the political. The home question can thus lead us from the confines of our own skin to the open spaces of worlds inhabited by others like and unlike me, to a politics of location.

In this chapter I discuss the notion of home in connection to the ideas of location, and belonging in light of the experience of multiplicitous selves. In the first section, I point out that the notion of home may be connected to a politics of location that reaffirms so-called authentic identities and serves to exalt those identities by negating those who are deemed as not belonging. Home may become the "barred room" that Bernice Johnson Reagon warned us about in her now-famous speech on coalitional politics (1983, 356–368). I illustrate some difficulties that arise when considering the meaning of belonging given the multiplicity of the self. We will see that given this multiplicity we cannot adhere to a notion of belonging that privileges so-called authentic or primary characteristics of identity.

Informed by Michel de Certeau's analysis of tactics, in the second section, I introduce the notion of hometactics, practices that allow for a sense of familiarity with and a particular sense of "belonging" to a place, space, group, or world while avoiding the restrictive, exclusive elements that a notion of belonging might carry with it. Given my analysis of coalitional politics in chapter 5, which takes into consideration both location and relations with others, being and becoming-with, here I would like to reveal another part of the story of home, location, and belonging—the lived experience of multiplicitous selves, the small yet important everyday practices of those selves as they negotiate their multiple and complex identities and attempt to get a sense of connection to those worlds, what we may call micropractices of lived experience.

Belonging, Location, and Multiplicitous Selfhood

Following Aimee Carrillo Rowe, I see the notion of belonging as a point of departure for understanding, naming, and imagining location (2008, 29). In other words, the notion of belonging is intimately tied to a politics of location, location here meaning not just spatial but also social location.[2] Carrillo Rowe asks that a feminist politics of location theorize the conditions for the possibility of belonging rather than assume an individual subject as already belonging to a location (2008, 25–46). While Carrillo Rowe ultimately moves away from a politics of location to what she terms a "politics of relation," in which locations are formed by a series of affective and political ties with others, her insistence that we understand conditions for the possibility of belonging is key to an analysis of the relationships among home, belonging, and location.

A politics of location that merely assumes individual subjects as already belonging to a location is indeed problematic because belonging is quickly interpreted by way of specific identity markers. Rather than understanding the complex ways in which an individual is said to belong to a social location—the ways personal identity markers as well as relational aspects are linked and negotiated—such a politics of location might quickly turn into a "home" for some members but also a "barred room" for those who are deemed not to belong. In other words, when belonging is a matter of satisfying particular conditions of identity, which in turn become homogenizing conditions, home serves to block out those who are not like us or whom we deem are not like us. Our bodies, our selves, are thus blocked from the entrance of that special room that is home for some but not others, the barred room that Bernice Johnson Reagon warns us about.

As Mohanty notes, Johnson Reagon's concern lies with the problematic spaces created by oppositional political movements that provide a "nurturing space" for a while but ultimately provide only the illusion of community and a freezing of difference (Mohanty 2003, 117). Johnson Reagon is concerned with the idea that a coalition should be as safe as a home, when in reality it is not safe or comfortable. The barred room of those who believe in narrow identity politics and who are seduced by overly nationalistic tendencies might serve as a nurturing space, but not for long. Questions arise as to why I don't belong in that room, or why doesn't he or she belong? Why have others been let in and not me? Don't I satisfy the conditions of belonging? Am I not one of you? And, soon enough, the walls of that room become too thick. That nurturing space reminiscent of the mythic, safe home is transformed into an illusive community in the attempt to reify our difference as Latinos, as Asians, as African Americans, as lesbians, and so on[3] Yet, as Johnson Reagon says, "The room don't feel like the room no more. And it ain't home no more" (1983, 359).

According to Johnson Reagon, community doesn't mean those that are or look like me. Spaces that have been created to reify certain characteristics can be modified when we take into consideration the heterogeneity within our group. I will then have to open the doors for others to get in or for me to get out of my zone of comfort. In the same way, we all have to leave the safety of the home at some point so as to not hide from the rest of the world and others in that world—not to mention those for whom home has never been safe or comfortable and those who have known better.

In order to problematize further the notion of home as connected to a particular kind of belonging, what we might call "authentic belonging," let us consider the experience of multiplicitous selves. As noted in chapter 2, all of us are multiplicitous selves, but there is a crucial difference between those who are comfortable and at ease in various worlds and those whose experience is marginalized, oppressed, or alienated in some way and who have to world-travel constantly. So, it is key to remember that multiplicity is more at issue for some selves than others, depending on the different ways in which their positionalities are perceived or negotiated given specific social, economic, and cultural contexts as well as power relations. For example, recall the way in which economic, social, and cultural issues related to the North-South border affect the new *mestiza* self and lead her to feel the contradictory aspects of herself and to be in-between worlds. Consider the way in which such power relations and social and cultural issues affect a newly arrived immigrant to this country who does not speak the language and who is marginalized, as opposed to the way in which these factors affect the life of someone who is part of the mainstream and whose experience is for the most part one of being-at-ease.

Multiplicitous selves are constantly negotiating their multiple social locations. They are also constantly world-traveling. As noted earlier, I, as a Nicaraguan-born, bilingual, lesbian, academic Latina living in the United States, have to constantly negotiate the multiple aspects of myself and travel to the different worlds associated with my various social positions. Yet, despite my status as a multiplicitous self, I also find myself asking the home question—a home question that comes in terms of geography—is Managua, Nicaragua, really my home, or is it Los Angeles, or Cleveland? And also in terms of associations with others—do I belong with US Latinos, Chicanos, Latin American exiles, or women of color?

The home question is particularly difficult for the multiplicitous self whose life and context are such that she has to continually world-travel, and thus the home question becomes a question of *homes*. Reflection on such a question paradoxically shatters any illusion of there being a definite place of belonging, while it also shatters the very multiplicity of our selves by way of a feeling and a questioning—that feeling of wanting to come home and that question of whether there is a home (or even homes) for me—as if there were a will to belong in the same way that Nietzsche claims there is a will to truth that inspires us to many a venture.[4] It cannot be denied that even for those multiplicitous selves who are border-crossers and world-travelers, the home question is still a question. Perhaps it is even a more painful question precisely because that home seems harder to find or cannot be found given one's multiplicity. Yet, despite the determination of this will to belong that might provide a feeling of security and comfort, we cannot avoid recognizing the limits and pitfalls of such security, namely, the reification of certain identity categories as opposed to others and thus the expulsion of those who do not fit a version of authentic belonging.

Let us look at María Lugones's early essay "Hispaneando y Lesbiando: On Sarah Hoagland's Lesbian Ethics," in which Lugones replies to the call of lesbian separatism (1990). In this essay, Lugones describes the contradictory nature of her lived experience as she asserts her identity as both a Latina and a lesbian in the context of Nuevomejicano culture. While she finds it empowering to participate in keeping the Nuevomejicano culture alive by being part of its community, she realizes that she cannot be openly lesbian there, and thus she feels that her self is diminished in that environment. As she says, "These communities do not recognize us as fully their own if lesbian. The culture is heterosexualist. It does not recognize the possibility of women loving women unmediated by male domination" (1990, 142). Yet Lugones still cannot follow Sarah Hoagland's advice to render the homophobic culture meaningless and agree to lesbian separatism, because this would entail her becoming an "obsolete being" or assimilating into another culture that disregards the needs of lesbians who are not white. Lugones concludes,

> Such a lesbian must, for her own survival and flourishing, acknowledge herself as needing more than "one world." Her ability to inhabit both a world where radical criticism of her culture is meaningful and to inhabit the world of her culture constitute part of the possibility of her future as a creative being. (1990, 144)

Lugones then inhabits both the Latina and the lesbian worlds. In each world she is lacking, and, as a border-dweller, she is not completely in either world. Inspired by Anzaldúa, she continues to have the perspective of the crossroads or the borderlands, a position that allows her a critical edge from which to interpret the multiple worlds she inhabits. She asserts her Latina and lesbian identities without accepting the homophobia present in the context of Nuevomejicano culture and the ethnocentrism present in the Anglo lesbian community.

Like Lugones, I have also found myself wanting to belong in the Latino community and yet being hurt as I experienced the Latino community's homophobia as well as alienation in the Anglo lesbian community. My identities as lesbian and Latina cannot be easily reconciled. In many cases these two identities appear as mutually exclusive. Consequently, I might experience a thick feeling of not being-at-ease or an existential crisis about my selfhood given that in dominant Latino culture lesbianism is generally not accepted. I will not be accepted within the Latino community unless I hide an important aspect of myself or I confine myself to a smaller Latino community, that of Latina lesbians, yet another barred room. As Lugones so aptly puts it, "Pluralism also requires the transformation of those 'home' cultures so that lesbians can be rid of 'homo-phobia' in Anzaldúa's sense: 'the fear of going home'" (Lugones 1990, 143). Yet, like Anzaldúa and Lugones, I still want to be part of the Latino community. This example and countless others (consider Anzaldúa's own example about the difficulties of being Chicana and American, Chicana and lesbian; W.E.B. Du Bois's example of being an African American and an American; Audre Lorde's example of being lesbian and African American) illustrate why the experience of the multiplicitous self might be complicated and fraught with painful moments of what Anzaldúa describes as "intimate terrorism." It also illustrates the need that even the multiplicitous self has of belonging and the drawbacks that such a need generates. As we have seen, ambiguity and contradiction are part and parcel of a life of in-betweenness and being-in-worlds. The difficulties and pain encountered can, as Anzalúa and Lugones have taught us, lead to creative ventures and critical resistance. While many women of color agree with Anzaldúa's claim that the ambiguities and contradictions of the self of the borderlands can open up constructive possibilities, others wonder whether all that the multiplicitous self can do is be tormented by the contradictions and ambiguities brought about by its multiplicity. What can multiplicitous selves do except feel the cactus needles embedded in their skin?

In *Wealth of Selves: Multiple Identities, Mestiza Consciousness, and the Subject of Politics*, Edwina Barvosa tackles critics of what she calls the multiple self and attempts to show that it is in fact this multiple self with its ambiguities and contradictions that can become an agent capable of political critique and social transformation (2008). Barvosa's strategy is to explain the ways in which a multiple, socially constructed self constitutes a cohesive whole that is capable of shifting its social identities in different contexts and of using ambiguity and contradiction to form a critical stance capable of being deployed for political activism. While Barvosa provides an interdisciplinary, complex explanation of the multiple systems at work in what she calls the multiple self, I would like to concentrate on the way she explains Lugones's experience of being a Latina and a lesbian. This example turns out to be as informative as Lugone's example of being playful and unplayful in different worlds.

According to Barvosa, Lugones integrates her mutually exclusive identities as a result of a conscious "self-integrative life project" rather than the usual rank-ordering of identities, as some philosophers suggest multiple selves should do. A self-integrative life project is one in which "self-chosen endorsements are loosely interwoven into broad self-guiding projects that serve as the basis for integrating the self" (Barvosa 2008, 141). For Barvosa, it is precisely the experience of contradiction, ambiguity, and ambivalence that plays an important role in the project of self-integration. Thus she sees Lugones as being able to integrate her different identities of Latina and lesbian because she has a life project of antiracism, anti-ethnocentrism, and anti-heterosexism. Because of this life project, Lugones remains highly identified as a Latina and a lesbian while at the same time using different identity markers at different times to claim a group identity ("selective identification/differential self-presentation"), for example, not including the issue of her sexuality in the Latino context. Thus Lugones's own ambivalence about belonging to the Latino group given its homophobia represents a strategy to hold her multiple identities together (Barvosa 2008, 151). Through having a life project, Lugones, according to Barvosa, can form intersections between her mutually exclusive identities and can claim a space in both communities.

Like Moya, Barvosa calls for integration of the self's various aspects or identities, although her conception of integration is more open to instances of ambiguities and contradiction. As we have seen, the experience of contradiction is key in Barvosa's account because it allows not only for the formation of a critical stance but also for the possibility of integration. As she states,

> I argue that while self-chosen rank-ordered endorsements, narrative unity, and self-fulfilling authenticity may have roles to play for some individuals in their particular processes of self-integration, these three elements alone are inadequate to contain the complexity of self-integration of multiple identities. This inadequacy is especially acute under those circumstances of

conflict or contradiction in which a person's multiple identities are socially constructed as mutually exclusive, or when their life projects have become contradictory due to social, political, or interpersonal conflicts beyond their control. Under these circumstances, enduring contradiction, ambivalence, and ambiguity can play important roles in the self-integration of multiple identities (141–142).

While appealing to integration, Barvosa recognizes that not all multiple selves can achieve integration and thus states that in her view "the self permits degrees of cohesion from a bare and highly fragmented minimum to highly self-integrated identities' (20). I see the value of Barvosa's appeal to a strategic, self-integrating life project as it is something that might be helpful as multiplicitous selves carry on with their lives. Yet it should not be understood as the preferred or necessary practice guiding multiplicitous selves as they negotiate their multiple positionalities. Despite the advantages associated with practicing a strategic, self-integrating life project, not all multiplicitous selves have such a project or desire it. Many prefer to give up the illusion of integration and be willing to live with the ambiguities and contradictions that their multiplicitous selfhood entails; many will be in circumstances in which integration is not possible. Moreover, given Lugones's own characterization of her experience, her appeal to ontological pluralism, as well as the experience of world-traveling in general, it is unclear that she would call for integration, even in Barvosa's sense. Nevertheless, Barvosa's explanation of a multiple self's negotiation of its various and sometimes mutually exclusive identities by way of a self-integrating life project is illustrative of the complexity of the notion of belonging. What we learn from examples such as Lugones's and from Barvosa's attempt to deal with the contradictions inherent in multiplicitous selfhood is that, given the complexity of the selves as well as the complexity of spaces of belonging (in terms of their members as well as criteria for membership), there is no sense in which one can be said to *fully* belong. There are only different senses of belonging depending on which markers of identity are chosen. Full membership and belonging—the safe, comfortable home—is indeed an imaginary space in need of demystification.

In both its personal as well as political instantiations, "home" can easily become a space of exclusion despite its many possibilities of providing nurture and inclusiveness. The childhood home might awaken not only our sense of comfort and love, if there was love and comfort within its walls, but also the sense of insecurity and bitterness at being merely a child who does not know better and a sense of alienation from the outside world. The political "home," the space to nurture our identities, not only affirms us and empowers us as group members but can also deny entrance to others not deemed as belonging unless they silence themselves. When thinking of the case of Lugones strategically choosing different identity markers in different situations, I see how, despite being able to claim both identities as Latina and lesbian, when she joins the Nuevomejicano communities she has to follow their rules/practices/norms and is making herself vulnerable to them. She embeds herself within a regularized location, and silence about her sexual identity is probably the best approach if she is going to participate and build community in such a location. While she may have the possibility to negotiate her identities by way of a self-integrative self-project or by way of differential or *mestiza* consciousness, she remains between worlds and various aspects or identities are actively (or passively—due to outside circumstances) highlighted or covered over. I cannot speak for Lugones here. Yet there are times when I would like to be with Latinos as a Latina lesbian. Clearly, reconsiderations, reframings, remappings of the notions of home, of location, of belonging are necessary.

Hometactics

As we have seen, despite the problems associated with the notions of home, belonging, and location, there is no denying the power that the notion of home has in producing sentiments of safety, comfort, and belonging. But there is also no forgetting its mythical, "unreal" qualities. The reality of the notion of home is many times quite different from our imagined home, both in its personal and political instantiations. I wonder, though, whether we can go beyond the myth of home and move toward a decentered praxis of home-making and belonging, one that gives up the possibility of full belonging and allows for the possibility of not longing to be on one side or site of belonging.[5]

Here I would like to introduce such a praxis as "hometactics." Importantly, I am not suggesting that we should give up all notions of belonging connected to a politics of location, as in Mohanty's work, or to a politics of relation, as in Carrillo Rowe's work. My own position, coalitional politics, is a practice mindful of both location and relation. I am also not suggesting that we should give up all attempts at projects of self-integration, as in Barvosa's account. There is room and necessity for larger political projects of co-belonging as well as moments when it might be necessary to integrate certain aspects of our multiplicitous selves. Yet I would like to add another layer to our attempt to understanding home, location, and belonging, a layer that is many times overlooked as we emphasize the grander project of forging a politics capable of generating resistance to oppression or projects that emphasize unity or integration. This layer is that of the lived experience of multiplicitous selves that are being-between-worlds and being-in-worlds and that find themselves constantly negotiating their multiple identities in light of both ambiguities and contradictions but also in light of what I have referred to here as a will to belong. Thus my introduction of the notion of hometactics is an uncovering of what multiplicitous selves are already practicing in their everydayness, a disclosure of that which is *already* happening in our lived experience.

As opposed to strategies, which de Certeau sees as bound up with regulations or set ways (norms/practices/laws) upheld by a dominant order, de Certeau sees a tactic as "a calculated action determined by the absence of a proper locus" and as the "art of the weak" (1984, 37). Tactics are creative, inventive, combining different elements of a system (or a set of strategies) "blow by blow," and cannot be easily traced or mapped. In terms of their relation to specific spaces, unlike strategies that impose and place limits on spaces, tactics divert spaces. According to de Certeau, tactics use time in a clever way, produce alternative opportunities, and introduce play into the foundations of power (1984, 38). In short, tactics are temporal interventions aimed at producing favorable situations but not necessarily at abolishing a system of power.

De Certeau's classic example of practicing tactics is walking in the city (he also considers reading, storytelling, and cooking)—the different ways in which we improvise when we walk—walking in the city without a set map, getting a sense of the city despite its largeness and foreignness (the pedestrian reading the city but also writing it through her walking). For example, de Certeau discusses the example of a migrant of North African descent now living in Paris and walking this city's streets, the way he dwells in his housing development and uses his environment with plurality and creativity, and thus "by an art of being in between, he draws unexpected results from his situation" (1984, 30). According to de Certeau, he develops modes of use or "re-use" as he acculturates in his new environment.

Although I realize the difference of the context within which de Certeau introduces the distinction between strategies and tactics, an analysis of capitalist modes of production and consumption, it is possible to apply it to the context of an examination of the notion of belonging in light of the experience of multiplicitous selfhood. As we shall see later, Lugones has already engaged de Certeau's distinction to analyze the possibility of resistance on the part of those who are marginalized, although my discussion and hers have some significant differences. Hometactics share some of the characteristics described earlier by de Certeau, but not all. For example, while I doubt de Certeau would want to circumscribe tactics in this manner, I see hometactics as a decentered praxis that is at the same time capable of having a general aim or result. The aim of hometactics can be understood as the production of a sense of familiarity in the midst of an environment or world in which one cannot fully belong due to one's multiple positions and instances of thin and thick not being-at-ease. Such a sense of familiarity is, of course, not to be associated with the problematic idea of belonging that leads to barred rooms generally associated with so-called authentic markers of identity. And while hometactics can be said to have this general aim, no specific, set formulation of what these practices look like is possible, since one of the main features of tactics are precisely their unmappability and their working "blow by blow," taking advantages of opportunities as they present themselves.

In "Tactical Strategies of the Streetwalker/Estrategias Tácticas de la Callejera," Lugones problematizes de Certeau's dichotomous distinction between tactics and strategies (Lugones 2003, ch. 10). Lugones believes that de Certeau's view cannot offer the possibility of theorizing resistance from the point of view of the oppressed and from what she terms a concrete body-to-body engagement, because the strategist is not able to understand the logic of the tactical, and the tactical is seen as "haphazard, happenstance, disjointed intrusions on dominant sense, a troubled sort of passivity" (2003, 216). Lugones thus proposes "tactical strategies" in order to disrupt the dichotomy between strategy and tactic and to offer a position in which a liberatory project is not guided by a mastermind or strategist. Instead, the liberatory project is intersubjective and based on concrete, embodied subjects at the street level (tactical strategists, "streetwalkers," or "active subjects") who perform acts that go beyond merely "making do" (2003, 207–209, 216). As Lugones states, "As we move from tactics to tactical strategies we move from ephemeral contestatory negotiations of sense to more sustained engagements" (2003, 218).

For Lugones, such sustained engagement is connected to the resistant practice of hanging out, which, as we have seen, allows the tactical strategist to develop a sense of the spatial context so as to see new possibilities in it. This sense of the spatial context available to the streetwalker or tactical strategist, is, according to Lugones, neither the "nowhere" of de Certeau's tactician nor the "proper" space of the strategist. It is constituted by hang-outs, which are fluid spaces that allow for multivocal sense and critical interventions against structures of domination (2003, 221). In effect, then, while problematizing de Certeau's distinction between strategies and practices, Lugones provides a "spatial politics" (2003, 220).

Lugones's emphasis on spatiality is one aspect of her analysis that I find particularly important and helpful. I agree that de Certeau's analysis misses the significance of spatiality as it is connected to tactics. While de Certeau's own characterization of tactics as opposed to strategies prioritizes the importance of time to that of place, in my view it is possible to understand tactics as giving meaning to both time and space without necessarily reifying them. De Certeau notes,

> Tactics are procedures that gain validity in relation to the perti-
> nence they lend to time—to the circumstances which the precise
> instant of an intervention transforms into a favorable situation,
> to the rapidity of the movements that change the organization
> of a space, to the relations among successive moments in an
> action, to the possible intersections of durations and heteroge-
> neous rhythms, etc. (1984, 38)

According to de Certeau, tactics prioritize time because of the way in which our actions create possibilities that might be favorable to our lives. Yet it is possible to think how creating such possibilities might allow us to get a sense of connection to a particular location while we traverse the complicated world of multiplicitous selfhood without necessarily having a particular location designated as our home.

Lugones is right on the mark to expose the weaknesses of de Certeau's characterizations of strategies and tactics in light of the possibility of a more sustained liberatory project, or a "spatial politics." I welcome her proposal for a more intersubjective, fluid, spatial politics attentive to difference and leery of clearly marked dichotomies. My account of hometactics, however, does not emphasize a larger spatial politics, not because of lack of interest but because here I wish to bring to light the more personal day-to-day practices of multiplicitous selves as they struggle with the home question. While I realize the connection between the personal and the political, here I am pointing to daily practices connected to the home question that are not necessarily aligned to an explicit political project.

Importantly, Lugones does not have any affinity to the notion of "home." Consider a footnote in her tactical strategies chapter:

> Streetwalkers include women who are at odds with "home." The home-shelter-street-police station/jail/insane asylum-cemetery circle, in ever so many permutations, is their larger understanding of home. Home is lived as a place inseparable from other places of violence, including the street. One could punctuate any other place in this circle. I count myself more skillful at dodging violence in the street. (2003, 209)

For her, home is more reminiscent of violence. There are no magical conjurations in this concept, no appeal to comfort and ease. It is another chapter in yet another unfortunate dichotomy of public/private that Lugones also wishes to dismantle in her analysis of tactical strategies. For me, however, the question of home and the will to belong associated with it are still issues, deeply personal issues, despite my clear understanding of the dangers of the myth of home and my understanding of the larger political questions associated with the home question. It is precisely this paradoxical position that motivates this discussion. My account of hometactics is my response to the paradoxical will to belong while understanding the mythical, magical, and thus unreal, aspects of home. It is also my disclosure of what multiplicitous selves are already doing in their everyday experience. I clearly do not oppose grander and more sustained political projects, but I do not wish to overlook or forget those moments when multiplicitous selves struggle with everydayness and find ways, yes, to "make do," to feel comfortable in spite of a clear understanding of the ways in which power relations are bound to undermine, to hurt, to alienate.

In my view, hometactics can be deployed at a personal or relational level. They are everyday practices that multiplicitous selves can perform in order to have a sense of familiarity, ease, or sense of belonging in a space or location, even though that space is a new or foreign one, or in a social gathering or community, despite the fact that a community might be made up of members claiming different identities. Hometactics are practices that we might suddenly recognize as granting us new possibilities of belonging in a location and a sense of identification with others with whom we may or may not share social identities, all without the appeal to a fixed home location, an intentional self-integrating life-project, or a set of so-called authentic identity markers.

Since hometactics are everyday practices in which we literally "make do" with what we have, they do not form a robust sense of belonging or familiarity, whether it is associated with a location or a group, and thus they might not be capable of forging strong political coalitions that can establish practices of resistance. Yet, what can be viewed as a lack of political functionality or strength does not undermine their importance in terms of the lived experience of multiplicitous selves. The sense of individual or group "belonging" that they might provide is a great source of comfort in the midst of the complex, sometimes ambiguous, sometimes contradictory lives of multiplicitous selves. Such a comfort is not based on a great myth or conjuration, such as the traditional notion of home, or on a grand self-integrating life project, but on particular everyday practices of "making do" with the incredibly complex and thorny yet creative and resourceful lived experience of the multiplicitous self.

How multiplicitous selves "make do" in their everydayness, how they engage in hometactics, is an important issue that we need to consider if we are to understand the phenomenology of multiplicitous selfhood. What I am calling hometactics, microtechniques of lived experience, is already being put in practice by these selves and might prove to be useful for those who are not already doing it. Important questions as to the extent to which such hometactics might be found to be too opportunistic within dominant schemas, might be representative of not just making do but of "selling out," might be too passive, might be too complicit in dominant schemes, or might or might not preclude the possibility of more sustained political projects need to be examined. That is, some could claim that hometactics could create a certain comfort or a being-at-ease while we are in worlds that might take away our critical attitude or possibilities of resistance to dominant norms, thus minimizing the desire or need to world-travel. This is an important concern that needs to be taken into consideration when thinking about hometactics. Yet my point here is to emphasize the fact that, given the complexity and difficulty of the lives a multiplicitous selves, these selves are *already* engaging in practices that allow them to have a sense of comfort within worlds in which they are not welcomed. Engagement in these practices does not preclude the possibility of critical world-traveling or a more sustained, resistant political engagement

Hometactics are practices that we develop as we travel our various worlds and that we can later repeat or maintain. Such practices are varied and depend on the specific experiences and locations of the selves that deploy them. They might range from painting the walls of your apartment with bright colors, such as the ones that remind you of a childhood home or your country origin; "reusing" your environment in various ways so as to make it more welcoming; making and sharing foods you used to eat in your past by improvising with ingredients that are available (here I pause to reflect on how satisfying it was to eat a *nacatamal*, a Nicaraguan tamale, in Cleveland); to rethinking, refeeling the meaning of family by developing new relationships with a neighbor, getting so close that he becomes family, too. Hometactics also include finding ways of relating to members of other groups with whom one was not associated before. There are linguistic hometactics as well, switching languages in different contexts or integrating words from familiar languages to feel more at ease.

An example of this latter case regarding linguistic practices is the way in which I immediately switch to speaking Spanish as soon as I find out that someone I have been introduced to speaks the language, or the way in which I add Spanish words while I am speaking in English. I still feel tremendous pleasure when speaking Spanish, and it gives me an incredible sense of comfort. As I live in an area where there are few Latinos, and I work at a university with very few Latinos, speaking Spanish becomes a treat, a joy. However, critics concerned with the deployment of hometactics that might lead to a "selling out" or to a too comfortable position within a dominant schema would have a different concern regarding linguistic hometactics. They might point out the way in which some immigrants might adopt the new language and prioritize it in order not just to feel more at ease but also to assimilate to the dominant culture. This might be a concern, although language assimilation is a lengthy process and might go well beyond "making do." Yet, as noted, an important aspect of hometactics is that they are micropractices used in different ways by different people. My view is that they do not necessarily have to be used in such a way to become complicit with dominant norms (e.g., passing, acting white, etc.). Although they may be used in this manner, what I find most interesting and meaningful about hometactics is the manner in which we deploy them in order to feel comfortable in strange or unwelcoming worlds, while at the same time being deeply aware of the oppressive nature of dominant norms in those worlds. Ultimately, I am appealing to the existential dimension of hometactics, to the manner in which they can facilitate my everyday being-in-worlds despite the ambiguity connected to my ability to find a sense of belonging while being aware that such belonging is not possible.[6]

There are many hometactics that we can practice and are already practicing in order to make our lives more comfortable, to alleviate the stress, pain, anxiety that can arise from a life of in-betweenness and world-traveling. As noted, these practices might be connected to remaking "home" within a new environment or performing activities reminiscent of the place/space/culture/people we once associated or currently associate with "home." Such practices make my new context easier to navigate. They are connected to our particular histories, desires, contexts, and abilities to make a better life in spaces in which we do not quite fit. These practices are varied and are usually not planned in advance. They are developed in the midst of, as Heidegger would say, our "throwness" in our various worlds and borders. While some of these practices might provide being-at-ease, comfort, and a sense of belonging, they do not necessarily preclude a critical, resistant attitude in the worlds we traverse.

As noted in earlier chapters, the multiplicitous self's creative as well as resistant potential is tied to her very liminality. While multiplicitous selves at the margins may deploy a number of hometactics to gain a sense of comfort in their lives, I suspect that given their condition as multiplicitous, as marginalized, as not being part of dominant groups, they will also encounter many instances of what I have referred to as thin and thick not being-at-ease. That is, they will experience every day the breaking down of equipment or norms as well as more existential crises related to their identities that will continue to make them more aware of their liminal condition. Even when performing the dominant norms expected of dominant culture, we will be somehow reminded that we do not belong. It is not possible, then, to say with certainty how and whether hometactics are going to make us too complicit with dominant norms and practices as they will be deployed in various ways. Here my aim is not to provide a theory of hometactics that fully explains how they work and the specific roles that they play in the lives of multiplicitous selves. I am trying to bring to light practices that I already employ in my everyday existence in order to have some comfort in my life, practices that I suspect many multiplicitous selves are also engaging in as they negotiate their complex lives in worlds where they might not be wanted, respected, or even seen.

While I was inspired to think about hometactics as I examined my own lived experience and how I tried to find more comfort in unwelcoming worlds, I realize that my discussion has been limited to their use by multiplicitous selves who are alienated or marginalized. What about those multiplicitous selves that find themselves in more dominant positions? Given my view that all of us are multiplicitous selves, there arises the possibility that members of dominant groups or those occupying positions of power can engage in hometactics due to their not feeling comfortable in certain contexts. Given our multiplicity, it is very possible that members of dominant groups don't experience being-at-ease in all aspects of their lives, and so it is very likely that they also have to deploy hometactics in different contexts and worlds. As we have learned from Lugones, the simple dichotomy of dominant/marginalized, oppressor/oppressed is not enough to explain our lived experience. Recall that all multiplicitous selves are oppress-ing/being-oppressed ⇔ resisting. That is to say, given our multiplicity and the various worlds we inhabit, we may gain a great deal of advantage by virtue of some of our social identities but not others. In some worlds we are more marginalized than in others, and in some worlds we fall on the side of the dominant. For example, as a light-skinned, educated Latina, I have many more privileges than many other Latinas who have not had the opportunities that I have had. Yet this does not erase the fact that for many multiplicitous selves, for many *atravesados*, life continues to be difficult in many areas. It is understandable, then, how even multiplicitous selves that can be seen as being part of dominant groups, or that have a privileged position, might make use of hometactics under certain conditions.

Nevertheless, the worrisome issue is the possibility of these selves in dominant positions using hometactics to satisfy and carry forth colonialist and imperialist desires. Another way to make the point is by asking whether the colonizer can engage in hometactics if he does not feel at ease in spe-cific contexts of the colonized society, and whether he can engage in those practices as a way of imposing his home in the new territory.[7] Here many images come to mind, including images of the British, Spanish, and other colonizing countries bringing their home with them to the new places of conquest, transforming these new territories so as to fit their customs and desires rather than adapting to their new land and customs. While initially some of the practices might be in fact a matter of being more comfortable in unfamiliar environments, one can easily see how these practices become impositions. In these cases, I would say that those practices the colonizers used in order to bring their homes with them cannot be seen as hometactics in the sense described here. They do not represent ways of "making do" in unfriendly, unwelcoming environments for the purposes of creating comfort in a life filled with difficulties due to one's in-betweenness, marginalization, and oppression. They are sustained, intentional practices with the specific purpose of imposing one's way of life on a world that one considers inferior and inhabited by inferior beings. These practices become strategies inten-tionally deployed to undermine, demoralize, and chip away at the fabric of a society that is not regarded as worthy of respect.

Hometactics, understood as practices deployed by multiplicitous selves in order to gain comfort and ease in a life of liminality and in-betweenness, a life that is not a stranger to oppression and marginalization, remain an important aspect of the lived experience of these selves. Yet given the open-ended and unmappable character of these practices, it is not possible to make *a priori* claims regarding what multiplicitous subjects are up to or what they always ought to be doing when they deploy these hometactics. For me, hometactics have been a way of not just surviving in my travels across worlds but of feeling a sense of much-needed familiarity and relief in the midst of an existence filled with contradictions and ambiguities that led both to moments of intimate terrorism—cactus needles embedded in the skin—and to exciting moments of creativity and resistance.

I would like to conclude with another confession. I am a philosopher working in an academic environment that continues to privilege maleness and whiteness and writing by maleness and whiteness, the two attributes still considered by many as the bearers of philosophical excellence. Recall how Hegel wrote that women are like plants and that Africans could not arrive at *Geist*—Hegel's views of women and people of color being just two of the many reminders of the narrow, restricting, and alienating intellectual space of philosophy, a space that I precariously inhabit. There have been changes; there has been growth. Talk of inclusiveness, talk of justice. But the writing that comes from the white female hand is still more important even within feminism, the movement pushing philosophy and others to see farther, to understand more. So what can I do? I take what is given to me and make it my own . . . with words, with ink, with my lived experience. I offer you these words, these thoughts. I carve out a space for me in this philosophy that was never meant to be a home for me—this is one of my hometactics.

When I write it feels like I'm carving bone. It feels like I'm creating my own face, my own heart.

—Gloria Anzaldúa

It must be noted, however, that each woman of color cited here, even in her positing of a "plurality of self," is already privileged enough to reach the moment of cognition of a situation for herself. This should suggest that to privilege the subject, even if multiple-voiced, is not enough.

—Norma Alarcón

Sed de Saber/Thirst to Know, acrylic, 24 x 24 inches, by Mortega

Afterword

Mañana estará seca la sangre. Ni sudor, ni lágrimas, ni orina podrán llenar el hueco de un corazón vacio/Tomorrow the blood will be dry. Neither sweat, nor tears, nor urine will fill the hollow of the empty heart (text in purple background by Joaquin Pasos). Este es el ser. Este es el corazón. Hay que vestirlo y bañarlo/This is being. This is the heart. It must be dressed and bathed (text in red background).

I come back to Anzaldúa's words. When I write I am carving bone, making my own face, my own heart, my own hearts. Trying to make a space for me, my thoughts, my black and red ink, in an unfriendly world. I surprise myself. Wounding questions sometimes return, "Where is your green card? Did you come on a boat?" How did I move forward? A song by a Nicaraguan poet remains in my head. "Song of the War of Things" tells about the hearts that will remain hollow from the ravages of war. A revolution brought me to the world of English language, strip malls, and Thanksgiving dinners, and to this world of philosophy. Philosophy both negates me and gives me new ways to see, to understand, to feel, to be. This is my hometactic. But there are many worlds, painted yellow, blue, multicolor. They wait for me, inviting me to explore, to learn. To suffer in them. I taste their blood, fill my heart—don't let my heart become hollow. I am in-between worlds; I travel worlds. New possibilities, new becomings-with you. Thank you for traveling with me in a journey of unlikely companions. Anzaldúa and Lugones go hand in hand. Heidegger and Anzaldúa and Lugones have yet to know one another. This is a start.

A Final Note: From Love of Exclusion to Love of Wisdom and an Invitation

While my philosophical analysis has led me to offer a *theory* of the multiplicitous, in-between self, I hope that this theory is more attuned to our complexity, multiplicity, and to our many intersecting, intermeshing social identities—and to the experience of those who remain in the margins due to hate, prejudice, greed, ignorance, or thirst for power. I have not, as Calvino would say, eliminated all the flesh and bones from the self, but I have also not deeply engaged with that flesh. More philosophical accounts informed from other horizons specific to our race, sexual orientation, class, and ability need to come to light. Yet I wish to open new roads for phenomenological accounts and to raise the voices of Latina feminist phenomenologies. The crossroads between existential phenomenology and Latina feminism have much to offer as we provide more inclusive theories, as we try to avoid the pitfalls of great thinkers who nonetheless covered up, erased, excluded the lives of so many.

This is a project of *mestizaje*, of disclosure—of making visible, audible, and perceptible the works of Latina feminist phenomenologists. We are in need of works that disclose rather than make invisible, cover up, or distort the lives of *los atravesados*, of those who have been excluded or left at the margins of philosophy, the so-called love of wisdom that has really been a love of exclusion. How have grand theories such as liberalism been tied to ignorance (Mills 1997), to racism (Sheth 2009)? How has philosophy turned women of color into "others, "outsiders," like Alcibiades rejected by Socrates (Marcano 2012)? How has it undermined so many? By assigning them with barbarity, stupidity, dependence, childishness. But some works do not hide the elephant in the room; they do not let us forget philosophy's racism (Bernasconi & Cook 2003; Eze 1997; Park 2013). Eze's reader *Race and the Enlightenment* brings to light the following statements by some of our most admired thinkers, statements that we cannot and should not forget:

From Hume's *Of National Characters*:

> I am apt to suspect the negroes and in general all other species of men (for there are four or five different kinds) to be naturally inferior to the whites. There never was a civilized nation of any other complexion than white, nor even any individual eminent either in action or speculation. No ingenious manufactures amongst them, no arts, no sciences. On the other hand the most rude and barbarous of the whites, such as the ancient Germans and present Tartars, have still something eminent about them . . . (Qtd. in Eze 1997, 33)

From Kant's *Observations on the Feeling of the Beautiful and the Sublime*:

The Negroes of Africa have by nature no feeling that rises above the trifling. (Qtd. in Eze 1997, 55)

From Hegel's *Letters on the Philosophy of World History*:

The characteristic feature of the Negroes is that their consciousness has not yet reached an awareness of any substantial objectivity—for example, of God or the law—in which the will of man could participate and in which he could become aware of his own being. . . . The Negro is an example of animal man in all his savagery and lawlessness, and if we wish to understand him at all, we must put aside all our European attitudes. We must not think of a spiritual God or of moral laws; to comprehend him correctly, we must abstract from all reverence and morality, and from everything which we call feeling. . . . For this very reason, we cannot properly feel ourselves into his nature, no more than into that of a dog or of a Greek as he kneels before the statue of Zeus. (Qtd. in Eze 1997, 127)

A look at Beverly Clack's reader *Misogyny in the Western Philosophical Tradition* illustrates how the philosophical tradition has described women, consequently excluding their thought. The most well-known example here is from Hegel's *Elements of the Philosophy of Right*:

Women may be well educated, but they are not made for the higher sciences, for philosophy and certain artistic productions which require a universal element. Women may have insights, taste, and delicacy, but they do not possess the ideal. The difference between man and woman is the difference between animal and plant . . . (Qtd. in Clack 1999, 177)

Racist, sexist, and deeply offensive remarks are many, but it is interesting to note that were it not for a feminist or a critical race theory approach to philosophy, these remarks themselves would remain invisible and in a sense present in their absence in philosophy classes. The virtues of deontological ethics and the beauty of the concept of *Geist* are taught without regard to the racist and sexist ideas contained in philosophical greats such as Kant and Hegel. The *Angst* of *Dasein* is pondered without comments on Heidegger's Nazism. And what do we call this utter disregard of racism,

sexism, and political reactionary views? We call it philosophy—love of wisdom! It is astonishing to think that countless students are taught philosophy
in a way that undermines or makes invisible so many. How many texts
written by women and men of color are read in philosophy classes? How
many of these texts are taught in the courses Introduction to Philosophy
and Continental Philosophy? When Hegel or Kant or other great figures of
philosophy are taught, are their inappropriate, racist, sexist remarks taught
as well? "Ah . . . but those views were characteristic of his time," many
will say. Many more will complain about imposing contemporary attitudes
concerning oppression to historical periods when these concerns found no
expression. And there will be the ones who say that the type of philosophy
they teach just "doesn't have anything to do with particularity"—so universal
are their concerns that there is no need to bring cultural, historical, or social
considerations or issues of social identities—"Let those who teach literature,
psychology, and sociology do that work." Let *them* digress. Or, "There are
just not that many works by people of color or women that could be used."
Or, "I just do not know that literature; I need to ask a person of color to
give me the information."

There are many excuses and many reasons given, some of which do not
have to do with claims to ignorance but with arrogance and gatekeeping, for
continuing the practice of philosophy as a single axis—the discipline that
highlights and prioritizes the thought of white men, old and young—and
if not white men, white women. How does the feminist who is sickened
by the previous quotations still, following Kant, Hegel, and other philosophers, disregard, fear, or hate the other, even if in more subtle ways, even
if lovingly (Ortega 2006a)? What can we do to make philosophy wiser?

I propose that we develop a praxis of intersectional philosophy, to
practice philosophy in a way that is mindful of both how philosophical
texts, traditional or contemporary, can be read in light of concerns related
to race, class, gender, sexual orientation, physical ability, nationality, and
so forth, and the way these are intermeshed or inform one another and in
light of how philosophical texts intersect with texts from other disciplines.
It will require that we see philosophy anew and leave behind its many
claims to purity. It will require that we be creative and that we read texts
through new lenses.

It will require that we learn from the wisdom of women of color.
Patricia Hill Collins calls for an understanding of intersectionality both
as an interpretation of the social world and as a form of critical inquiry
(Intersectionality Symposium at Michigan State University, April 2013).
This critical inquiry involves both a diagnostic project (methodologies that

critique the current social world) as well as a creative or constructionist project (methodologies that create new possibilities). Practicing intersectional philosophy would thus require us to read philosophical texts not merely to dissect them for the sake of knowing what Kant, Hegel, Arendt, Beauvoir, Fanon, and others said, but with both the diagnostic and constructionist projects in mind, with an attunement to how these texts can be connected to our current social world and how they can help us create new possibilities within our discipline and in the worlds in which we dwell. Both projects would be attentive to the interlocking nature of race, class, age, sex, gender, sexual orientation, bodily ability, nationality, and so on. While some philosophers, particularly critical race theorists and feminist theorists, are engaging in such projects already, more needs to be done.

While introducing this intersectional approach to our philosophical practices might yield what I would consider a wiser practice of philosophy, a wider opening of our philosophical eyes by taking into consideration not just one subjecthood—the white male—and not just analytic, intellectual concerns but also attention to social justice, this approach is not without its problems. As Kimberlé Crenshaw reminds us, there are also intersectional elisions—that is, even within attempts that have paid attention to intersectionality, invisibility and exclusion take place. A notable example is the feminist movement, which, as we are well aware, excluded women of color and their concerns, concentrating in the single axis of white middle-class women, and which, even when it became aware of this exclusion and modified itself so as to include women of color, continues to engage in internal exclusions. While there is some attention to the lives of women of color, and a few texts by women of color have become standard, there is still a lack of in-depth analyses of the work of women of color. The infatuation with the work of white European women such as Beauvoir, Irigaray, Kristeva, and others continues. The epistemic violence as well as the loving, knowing ignorance concerning the lives and works of women of color continues (Dotson 2011; Ortega 2006a). Women of color continue inhabiting a "negative socio-economic space" and being "socialized out of existence" (Dotson, unpublished manuscript).

Let us then keep practices of *mestizaje* and intersectionality as we engage in philosophical work. Intersectionality may be helpful not only in the way we approach philosophical texts but also in how we view ourselves as philosophers. When referring to group identities, Crenshaw notes that they are "potential coalitions waiting to be formed" (1995, 377). Can we see ourselves as philosophers open to other philosophers of different identities and philosophical schools, as well as to theorists from other disciplines, and consider the possibility of coalition in our quest for knowledge and social justice? Let us return to María Lugones for a moment. When she tackles the difficult question of coalitions and suggests the model of *deep coalition* calling for *complex communication*, she appeals to the work of Humberto Maturana and his reading of the story of the Tower of Babel. She states,

> The Christian Holy Book has it that the Tower of Babel was being built so as to reach heaven. The Christian god disrupted that project by disrupting the original, unified language. It produced a division among people by creating linguistic division. Maturana suggests that the introduction of the 72 languages will not have created the division unless one adds a disposition against understanding each other's way of life. It is this disposition, an openness to learn each other's meaning, that we are often lacking and that we need to understand each other in a coalitional limen. (Lugones 2006, 84)

While I see Lugones's model for deep coalition as being far from attainable in the current state of philosophy and given the number of dominant subjectivities that make up part of the profession, I want to leave you with the question prompted by Maturana and Lugones: As philosophers, do we lack the disposition to understand each other's way of life? If we do, let's remember Collins's call for an intersectional, critical, and constructive project; let's remember Anzaldúa's creative *mestizaje*; let's reconstruct the way we do philosophy; let's drop the false idols and break the imposing statues that are gatekeepers of the profession; and let's ignore the empty promises of justice and neutrality and not allow those who have no disposition for understanding each other's way of life define what really should be a love of wisdom, not of exclusion.

Notes

Introduction: Latina Feminism,
Existential Phenomenology, and the Self

1. Philosophical discussions on "identity" are varied and include analyses of a number of issues, notably the problem of "personal identity," or finding the criterion/a that makes it possible for a person to be the same over time or to have numerical identity. One of the most important views of personal identity is John Locke's, which takes the main criterion for personhood to be memory (Perry 1975, 33–52). See Perry (2002) for explanations of the different philosophical treatments on the issues of identity and self, many of which have had to respond to the Lockean memory criterion. However, the notion of "identity" may also be used to discuss social, political, or national identities. The concept of "selfhood" is understood in a broader sense—that is, it has to do with the different general characteristics that make up a self. "Subjectivity" is yet another philosophical term associated with discussions regarding the metaphysical and epistemic status of human beings—for example, the Cartesian account of epistemic subjectivity, which posits a subject that has a primarily epistemic relationship to the world via mental representations, and the Kantian transcendental account of subjectivity, which explains the conditions for the possibility for the unity of experience. Here I do not follow the traditional philosophical line of inquiry about personal identity. Instead I discuss the more general notion of selfhood. I am interested in an analysis of selfhood that is attuned to both metaphysical and existential concerns.

2. Phenomenology is a 20th-century philosophical movement concerned with the study of structures of consciousness and experience as understood from a first-person perspective. Important figures in this movement include Edmund Husserl, Martin Heidegger, Jean Paul Sartre, Simone de Beauvoir, and Edith Stein. While Husserl, considered the founder of phenomenology, developed a method for *transcendental* phenomenology, or the study of structures of consciousness, Heidegger, Sartre, and others developed the study of *existential* phenomenology, which is characterized by an analysis of the structures of being human. One of the characteristics that these existential phenomenologists share is the view that human beings have a primarily nonreflective, practical orientation in the world. Merleau Ponty is recognized for his explicit analysis of embodied subjectivity in his influen-

tial *Phenomenology of Perception* (2003), which remains one of the most important philosophical discussions of embodiment. Merleau Ponty proposes a new vision of an embodied subjectivity in which there is an intertwining between the mental and the physical and discloses the primacy of perception. In this view, the body is not merely a sum of parts but a synthesis or nexus of living meanings (part I, ch. 4). Nevertheless, despite his interest in embodiment, Merleau Ponty fails to discuss issues concerning race and gender. Contemporary philosophers are thus applying his phenomenological insights about embodiment to discussions regarding various social identities. For example, see Al Saji (2014) for a discussion of Merleau Ponty and racializing vision; Linda Martín Alcoff (2006, ch. 7) for a discussion of the relationship between the habitual body and racist practices; Olkowski and Weiss (2006) for an important compilation of feminist interpretations of Merleau Ponty; Weiss (2008) for a view inspired by Merleau Ponty about the manner in which race, class, sexuality, gender, ability, age, and ethnicity inform ordinary experience and how such experience can be reconfigured; and Young (2005) for some of the most influential discussions in feminist philosophy about female embodied lived experience. While in this work I do not engage explicitly with Merleau Ponty's phenomenology, my discussion of multiplicitous selfhood follows Merleau Ponty in his understanding of the self as fundamentally embodied and as having an existential sense of spatiality in terms of the self's specific situations and activities. See Aho (2010) for an interesting discussion on the manner in which Heideggerian philosophy, which is usually criticized for not considering the body, can be seen as contributing to theories of embodiment. For a classic, historical introduction to the phenomenological movement see Spiegelberg (1984).

3. There are numerous writings by women of color that have been highly influential in feminism and that opened many new doors to me as a philosopher and that continue to inspire me: Alarcón 1991; Martín Alcoff 2006; Alexander 2005; Anzaldúa 1987; Bambara 2005; Collins 2008; Crenshaw 1989, 1995; Davis 1983; García, 1997; Guy-Sheftall 1995; hooks 1981; Hull, Bell Scott, & Smith 1982; Lorde 1984; Lowe 1996; Lugones 2003; Minh-ha 1989; Mohanty, Russo, & Torres, 1991; Moraga & Anzaldúa 1983; Narayan 1997; Pérez 1999; Sandoval 2000; Schutte 1993, 1998; Smith 2005; and Trujillo 1998. For a recent important collection on women of color feminist philosophy, see Dotson 2014.

4. For a discussion of Heidegger and the political question, including his endorsement of National Socialism, see de Beistegui 1998; Farías 1991; Faye 2009; Lacoue-Labarthe 1990; Radloff 2007; Rockmore & Margolis 1992; Wolin 1993; and Young 1998. (Note that Farías and Faye have both been highly criticized for their approach to the issue.) The release of Heidegger's *Black Notebooks* further confirms Heidegger's endorsement of National Socialism and has sparked more debates on the issue. Unfortunately, the debate is simplified by interpreters who feel that they have to fight for the right to read Heidegger (Marder 2014) and those who oppose reading Heidegger at all because of his anti-Semitism. In a 2014 blog, John E. Drabinski makes an important point when he states,

Who are we in relation to the text? If we take suspicion seriously, suspicion that these texts are entangled, then we begin the process of critical dismantling—searching for what Levinas called "the echo of that evil" in the entangled text. (Of course Levinas never heard the echo of evil in his own work, but that's another story.) If we are afraid of that entanglement and hold fast to our provincial concerns, casting the entire issue in terms of "right to read" and "censorship," then who are we? What kind of scholars have we become? (2014)

5. For those not familiar with Heidegger's work, *Dasein* is the term that he uses instead of traditional philosophical terms such as "self" or "subject"; Heidegger creates his own terminology in order to avoid metaphysical and epistemological assumptions associated with traditional philosophical terms. *Dasein* is a combination of the German adverb *da*, meaning "there," and *sein*, the infinitive form of the verb "to be." Thus, *Dasein* literally means "therebeing," or we can think of it as "the being of the there" (182 [142]) or "the there of being" (Heidegger 1962, 173 [135]) (page numbers in brackets refer to Heidegger's original text). As Frederick Olafson notes,

Both of these locutions characterize the kind of entity that *Dasein* is by reference to the fact that it is the entity for which entities are *there*; but they do so in different ways. The first, *Dasein* as the being of the There, says that when *Dasein* exists (and there is no necessity that it should), it does so as a kind of place—the kind best described as a "clearing" (*Lichtung*), in which entities present themselves as entities. . . . When *Dasein* does exist, however, one can say that there is a "There is," and what this expresses is the fact that there is a place—a "There," or clearing—in which entities show themselves as entities. (1987, 62)

Here I concentrate on Heidegger's early work, which is characterized by an investigation of the ontological characteristics of *Dasein*. His later works are influenced by a "turn" away from an emphasis on the question of subjectivity or a reorientation of his discussion from analysis of human subjectivity to an exploration of the relationship of language to being.

6. I have previously tried to engage with Heidegger's work in a constructive way, for example, by trying to investigate the question of ethics in Heidegger's early work (Ortega 2005), but I have given up on such a project. Even though it might be possible to find some elements for a positive ethics in his work, it is extremely difficult, given Heidegger's own view that ethical investigations were not part of the type of ontological project (the investigation of the question of the meaning of being) that he was proposing. It is also difficult due to Heidegger's own political and personal choices and the question of whether the content of his work is itself tied to National Socialism. I still find Heidegger's work to be useful in attempts at understanding the notion of selfhood. But as this work will show,

such a project requires that we take Heidegger's account of self beyond Heidegger's own characterization of *Dasein*.

7. In many philosophical circles even Heidegger is a marginal figure.

8. It is important to note that feminists in general have not always aligned themselves with phenomenology because they considered phenomenology to be masculinist and essentialist (Fisher 2000, 22–32). As Helen Fielding notes, the intersection of phenomenology and feminism arises in second-wave feminism in the 1960s and 1970s, and while some claim that Edith Stein is the first feminist phenomenologist, Simone de Beauvoir's *Second Sex* is recognized as one of the core early texts by feminist phenomenologists (Fielding 2012, 519). See Fisher & Embree 2000, a key anthology that paves the way for the study of constructive connections between phenomenology and feminism. There we find an early alliance between phenomenology and Latina feminism in Linda Martín Alcoff's "Phenomenology, Post-structuralism, and Feminist Theory on the Concept of Experience." She notes that phenomenology "offer[s] to feminist theory the beginnings of an expanded conception of reason and knowledge, one which is not predicated upon the exclusion of the feminine, the concrete, or the particular" (Alcoff 2001, 51).

It is also important to note that feminists have been especially wary of Heideggerian phenomenology. As Patricia Huntington states,

> It would be a laughable exaggeration to claim that feminist theory and praxis in the United States has sought out and mined Heidegger as a central resource. The reasons that feminist scholars shy away from Heidegger stem from the suprapolitical, seemingly esoteric, and nonempirical nature of his thought. (2001, 2)

It is not until 1970 that we find an explicit feminist engagement with Heidegger's thought by way of the work of Sandra Bartky, which condemned Heidegger's thought as being too abstract (Huntington 2001, 4). It was only in the 1990s that important work with a "seriously Heideggerian-inflected feminism" appeared (5). Although the connection between feminism and phenomenology has expanded considerably, especially as it pertains to the work of Merleau-Ponty, connections between feminism and Heideggerian phenomenology are still sparse. Intertwining Heideggerian phenomenology and Latina feminism is thus a novel project. See Ortega 2006b for an earlier discussion linking phenomenology with US Latina feminism as well as Latin American feminism. See Vallega 2013 for a discussion on Heidegger in the context of Latin American philosophy. Other volumes on phenomenology and feminism include Heinämaa & Rodemeyer 2010; Schües, Olkowski, & Fielding 2011; Simms & Stawarska 2013; Stoller, Vasterling, & Fisher 2005; and Zeiler & Folkmarson Käll 2014.

9. See Saldivar-Hull 1991 for an important early critique of the "blind spots" of white feminism and whether Chicanas can consider themselves part of the "sisterhood." Saldivar-Hull expands her discussion in *Feminism on the Border: Chicana Gender Politics and Literature* (2000). See another important early critique by Aída

Hurtado (1998). While more Latinas are willing to call themselves feminists, issues raised by Saldivar-Hull and Hurtado remain relevant for many Latinas, especially the tension between staying connected to issues facing poor and working-class Latinas and occupying the privileged position of an academic.

10. Writings disclosing lived experience at the intersection of multiple axes of oppression such as gender, race, and sex, were at the heart of black women's writings. See, for example, the work of Sojourner Truth, Anna Julia Cooper, and later writers such as Frances Beale, who discusses the "double jeopardy" of being black and female, and Deborah King, who discusses her "multiple jeopardy" (Beale 1995; King 1995). Writings by Latina women have also been deeply intersectional; Anzaldúa's groundbreaking *Borderlands/La Frontera* (1987) is an important example of a discussion inspired by the intersections of class, gender, sexuality, race, nationality, and geography. Latina feminists are working on tracing intersectional analyses in early Latina feminism.

11. Ahmed concentrates on a discussion of *orientation*—of our orientation toward objects and others. She is interested in the question of how our actions create lines of directions that lead to particular objects and people and what happens when queer bodies turn toward objects that are not in line, that don't follow heteronormative practices (2006). My reading Anzaldúa, Lugones, and Heidegger together is a change in the lines of direction that usually lead philosophers to particular canonical texts written primarily by white males. It is also a change in the lines of directions in which Heidegger's texts are taken. In this sense, my discussion might be (dis)orienting and "queering." While the extent of such queering might vary given the reader's own philosophical orientations, at the very least I suggest a different orientation for doing philosophy and for engaging with Heidegger's thought. While I think that engaging solely with philosophical works is intellectually stimulating, I am frankly not sure how helpful it is for philosophers to continue to carry out overly narrow investigations, or to put Heidegger (or another philosopher) on such a high pedestal that our interests are confined only to in-depth examinations of his or her work.

12. The question of the relationship between the ontic and the ontological is complex. While Heidegger claims that the ontological has to be confirmed by the ontic, he is first and foremost an ontologist that emphasizes a discussion of the ontological or existential categories of human beings. Heidegger understood himself as developing a fundamental ontology and objected to being called an existentialist. Here I understand the notion of the ontological as always connected to the ontic, and I have no pretense to engage in fundamental ontology. I am deeply interested in the way in which Heidegger's analysis of *Dasein* does point to existentialist concerns.

Chapter 1: The New Mestiza and La Nepantlera

1. In *Borderlands/La Frontera*, Anzaldúa italicizes words in Spanish. In her later work, she preferred not to follow this practice in order not to "other" the

Spanish words and phrases (Keating & González-López 2011, 16). Here I italicize Spanish words as Anzaldúa did in *Borderlands/La Frontera*, but I don't italicize them when quoting from her later works.

2. Anzaldúa's work is intersectional in that it does not emphasize only one category of analysis but, instead, recognizes the ways in which various social identities that can be understood as sites of oppression intersect and play a role in one's experience. Here I follow María Lugones in her understanding of social identities as "intermeshed" rather than "interlocked." While Lugones does not appeal to the notion of intersectionality, given that in her view theories of intersectionality presuppose the separability of the categories, I hold on to the notion of intersectionality as described by Collins, in which social categories marking axes of oppression are mutually constituted (Lugones 2003, 231; Collins 1998, 205). Following Lugones, Michael Hames-García also appeals to the notion of intermeshedness instead of intersectionality (Hames-García 2011, 10). I discuss the notion of intersectionality further in chapter 2. Commentators such as AnaLouise Keating, however, point out that Anzaldúa's view moves beyond intersectional frameworks (Keating & González-López 2011, 12). See Keating 2013 for her discussion of the limits of intersectionality. In her view, intersectionality "leads to restrictive understanding of personhood, narrow identity-politics and binary-oppositional tactics" (2013, 37). In my view, however, an intersectional approach does not necessarily lead to narrow identity politics, especially when considering the mutual constitution of social identities. I introduce a view of coalitional politics in chapter 5.

3. Given her tremendous influence in numerous fields, Anzaldúa and her work have been tokenized, simplified, and romanticized too many times. See Castillo 2006 for a brief analysis of the manner in which Anzaldúa's work has been used in academia, especially in American studies.

4. As noted in the introduction, Anzaldúa uses *autohistoria-teoría*, biographical writings that inform theory. Anzaldúa also uses the notion of *autohistoria*. As Keating notes, "Both *autohistoria* and *autohistoria-teoría* are informed by self-reflexive self-awareness employed in the service of social-justice work. *Autohistoria* focuses on the personal life story but, as the autohistorian tells her own life story, she simultaneously tells the life stories of others" (Anzaldúa 2009, 319). *Autohistoria-teoría* includes both the life story and self-reflection on the process of storytelling.

5. Anzaldúa's writings have a deep spiritual dimension and an account of "spiritual activism" that, as Keating notes, is not always recognized or discussed (Anzaldúa 2000, 6). Yet her work has led some of her readers and admirers to construct altars in her honor. There is a web altar to her at http://gloria.chicanas. com/index.html. It is significant that Anzaldúa's work has been received with such intensity and devotion, to the point that candles are lit to her words, to her image, to her relentless quest for spiritual-corporal-intellectual wisdom. According to Laura Pérez, "The altar has been a site for the socially and culturally 'alter,' or other, to express, preserve, and transmit cultural and gender-based religious and political differences" (Pérez 2007, 91). Pérez notes that Anzaldúa's works can be thought of as *ofrendas*, offerings, but also as textual altars that "figure the imbrication of the

artistic, the spiritual, and the political"—and I would add the philosophical (Pérez 2007, 92).

6. It is interesting to note that many commentators concentrate on Anzaldúa's 1987 *Borderlands/La Frontera* and neglect her earlier and later work. For a discussion of why *mestiza* consciousness became more popular than Anzaldúa's later characterization of self, *la nepantlera*, see Koegeler-Abdi 2013, 83. Anzaldúa herself noted that even the reception of *Borderlands/La Frontera* was selective in that commentators appropriated and used the "safe" elements of the text, such as history and borders, but not the "unsafe" elements, such as the relationship between body, mind, and spirit (Anzaldúa 2000, 7). In other words, Anzaldúa thought that readers of *Borderlands/La Frontera* had missed the text's spiritual component. Nevertheless, various commentators are now engaging this aspect of Anzaldúa's work. For an interesting and important development of Anzaldúa's "spiritual mestizaje," or an embodied spirituality that resists oppression, see Delgadillo 2011. For a fascinating discussion of a Chicana culturally hybrid aesthetic and spirituality inspired in part by Anzaldúa, see Pérez 2007.

7. One of the most interesting and poignant aspects of Anzaldúa's *Borderlands* is the way in which her writing illustrates and embodies her own struggles. Writing is her way to deal with the difficulties of a life in the borderlands. Yet, not only does her text show Anzaldúa's struggles and her attempts to understand herself, it also invites the reader to follow Anzaldúa's journey in a path of self-discovery. Consequently, *Borderlands* has had tremendous personal significance for a great number of readers.

8. As noted in the introduction, traditional philosophical discussions on identity emphasize the question of "personal identity," which has to do with the specific issue of finding criteria to explain how the self remains the same over time. "Social identity" is understood as social location or the different markers of identity such as race, sex, class, gender, and so on; "subject" is associated with specific philosophical conceptions such as the Cartesian epistemic subject; "self" refers to a more general conception of characteristics of human beings. Latina feminists discussed in this work do not adhere to the specific philosophical meanings of these terms and sometimes use "self," "subject," and "identity" interchangeably. My discussion of their work reflects this wider use of terminology.

9. In her important discussion about identity, Linda Martín Alcoff points to the way in which critics blame identity for "balkanization" and asks the crucial question: "How did the legitimate concern with specific instances of problems in identity-based movements become a generalized attack on identity and identity politics in any and every form?" (Martín Alcoff 2006, 16).

10. See Keating 2005 and 2006 and Koegeler-Abdi 2013 for detailed discussions on Anzaldúa's "shift" from the conception of the new *mestiza* to *la nepantlera*, a more expansive and inclusive view of self. While Keating recognizes the importance of Anzaldúa's view from *Borderlands/La Frontera*, she is the primary commentator on Anzaldúa to stress the necessity to understand the way Anzaldúa's view changed since the publication of this influential text (Keating 2006, 7). See Keating 2013,

chapter 3, 105, in which Keating discusses the manner in which Anzaldúa expands identity by way of this retribalizing of *mestizaje* to the extent that she moves beyond the human and aligns herself with a "transhuman, planetary citizenship." Inspired by Anzaldúa's new expansive vision of self, Keating also develops a theory of "post-oppositional politics."

11. Anzaldúa took the term "new tribalism" from David Rieff, who criticized her for having a romantic and naïve vision of a return to her indigenous roots (Rieff 1991). She states that she "appropriated" and "recycled" the term (Anzaldúa 2009, 283).

12. Keating describes the "early writings" as work up to and including the second edition of *This Bridge Called My Back* (1983), the "middle writings" as work shortly before and after *Borderlands/La Frontera* (1987), and the "late writings" as work from the mid- to late 1990s until her death in 2004. Keating states,

> . . . Anzaldúa's writings from the early and late periods are broadly inclusive, at times positing a global citizenship of sorts, while some of her work from the middle period is less inclusionary, more focused on rigid identity labels and categories, and (therefore) more restrictive. (Anzaldúa 2009, 11)

Among Anzaldúa's inclusionary works, Keating includes "La Prieta" and "Let us be the healing of the wound." Among her less inclusionary works, Keating lists "Haciendo caras, una entrada," "Border Arte," and "Bridge, Drawbridge, Sandbar or Island." Keating also describes "The *New Mestiza* Nation" as an example of Anzaldúa's transition from an exclusionary to an inclusionary vision of self.

13. It is interesting to note how both Anzaldúa and Lugones reframe the idea of the collective "we." Anzaldúa appeals to *nos/otras* and reminds us of our otherness and our position as insider/outsider; and Lugones appeals to "I ⇒ we," symbolizing how the subject is always looking to meet others (Lugones 2003, 227). Lugones's view expands on Anzaldúa's view of *nos/otras* by appealing to the complexity of a subject that is both resisting ⇔ oppressing. She thus provides a view that allows for understanding ourselves in a complex manner as oppressed, oppressing, and resisting in different contexts.

14. Consider the Nahuatl phrase, *In Lak'ech*, translated in Spanish as "Tú eres mi otro yo" and in English as "You are my other me." This Mayan greeting has been an inspiration for many Chicanos and Latinos, most notably Luis Valdez, whose famous poem *In Lak'ech* from *Pensamiento Serpentino* continues to be an important call for unity among Chicanos and Latinos in the United States, especially after the 2010 signing of House Bill 2281 in Arizona, a bill that targets the Mexican American studies curriculum in Tucson.

15. Inspired by Anzaldúa, Keating first calls for an abandonment of identity politics, but she realizes that appealing to this position reactivates the oppositional binaries that she is trying to overcome. She proposes a "transformation identity

politics" (Keating 2013, 91). Such a "post-oppositional" identity politics allows for a more inclusive account of identities by denying binary oppositional understandings and appealing to interconnectedness rather than antagonisms (2013, 96).

16. Here it is important to note the difference between social identities. Consider issues regarding the undermining or elimination of racial categories, even when they are understood to be socially constructed as opposed to the critique of gender and sexual categories. Queer theory and feminist theory have made some positive contributions in the dismantling of the oppressive and essentialist aspect of gender and sexual identities, whereas theories that propose the elimination of racial categories are potentially harmful given the impact of the social reality of race.

17. Anzaldúa's work precedes the development of queer studies. Even though it has not always been included in queer studies (Pérez 2005), her work has contributed significantly to this discipline. As Ian Barnard notes, *Borderlands/La Frontera* "presages" many of the issues and concerns studied in queer theory. See Barnard 2004, chapter 2, for a detailed discussion of Anzaldúa's account of the new *mestiza* and queer theory. Linda Garber, on the other hand, does not identify Anzaldúa as a queer theorist but as straddling the divide between queer theory and lesbian feminism. See " 'Caught in the Crossfire Between Camps': Gloria Anzaldúa" in Garber 2001. See Phelan 1994 for a discussion of how Anzaldúa's *mestiza* consciousness helps in envisioning a lesbian subjectivity and political community that does not fall prey to essentialism. See Arrizón 2006, chapter 5, for a discussion of "queering" *mestizaje* and "mestiza-ing" the queer that shows how Anzaldúa's work points to the important connection between desire and race in the representation of the brown queer-lesbian body.

18. It is important to understand this tension between Anzaldúa's visions of selfhood as part of a process of self-understanding that Anzaldúa is not just writing about but also going through. That is, *Borderlands* discloses Anzaldúa's own struggles with understanding herself and her own transformation as she lives in the borderlands. Yet it is not only Anzaldúa who experiences this self-seeking. The reader is also being called to look for herself and to understand her own changes and transformations while reading the text. I thus see *Borderlands* as a deeply existential text that invites our thinking, being, and doing.

19. My view is that while her Chicana as well as queer and other identities are crucial in Anzaldúa's development of the new *mestiza*, her account is much more inclusive and allows for the possibility of those who are not Chicanas to attain a *mestiza* consciousness. Yet we must beware of appropriations of Anzaldúa's view and interpretations that overemphasize the metaphorical aspect of her discussion and miss the importance of the new *mestiza*'s situatedness.

20. For an analysis of the history of the notion of *nepantla*, see Román-Odio 2013, 51–57. There are various theoretical approaches to the notion of the in-between. For a discussion of the in-between from a postcolonial studies perspective see (Bhabha 1994, 1996). Bhabha has famously introduced the important notions of "hybridity" and of "third space" in order to describe conditions that arise in a

space dictated by colonization. Anzaldúa's notions of the new *mestiza* and *Nepantla* as well as the view of in-between offered here share affinities with Bhabha's notion of hybridity in so far as both concepts are connected to the possibility of transformation and creation of new meaning from circumstances of oppression. Moreover they represent a move against so called pure, authentic, or essential identities. For a discussion of the in-between from a perspective of sexual difference theories, see Bloodsworth-Lugo 2007. Bloodsworth-Lugo develops a theory of lived, in-between bodies located in the in-between space of traditional oppositional binaries such as male/female, white/black. According to Bloodsworth-Lugo, such a space constitutes a site for meaning making and for the articulation of a dynamic identity and subjectivity that has practical and material implications for our understanding of sex and gender as well race. In this work I have chosen to concentrate on the notion of in-between as presented by Latina theorists given their vision of the self as occupying a more complex space than is prescribed by binaries such as colonizer/colonized, oppressed/oppressor, and thus always oppressing, oppressed, and resisting.

21. See Martinez 2014 for a discussion of borderlands in light of the Husserlian view of the *epoché*, the bracketing or suspension of the "natural attitude," the everyday commonsense understanding of the world. Martinez interprets a borderland or "an unnatural boundary" (Anzaldúa's description) as a possible suspension of the everyday world that may lead to "an experience of unplaced and disjointed energies that loosens the normative boundaries" that could lead to *mestiza* consciousness (226).

22. As opposed to the type of spiritual activism that leads some of Anzaldúa's followers to praise the way in which her work brings together the artistic, the political, and the spiritual, there are theories introduced to give their creator a godlike status. See Bird-Soto 2014 for a brief but moving appeal for Atheories, theories not meant to reify gods and establish standards for what counts as acceptable knowledge.

23. See Anzaldúa & Keating 2002, 540–578, for Anzaldúa's discussion of the path to *conocimiento*, which has seven interdependent stages that allow for transformation, and her later vision of a new tribalism, in which *nepantleras* "forge bonds across race, gender, and other lines" (574).

24. See Harding 2004 for several key discussions on "standpoint theory," the view that knowledge is situated and that marginalized groups have an epistemic privilege or advantage in that they can see from both dominant and nondominant perspectives. Anzaldúa is appealing to the epistemic, emotional, and spiritual advantage of *los atravesados*. However, residing in the borderlands does not guarantee a *mestiza* consciousness, or *conocimiento*. See Koegeler-Abdi 2013 for a critique of the view that Anzaldúa offers a standpoint theory. Koegeler-Abdi states,

> Anzaldúa is not really expanding standpoint epistemology to include mestiza experiences. Her constant quest to destabilize ethnic, gender, sexual, and other clear-cut standpoints as foundations of identities actually contradicts the possibility of fixed epistemological or political standpoints. . . . mestiza consciousness is not a conventional standpoint

because it is based on affiliations exceeding, and not exclusive to, Chicana ancestry or that of any other group. (2013, 74)

I agree with Koegeler-Abdi when she states that Anzaldúa's accounts of the new *mestiza* and *la nepantlera* "complicate any *easy* classification of Anzaldúa's legacy to standpoint epistemologies" (2013, 74; my emphasis). However, the material situatedness of her experience as well as her identity as Chicana are crucial aspects of the forging of a *mestiza* consciousness and provide a vantage point from which to look at the world. That the Chicana identity that Anzaldúa claims is more flexible does not preclude the possibility of her view being a standpoint theory (with the understanding that "standpoint" does not refer to essential, homogenizing categories).

    25. That her work is being considered in a discipline such as philosophy, even though by a small number of philosophers, is remarkable given what I call philosophy's "love of exclusion," this discipline's narrowness and its commitment to the thought of white European males in its traditional form as well as white European and American women in its more pluralist form. It is not yet possible to determine the extent of the contribution that Anzaldúa's new *mestiza* and later visions of self will have in philosophy, because her work is being read by a relatively small number of philosophers. As more women of color intervene in the philosophical terrain, we will increasingly see the ways in which women of color's ideas, including Anzaldúa's, can reshape, reframe, and reorient conversations on philosophical issues. The new *mestiza* embodies possibilities for transformation not only of her own self but for a discipline such as philosophy. Within philosophy there is already important work employing Anzaldúa's writings to various degrees. See Pitts 2014 for a discussion on Anzaldúa and the Mexican philosopher José Vasconcelos in the context of social epistemology; Rivera Berruz 2014 for an analysis of the relationship of language, space, and identity given the presence of Latina/o philosophers; and Cisneros 2013 for a discussion of "alien" sexuality in a Foucauldian context but informed by Anzaldúa. See Sushytska 2012 for an interesting discussion of the notion of "Eastern Europe" that employs the work of Anzaldúa, Heraclitus, and Merab Mamardashvili.

    26. Different Latina feminist phenomenologists provide different answers to issues regarding the unity, the continuity of the self, as well as the integration of the multiple aspects of the self—some embracing a kind of unity of the self (Moya), others suggesting a new vision of integration (Barvosa), while others (Sandoval, Lugones) question the possibility and necessity of unity or continuity as well as the value of integration. I appeal to the continuity of the self in terms of my account of multiplicitous selfhood in chapter 2. I discuss the issue of integration in chapter 6.

    27. Given this relational character of the self, Anzaldúa avoids the traditional philosophical problems of the existence of other minds and the existence of the external world, problems associated with the Cartesian epistemic subject and other philosophical accounts of subjectivity. Her vision of self is one of a complex self in process that becomes who she is through interaction with other selves and the world but who also has a sense of being one.

Chapter 2. Being-between-Worlds, Being-in-Worlds

1. As we will see in the next chapter, María Lugones rejects the traditional oppressor/oppressed dichotomy and introduces a vision of subjects as oppressing, being oppressed, and resisting within different contexts. As she states,

> All subjects can then be understood as active contributors to, collabora-
> tors in, creators of oppressive or resistant practices even when the logics
> of oppression constitute some subjects as passive. That is, resistance and
> oppression vie as constructions of everyday life. One way of putting the
> point is to think of particular subjects as oppress-*ing* (or collaborat-*ing*)
> or be-*ing* oppressed and as resisting. (2003, 200)

2. In the study of continental thought within US philosophical circles and in the European context, thinkers such as Sartre, Merleau-Ponty, Arendt, and Derrida are widely recognized as having been influenced by Heidegger's thought. However, less attention is paid to the connection between Heideggerian thought and the work of one of the most prominent, if not the most prominent, Spanish philosophers, José Ortega y Gasset. The reason for this lack of interest not only in the connection between Heidegger and Ortega y Gasset as well as in the work of Ortega y Gasset in general, has partly to do with the field's predilection for French and German theory and the lack of recognition of the Spanish language as philosophical. Thus there are exclusions in philosophy not just in terms of non-European thought but also "internal exclusions" within continental philosophy itself.

3. Despite the fact that Anzaldúa, Lugones, and other Latina feminists do not explicitly use the term "thrown" to describe the self's condition as already in the midst of a world, they underscore the importance of the self's situatedness and the importance of the circumstances they must face given their situatedness.

4. See Heidegger (1962, ch. 4, §27) for a full explanation of the "ways of being" of *das Man* or what Heidegger refers to as "publicness." For more on the different interpretations of *das Man*, see Carman 1994; Dreyfus 1991; and Olafson 1993. For an analysis of the important debate between Dreyfus and Olafson on *das Man*, see Egan 2012.

5. I discuss this view of identity as interpretative horizon in light of the issue of the multiplicity and sociality of the self in chapter 5.

6. La *facultad* is an unconscious "sixth sense" that is different from the non-reflective orientation of the self according to Heidegger. Anzaldúa is referring here to a deeper sense, a spiritual sense that the new *mestiza* has. It is possible, then, to understand how she can have this sense along with a more reflective orientation in her everyday existence due to ruptures in everyday norms and practices.

7. Since here I am appealing to the notion of being-at-ease and later to other notions such as being-in-worlds and being-in-between, it is important to recall my point made in the introduction that I always understand these ways of

being as connected to particular circumstances the self experiences. The ontological is always connected to the ontic.

8. Here I purposely choose examples of "everyday" norms and practices since one of the points of Heidegger's analysis is to describe the self in everydayness.

9. Heidegger connects nonreflective understanding of the world to our use of things that are "ready-to-hand" to us, things that we use as equipment and that are part of an equipmental whole (1962, chs. 2 & 3).

10. I do not mean to suggest that all existential phenomenologists are the same in terms of their recognition and their inclusion of the different axes of oppression affecting those who are marginalized. While Heidegger and Merleau-Ponty, for example, did not engage with the particularities of embodiment such as race and gender, Sartre and Beauvoir were more attuned to issues concerning race despite their problematic discussions on the issue. See Gordon 1995 for an important discussion in which Sartrean themes are effectively used to analyze issues of race and racism.

11. African American and other feminist writers have also connected their experiences with particular epistemic standpoints and epistemic privilege (Collins 2008; Harding 2004).

12. I read Heidegger as providing an account of the "they" that is normative. That is, he is criticizing the mode of being of publicness as it takes away responsibility for the self's choices. This reading does not preclude an understanding that there are also constructive aspects of the "they" in terms of issues of intelligibility and sociality.

13. See Dussel (2009) for a discussion of *ser-hispano* in terms of the Heideggerian idea of being-in-the-world. Dussel describes "being-in-the-*hispanic*-world" as being on the border of many worlds, the five historico-cultural worlds in which, according to him, every *hispano* lives. Unfortunately, Dussel's discussion lacks an in-depth consideration of issues regarding race and gender.

14. In the introduction to *Pilgrimages*, written after the well-known essay on world-traveling, Lugones compares her understanding of "world" to that of Danto's. She points out that Danto is mistaken in interpreting worlds as possible worlds and as set "cultures." By analyzing his example of a disordered room being a symbolic expression of a woman who does not want to conform to gendered norms about tidiness and to the possibility of a different world that is gender-just, Lugones points out that Danto does not consider the tense power relations that occur in multiple actual worlds. According to Lugones, not doing so precludes the possibility of resistance (2003, 25). Moreover, according to Lugones, Danto misses that the intersection between worlds is set up in terms of power relations in multiple actual worlds; he thus misses what Lugones calls the "social as heterogeneous in terms of multiple actual worlds" (2003, 25).

15. It is important to note that not all Nicaraguans or white US-born citizens will have the same experiences in a particular location. I do not wish to homogenize groups. I wish to emphasize the fact that we might have different experiences in

specific locations depending on our social identities and backgrounds as well as depending on our familiarity with dominant norms and practices.

16. Given the definition of "world" used in this work, we have to remember the world of Latinas or any other world as incomplete and subject to interpretation and reinterpretation.

17. Importantly, worlds are connected to social locations and thus to particular social identities that constitute shared horizons. In chapter 5 I discuss the question of social identity and elaborate on how my account of multiplicitous selfhood can be enhanced by Linda Martín Alcoff's understanding of identity as interpretative horizon, and I take up the question of the relationship between the self's various social identities and the question of identity politics.

18. Heidegger pays a great deal of attention to this third understanding of world as that wherein *Dasein* lives, although he is also ultimately interested in understanding "world" as "worldhood," an ontic-ontological concept that is prior to the three understandings of world that he presents.

19. Theorist Edwina Barvosa, who provides a theory of multiple identity based on the interaction of identity schemas, expands on Collins's and Crenshaw's view of intersectionality, which she believes mostly emphasizes the experiences of those that have multiple oppressions and thus provides analyses in which social identities "converge," what she considers "the additive type of intersectionality" (Barvosa 2008, 77). She consequently adds two other understandings of the way that intersectionality works: cross-cutting intersectionality, in which social identities produce cross-cutting meaning or influence (e.g., a Haitian woman who is treated differently than African Americans by whites and is thus not considered black by some of her African American friends), and overlapping intersectionality, in which social identities overlap and thus share group-specific meanings, values, and practices (e.g., a Haitian woman being able to speak in such a way that she sounds white and so demonstrating a common speech that could signify either Haitian identity or white identity (78). Barvosa also believes that intersectionality is not about social constructions only but about associations in the mind between social identity schemas, what she calls internal intersectionality (79). This analysis points to the complexity of the notion of intersectionality and to the different ways that this notion is theorized by women of color.

20. See Feder 2007 for an important discussion of the need to think race and gender together while at the same time appreciating the different ways in which each becomes salient in the context of the family.

21. I analyze Moya's argument in detail in chapter 6.

22. Even though Barvosa believes that a project of self-integration is completely optional, she suggests that it would be highly beneficial. As she states,

> Integrative self-craft thus presents an opportunity to balance the creative benefits of inner contradiction with the potential for agency and self-management of our otherwise unruly multiplicity. While individuals may choose to forego that opportunity, I argue that it is through the hard

work of self-craft that the potential for robust agency and *independent* critical reason are possible. (2008, 175)

23. In political terms, rather than appealing to what influential postcolonial critic Gayatri Spivak termed "strategic essentialism" or the idea that marginalized groups use the short-term strategy to appeal to group identity for political purposes, I introduce a notion of intersectional coalitional politics in chapter 5. This notion relies on tactical alliances rather than on temporarily claiming some "shared essence" in order to alleviate differences and carry out a political project (Spivak 1987, 205).

24. For a more in-depth account of the Heideggerian account of self and a discussion of the individual character of *Dasein* that explains the notion of mineness, see Ortega, "*Dasein* Comes after the Epistemic Subject, but Who Is *Dasein*?"

Chapter 3. The Phenomenology of World-Traveling

1. As noted in the introduction, Lugones's 1987 essay on world-traveling has special significance for me not only because it was one of the first essays written by a Latina feminist philosopher that I read, but also because of the way it captures my own lived experience as someone who saw herself as a displaced Nicaraguan in the midst of an unfriendly world. Her discussion of world-traveling remains an inspiration for me as I continue to think of the ways in which we can overcome our many failures in loving one another. While many commentators call for world-traveling as a way in which white women can learn to love women of color, I am also deeply interested in the way in which people of color can learn to love one another and resist the "divide and conquer" trap, which pits particular racial groups against each other. See Ortega 2009 for a discussion of tensions between the Latino and African American communities in the context of the aftermath of Hurricane Katrina, and see Ortega 2014 for a discussion of such tensions in the context of aesthetic representations of racialized bodies, particularly Afro-Mexicans.

2. When defining world-traveling as an epistemic shift, Lugones states that: (1) world-traveling is an epistemic shift from being one person to being a different person; and (2) world-traveling is an epistemic shift to other worlds of sense. While related, these two definitions convey different senses of epistemological shifting. The first seems to emphasize the self's understanding of herself as different, and the second underscores a different understanding of worlds in a more general sense. Moreover, her description of traveling as the shift from "being one person to being a different person" suggests more of an ontological rather than an epistemic shift.

3. It is important to note here that more explicit discussions regarding the multiplicity of realities are not part of the 1987 essay on world-traveling. In this early essay Lugones emphasizes the idea of "worlds of sense," although she is clear that, in her view, "worlds" are not abstract. Lugones uses the notion of "worlds" in quotation marks to separate her sense of the term from the traditional understanding of world. It is in the last three chapters of *Pilgrimages* in which she explicitly

introduces issues connected to spatiality and concreteness that she emphasizes the idea of multiple and intersecting cotemporaneous realities. She also notes that she prefers to keep quotation marks around "worlds" since she does not wish to reproduce an atomistic understanding of heterogeneous reality, given that worlds are permeable and they intersect (2003, 16).

4. In an unpublished draft of a presentation for the Society for Women in Philosophy Lugones introduces the idea of "long and wide selves," in which selves are presented as relational and as occupying concrete spaces. In my view, the unpublished manuscript offers an early vision of what would become "active subjectivity."

5. Interestingly, Lugones's methodology involves a circularity that is not vicious. Her approach is to use examples and stories, but those stories need to be interpreted in light of our own experience. As she states, "I exhibit the logic of the story/example with a possible modality in mind: oppressive, resistant, reactive, and so on. I used the modalities to have an edge into the story, but my task is really to enrich, complicate, give texture, and concretize the modalities, making them temporally and spatially concrete" (2003, 27). Her point is not to exhibit the story line in a temporal sequence but "through dwelling in the meanings that one can reveal going in this or that tactical strategic line" (203, 28). According to Lugones, her writing as well as her texts constitute a pilgrimage through the practice of *tantear*, tactically feeling one's way for meaning, for what she calls enclosures and openings of our praxis (2003, 1). In Heideggerian phenomenology, there is also a circularity. The circularity arises because to answer the question of the meaning of being, human beings are supposed to have a sense of the answer already, what Heidegger calls a preontological understanding of being (1962, 25[6]). Heidegger's existential analytic, or the account of the ontological characteristics of *Dasein*, can also be considered a pilgrimage, a long journey in which Heidegger is on the path of understanding the answer to the question of the meaning of being, a journey that can be traced to as early as 1919–1920 (Kisiel 1993, 16). In such a journey, Heidegger, like Lugones, is also interested is the situatedness and concreteness of the self and thus presents us with one of the most important explanations of a philosophical theory that is mindful of everyday experience. Heidegger, however, moves toward a very different goal than Lugones when he directs his investigation explicitly toward a fundamental ontology. See Kisiel 1993 for an explanation of the movement from what is considered the first draft of *Being and Time*, *The Concept of Time*, written in 1924, to the second 1925 draft, *The History of the Concept of Time*, to the published but incomplete 1927 final draft. See also Heidegger's *The Basic Problems of Phenomenology* (1982), which is interpreted as containing the final or third division of *Being and Time*.

6. This citation is from the introduction to *Pilgrimages*. Here Lugones uses "oppressed ↔ resisting," a more complex way of understanding the social position of the oppressed. As noted, rather than adhering to a simple dichotomy of oppressor and oppressed, Lugones rightly notes that those who are oppressed are involved in a double movement of being oppressed ↔ resisting. She explains that in her early essay "Structure/Antistructure and Agency under Oppression" (ch. 2 of

Pilgrimages), she was not writing from within the oppressing ↔ resisting tension, and thus her analysis lacks complexity and misses the way in which the interlocking of oppressions obscures the ways in which oppressions are intermeshed (2003, 31). By the end of the text, one can see the way in which Lugones works within this more complex understanding of the way the self stands in light of different power relations and social locations.

7. How great is the coincidence that does not happen by chance—the intimate relationship between the myths of univocity and the breaking of cracked mirrors that show us ripped, torn apart (my translation).

8. Here Lugones's discussion is based on a popular understanding of schizophrenia as a condition of being confused about oneself or having more than one self, given the traveling back and forth between worlds. It is interesting to note that, due to traditional understandings of self that emphasize unity, psychologists pathologize this experience of self-confusion. Rather than a diagnosis of Schizophrenia, a condition that may involve various symptoms including delusions and hallucinations, the confusion that Lugones describes could be better explained by what is now referred to as Dissociative Identity Disorder (previously named Multiple Personality Disorder) (American Psychiatric Association 2013). However, it would be interesting to explore the way in which philosophical conceptions of self that are more attuned to multiplicity could influence our understanding of Dissociative Identity Disorder and the ways in which an understanding of the self as more complex and open to ambiguity and contradiction might prevent us from pathologizing some of our experiences. I thank Brittan Davis for pointing out the differences between the diagnoses and the change of name for Multiple Personality Disorder.

9. Existentialism is one philosophical movement that highlights the ambiguous, contradictory, and paradoxical aspect of existence. As Simone de Beauvoir notes, the human being is characterized by freedom and yet is also "a thing crushed by the dark weight of other things" (de Beauvoir 2000, 7). Beauvoir posits this paradoxical aspect of existence as the starting point for a philosophy in which ethics really matters. Similarly, Lugones presents a philosophy that has its beginning in the recognition of our complexity and multiplicity. For Lugones, this starting point allows for the possibility of resistance that is not merely reactive or oppositional but that carries with it the promise of multiple visions of radical transformation against politics of the same or homogenizing politics.

10. Given our previous discussion of the self's decenteredness in chapter 2, I understand "character central" as meaning a characteristic or aspect of the self that the self prioritizes in being-in-worlds. It does not mean an essential or a priori central characteristic.

11. In her original comparative discussion of anger in light of Lugones and Zen Master Hakuin, Jen McWeeny notes that Lugones's view is "somewhere between a strong pluralism that holds that worlds are numerically distinct and a weak pluralism that simply having a 'different take' on reality is a sufficient condition for defining a world" (2010, 298). She proposes that we understand what Lugones means by worlds of sense as "structures" or practices, concepts and institutions that serve to

constitute persons, a notion introduced by Lugones in "Structure/Antistructure and Agency under Oppression" (Lugones 2003, 60). McWeeny notes that second-order anger (anger that is liberatory and resistant rather than merely reactive) happens at the limen, and that the angry self is not a fully formed self but an "in-between self" (2010, 298). She also recognizes the difficulty of holding a view that appeals to a self that is both one and many and thus productively engages Lugones by elaborating a response that can explain a pluralism that is neither strong nor weak. Yet I wonder what it means to be a fully formed self in this view. I also wonder how a recognition of the angry self as an in-between, partially formed self residing at the limen keeps Lugones's view between strong and weak pluralism, especially when Lugones's later writings place even more emphasis on the multiplicity of selves and realities and moves further away from what we may think as the individual aspects of the self. It seems to me that Lugones's pluralism has always been strong, and it is even stronger in her more recent writings. I read Lugones as a strong pluralist in terms of selves, even if not all the selves have resistant practices. I also read her as a strong pluralist in terms of worlds, as noted, and understand her vision of worlds as having both an epistemic sense (worlds of sense) and a metaphysical sense (multiple crisscrossing realities).

12. I find Lugones's use of I → we as quite interesting, since it can point to both the self being a multiplicity of selves and the self's relationality with others that is necessary for the possibility of deep coalition.

13. My appeal to a multiplicitous self that is being-between-worlds and being-in-worlds might seem problematic, since I appeal to one self but to multiple worlds. Yet, despite not positing an ontological pluralism of worlds in the sense that there are multiple realities (as Lugones does), it is possible to be a multiplicitous self that can travel various worlds, worlds understood as having an ontological dimension in which selves might inhabit the same space but have different ways of being in that space and possibilities of understanding worlds differently—so the multiplicitous self has access to various worlds both in having a sense of how she fares in the particular locations she inhabits and also has an epistemic relation to those worlds. She is capable of understanding features of those worlds and of understanding herself differently in different worlds, thus opening possibilities of resistance. In my view, the possibility of a resistance that is not merely reactive but transformative does not necessitate an appeal to multiple realities but it does require access to various worlds. It does not necessitate a pluralism of selves either.

14. I would like to thank Talia Mae Bettcher for pushing me to think further about the relationship between world-traveling, resistance, and multiple realities in Lugones's account and thus to be more mindful of the relevance of the fact that, given certain power structures, the self cannot animate or highlight certain attributes/characteristics that are necessary for resistance. See Bettcher 2013 for a critique of both the wrong-body and transgender approaches from a perspective that appeals to Lugones's view in terms of "multiple worlds of sense."

15. Note that while all of these resistant practices involve an epistemic component, not all of them are as attuned to spatial considerations. As Lugones notes in her introduction to *Pilgrimages*, the last three chapters of the text are "most frankly

spatial" and include the "production of spatial continuities and discontinuities and their liberatory and oppressive possibilities" (2003, 35). Lugones is deeply interested in the bodily component of resistance. In her later work resistance takes a more embodied dimension—we need to have a bodily, material sense of an alternative reality or the experience of being in spaces in which our lives matter and there is justice for us in reality, not just in our imaginations. While I agree with this need for bodily attunement to resistant possibilities and understand the multiplicitous self as engaged in embodied practices of resistance, we do not always have the possibility of experiencing a context in which my resistant possibilities come to light.

16. Trespassing includes "a vocabulary, an imagery, a set of practices, and exercises in praxical thinking designed to convey the complexities of resistances to intermeshed oppressions" (2003, 8).

17. See Alison Bailey's important discussion of how this notion of curdling/separation is visible in acts of "strategic ignorance." Bailey explains that such ignorance is based in ways in which members of nondominant groups can take advantage of a dominant group's tendency to see wrongly (Bailey 2007, 87–90).

18. I wonder whether Lugones herself is involved in the very dichotomous thinking that she often warns against when she circumscribes the logic of purity and the logic of impurity in specific ways that don't seem to allow for views of selfhood that are not prescribing a unitary subject (logic of purity) or a curdled self (logic of impurity). In her view the problem with dichotomies is that they don't allow us to see the intersections between worlds, and seeing these intersections is needed because it is in the limen that we are capable of doing so (Lugones 1983, 197).

19. In her comparative analysis about questions of selfhood in both Anzaldúa and Lugones, Zaytoun notes that Lugones's logic of fusion is partly a development of the previous account on curdling (Zaytoun, forthcoming). She explains that for Lugones the logic of oppression is connected to the logic of intersectionality that ultimately leads to fragmentation. Zaytoun discusses Lugones's claim that the colonial understanding of "the light and dark side" of womanhood leads to a false or ornamental account of sisterhood that in reality works to obscure white women's privilege. An important contribution by Zaytoun is her argument that Anzaldúa's account of la naguala adds to Lugones's critique of the logic of oppression by providing an account of a "knower" that is not dominated by the logic of narrow identity (Zaytoun 2013, forthcoming). Inspired by Lugones's view on active subjectivity, the logic of fusion, and complex communication, as well as Anzaldúa's vision of la naguala, Zaytoun develops an account of self-in-coalition that aims at providing a more expansive account of coalition and solidarity across differences.

20. I find that interpreters of Lugones's work do not usually discuss the meaning of multiplicity in detail. Some read her account of multiplicity as meaning that selves are multiplicitous, and others read it as meaning that selves are multiple. Still others use the terms interchangeably and do not discuss the metaphysical questions arising from the different interpretations of multiplicity.

21. Given Lugones's understanding of the tension, works such as *The Pedagogy of the Oppressed*, one of the most important analyses of oppression in Latin American thought, fall short (Freire 2000). From the point of view of Lugones's

explanation of the complex way in which oppression and resistance operate in our lived experience, Freire's dichotomous analysis of the oppressor and the oppressed does not fully account for the self's multiple positionings on the map of oppression. Despite the fact that Freire acknowledges that the oppressed tend to adopt the practices of oppressors, he nevertheless holds on to the oppressed/oppressor dichotomy in his analysis.

22. See Lugones 1992, in which she explains how Anzaldúa's account of *Borderlands* is strong in creating a theoretical space for resistance, although it prioritizes crossing-over as a solitary act and thus fails to reveal the sociality of resistance (1992, 36).

23. Being-in-the-world is Heidegger's alternative to a conception of subjectivity that is understood as having an intentionality that is directed from the "inside" to something "outside." However, Heidegger is well known for his rejection of the subject/object dichotomy. He rejects the view that the subject performs a mental act that is inside and directs it outward. Recall that he gives up the term "subject" and redescribes it as *Dasein* and being-in-the-world. As existing, the self already stands out in the world or "transcends" (Olafson 1987, 68).

24. Here Lugones is guided by Michel de Certeau's discussion regarding the strategist and the tactician. According to de Certeau, while the strategist has a vision of the street from above and creates abstract norms and rules, the tactician is on the ground subverting those rules day to day (Lugones 2003, 211).

25. See Hart 2013 for an analysis of immigrant domestic labor in light of Arendt and Lugones that shows how hangouts and hanging out disrupt the public/private dichotomy. While I am sympathetic to Hart's claims about the way in which immigrant domestic workers embody a defiance against the public/private dichotomy, and the way in which hanging out with others workers helps them make sense of their multiple worlds, I worry about the romanticization of workers' experience. That is, hangouts and hanging out do not always yield what Lugones calls "emancipatory sense-making" (2003, 65).

26. In order to make visible the fragmentation that occurs under views dominated by purity, and by interlocking oppressions, Lugones uses the virgule (/), for example, Latina/lesbian, Mexican/American. She uses a hyphen to indicate that these and other selves that are seen as fragmented under dominant logic are not fragmented under her view. I am particularly moved by Lugones's description of Latina/lesbians as having to get together in "some halfway spot between the bar and the closet, una penumbra" (2003, 171). Lugones provides an interesting discussion of the formation of Latina/lesbians within national and gay and lesbian movements. She states, "Can the cachapera gain voice in the Movement? Not unless we take seriously the need to question the geography in which the 'we are fa-mi-lí' is to be lived and the colonial induction of cachaperas into the traditions of Anglo-European sapphists" (2003, 177).

27. Consider the practice of "tagging," in which members of particular gangs use graffiti to claim certain areas of neighborhoods.

28. I think that there is an interesting tension between world-traveling and streetwalker theorizing. The resistance described as arising from world-traveling

appeals both to concrete practices and to memory, to the possibility of remembering oneself as different in another world, and is thus connected to a non-utopian visionary appeal. Streetwalker theorizing is even more connected to the concrete, in which the pedestrian theorist is in the midst of selves that are challenging and defying oppressive practices. Does she then not need to world-travel as much or at all? What is the relationship between the two?

29. Quijano provides an interesting explanation of the way in which a new model of power, colonial/modern Eurocentric capitalism, arose during the conquest of the continent of America and established racial categories for the purposes of domination and continued colonization. He points out that this new world system has three central elements that affect the daily lives of all people around the globe even to this day: coloniality of power (the structures of power and hegemony of colonialism), capitalism, and Eurocentrism (Quijano 2000, 544).

30. I understand Lugones's aim of "moving against the grain," a phrase that she repeatedly uses, as pointing to a position that is beyond or outside of modernity/coloniality. The call to move "against" the grain suggests an oppositional stance and thus a counterhegemonic position. However, her call for resistance as "responsive" rather than reactive suggests a more radical move.

31. There are various understandings and approaches to decoloniality. Here I am noting that I am in agreement with what are understood as some important general aims of the decolonial movement. Different theorists propose different visions of how these aims are to be achieved. See Mignolo 2011 and Maldonado-Torres 2011 for introductory discussions of decoloniality. See Martín Alcoff 2012 for an interesting discussion of the concept of transmodernity. She also provides a defense of Mignolo and Dussel from critics who claim that even their decolonial project does not escape the modern/colonial paradigm, because the notion of transmodernity involves a meta-narrative. In defense of Dussel, Martín Alcoff points out that not all meta-narratives are the same and, further, that the meta-narrative of transmodernity avoids the exclusionary and hierarchical effects of totalizing systems (2012, 65) and is not universalist or connected to objectivity and neutrality. It is attuned to perspectivism and revision (2012, 66). See Pérez 2010 for a critique of Dussel and an important reminder to decolonialist theorists to avoid "one-way" transnational exchanges of knowledge, what she calls "desencuentros" or dis-encounters between Latina American thinkers and U.S. Latino/a scholars, in which Latina American thinkers disregard the contributions of women of color and queer folk. As Pérez states, "It matters that we learn to walk our brave decolonizing talks" (2010, 123).

32. Mignolo describes border thinking as "moments in which the imaginary of the modern system cracks" (2000, 23).

33. I take it that delinking is an extremely difficult process, in that even resistant practices are informed by and take place in the dominant paradigm. Different decolonial projects will take different approaches and lead to visions that are to greater and lesser degrees connected to dominant languages, practices, and concepts.

34. This openness to a critical approach as well as to inclusiveness of "other" epistemologies *and* phenomenologies is of great importance in my account, and, thus, it has some affinities with a decolonial vision. As Martín Alcoff notes, the

possibility of transmodernity as conceived by Dussel rests on a critical and inclusive stance (2012, 63).

Chapter 4. World-Traveling, Double-Consciousness, and Resistance

1. As we have seen in the previous chapter, Lugones's account of self is complex. So is her appeal to a double-image of the self when world-traveling, as having a double image may mean seeing oneself as two different people or seeing two aspects of oneself.

2. Du Bois first writes about double-consciousness in 1897 (194) and later in 1903 (1999, 11). See Bruce 1992 for an explanation of the sources that might have influenced Du Bois to theorize about the concept of double-consciousness: European Romanticism, American Transcendentalism, and the writings of William James and other psychologists of the time.

3. See Adell 1994 and Zamir 1995.

4. Lugones uses the Spanish *tantear* (to feel, to test, to try out) and wishes to appeal to its "sense of exploring someone's inclinations about a particular issue and in the sense of 'tantear en la oscuridad,' putting one's hands in front of oneself as one is walking in the dark, tactilely feeling one's way" (Lugones 2003, 1).

5. I wish to be careful with this comparison between Du Bois and Lugones as both thinkers offer multifaceted discussions. Here I am suggesting that there is an element of playfulness and experimenting being suggested by Lugones that is not apparent in Du Bois's discussion. However, this view rests on how the notion of playfulness is understood. The spirituals that Du Bois presents in the text and that alert the reader of the tremendous spiritual contribution of African Americans to the United States can be understood as part of a resistant praxis, but the question is whether they can be understood as playful in the sense that Lugones suggests.

6. See Gooding-Williams 2009. Gooding-Williams provides an interesting interpretation that reads Du Bois's text as pointing to the experience of African Americans when they are not recognized by whites. Gooding-Williams distinguishes between second sight, double consciousness, and twoness. He describes second sight as the ability African Americans have of seeing themselves as whites see them and of seeing reality as whites see it; double-consciousness as a false self-consciousness that emerges when African Americans judge themselves with the views of racist whites, and twoness as African Americans' conflictual sense of being both American and Negros. When discussing double-consciousness, Gooding-Williams states,

> The feeling of being denied the normative status of membership in American society through the betrayal of the ideal of reciprocity is a feeling of a double-consciousness, or false self-consciousness, that results from exercising the power of second sight in the very American society

that has denied African Americans the normative status of membership. (2009, 81)

7. Allen argues that the notion of double-consciousness is not central in Du Bois's thought and that Du Bois brings it forth in *The Souls of Black Folk* for practical purposes, namely, in order to elicit sympathy from educated whites (Allen 2002).

8. James discusses the problem of the "double aspect of the self" in *Principles of Psychology* and the problem of the "divided self" or "divided will" in *The Varieties of Religious Experience*. See James 1981 (279) and James 1987(189). James's solution to the problem of the divided self is to unify the different aspects of the self or to order them hierarchically with the spiritual aspects being at the top.

9. Unfortunately, there is not much literature analyzing the notion of double-consciousness in the context of Latino/a lived experience. Two examples are Roof 1996 and Saucedo 1996. In the latter, Saucedo gives up the desire to merge both selves. He describes not his double but triple sight in light of the fact that he is a Mexican Irish American. He doesn't provide an in-depth analysis of double-consciousness or triple sight. Instead, he concentrates on providing an account of his lived experience as someone who feels an outsider from the mainstream, white, American society. Saucedo concludes by saying, "It is a vain attempt to search for a place in a white society that will continually deny you. But it is even more vain yet to try an escape from a culture that has an unyielding grasp on your soul" (1996, 100). Saucedo, who at some point tried to move away from both his Chicano self and from white society, is left knowing the importance of both Chicano and white American cultures, while understanding that he doesn't have the possibility of integrating both. In a statement that can be seen as opposed to Anzaldúa's and other Latina feminists' endorsement of in-betweenness, he states, "That duality in life is something to resist against, because ultimately those who stand in the middle are torn apart by either side" (1996, 100). Unfortunately, Saucedo seems to recognize only two modes of being for his multiplicitous self, integration or complete fragmentation.

10. Recently, in his work on epistemology and resistance, José Medina has introduced an account of "kaleidoscopic" consciousness and social imagination that takes into consideration a plurality of publics that are heterogeneous and that can allow for a more robust notion of epistemic justice (Medina 2013, 44, 24). Despite having worked separately on our respective views, both of our projects see the necessity of moving beyond an account of "double-consciousness," given the complexity and multiplicity of the social world and of our selves. While Medina underscores the way in which kaleidoscopic consciousness might help us develop epistemic and social practices that allow us to engage in solidarity across differences, what Medina sees as "pluralistic forms of solidarity/network solidarity," my account highlights the existential dimension of having multiplicitous imaging or consciousness. That is, while I am also concerned about epistemic issues, I am particularly interested in the manner in which having a multiplicitous imaging affects my sense of self and how I am faring in my everyday experience.

11. See Heidegger's discussion of distantiality, averageness, and leveling down as three elements that characterize publicness (1962, ch. 4).

12. I am here reminded of Rebeca, one of the characters from the brilliant novel, *One Hundred Years of Solitude*, by Gabriel García Márquez. Rebeca arrives at the Buendías's household in Macondo carrying a bag with her parents' bones, carrying her past, her history. What bones do we as multiplicitous selves carry as we move from world to world?

13. Despite my uneasiness with Lugones's emphasis on playfulness when world-traveling, I understand the value of play in feminist theorizing, as it allows feminists to look for alternative practices against oppression. See Nagel 2001 for an interesting discussion that criticizes Heidegger's appeal to play in *Being and Time*, as *Dasein* remains "a radically isolated, monologically positioned player whose ultimate game is projection of possibilities towards anxiety and death" (2001, 291). Contra Heidegger, Nagel proposes that the inauthentic modes of *Dasein*, such as curiosity, ambiguity, and gossip, can be used in order to develop a playful dwelling-in-the-world. I agree with Nagel that the notion of play can be read in the Heideggerian view of "throwness," but ultimately Heidegger's discussion paints a *Dasein* that turns dead serious or becomes agonistic in the turn toward authenticity. However, I question her claim that *Dasein* "never is in a meaningful relationship with others," as it underscores Heidegger's critique of the deficient, inauthentic mode of solicitude and ignores the possibilities for constructive sociality under authenticity (2001, 301). It would also be helpful if Nagel provided a more in-depth discussion of the manner in which the inauthentic modes play a role in a feminist ethics of play.

14. For an analysis of the role of unconsciousness and racism, see Sullivan 2003a, 2003b, and 2006, as well as Linda Martín Alcoff's important analysis of the tacit habitual bodily practices deployed at visible identities (Martín Alcoff 2006, ch. 7).

Chapter 5. Multiplicitous Becomings, On Identity, Horizons, and Coalitions

1. Some important analyses on identity and identity politics are Alarcón 1991; Martín Alcoff 2006; Anzaldúa 1990; Brown 1995; Butler 1990, 1997; Collins 2008; Combahee River Collective 1979; de Laurentis 1990; Gilroy 2000; Hekman 1999, 2000; hooks 1981; Kruks 1995, 2001; Lloyd 2005; Meyers 1994, 2004; Mohanty 2003; Muñoz 1999; Phelan 1989, 1994; Spivak 1990; Weir 1996, 2008; Young 1997; Zerilli 2005. For a useful edited collection about identity politics that is inclusive of women of color perspectives, see Ryan 2001.

2. Given that I hold onto the notion of identity, it is important to reiterate that, in my view, the "I" is always situated. The multiplicitous self as being-between-worlds and being-in-worlds is a self in process that has various social identities that are grounded on particular material conditions (spatial, political, social, historical, cultural, relational) as well as on discursive considerations.

3. Hekman prompts us not to go so far as Butler who, in her view, does not consider the middle ground between the extremes of a deep self and no self and does not explain the "being behind the doing" (1995, 18). Hekman, however, still does not support the idea of identity, especially as it concerns identity politics (23).

4. Martín Alcoff lists other metaphysical assumptions that drive the critique: identities are considered the product of oppressive practices; they are seen as pathological, inaccurate, and they are believed to manifest an alienation in which categories are imposed from outside (2006, 80).

5. Martín Alcoff recognizes the importance of the relational aspect of identity and the interaction with the other as needing to be not just an addition to the self but a constitutive part of the self. In her view, others are part of the self's own identity. She consequently questions views such as those by Ricoeur, Brison, and Code, in which, despite the fact that they consider the other as important for the self's understanding of itself and its autonomy, the other ends up being a "temporary engagement" (in the case of Ricoeur) and having the role of "effective listening" (in the case of Brison) (Martín Alcoff 2006, 59–62).

6. Weir does not deny claims by Butler and others that point to the manner in which identities serve to subjugate the individual. However, she wishes to go beyond a categorization of identity that emphasizes this fact and to provide a more complex account of identity that recognizes other key points about the process of identification, for example, that (1) not all identities are forged through subordinating power regimes; (2) identities are produced by multiple logics and intersubjective affective relations that are not reducible to relations of subjugation; (3) identities are not fixed but heterogeneous and unstable; and (4) understanding identities as categories obscures the manner in which identities can yield connections to ourselves, others, places, and to our ideals (Weir 2013, 8–11). I welcome Weir's analysis, as it reframes the discussion on identity in such a way that we do not get trapped in the subjugating operations of identity. While we cannot deny these operations, they are not the sole product of the process of identification. Yet, this reframing makes it difficult to make general claims about the negative or positive/transformative aspects of identities, or to assess the relationship between the two.

7. I must be careful to point out that in my discussion of the "they," I am also adding ontic relations with others. As previously noted, Heidegger emphasizes the ontological aspect of the "they" and considers it a way of being of the everyday self.

8. In no way do I wish to suggest that, in the case of particular horizons associated with specific groups, there is a set number of views and interpretations that all members of that group share. While it is the case that members of groups share horizons insofar as they are able to interpret their experiences through the lenses of their particular social identities, these horizons are not exactly the same or static. Heterogeneity within groups needs to be considered.

9. See Weiss 2011 for an interesting discussion of "sharing time" across "unshared" horizons, for example, the horizons of disabled and able-bodied individuals (173). While agreeing with Martín Alcoff's points about the manner in which

horizons are lenses through which we understand our experiences, she questions Martín Alcoff's emphasis on visible identities, making the important points that religious and ethnic identities may sometimes be more visible than race and gender and that the work of disability scholars such as Robert Murphy shows the way in which the visibility of a wheelchair erases race and gender (Weiss 2011, 181). By appealing to the notions of horizon and we-relationships, Weiss sees the possibility of sharing a present and ultimately developing a ground of mutual respect for the differences between our identities (2011, 183). She notes that such a ground, however, cannot be developed if the different horizons involved are understood to be incommensurable (2011, 183). Weiss is right in bringing to light the fact that there will be cases in which there will be no possibility for sharing time across different horizons, and thus coalitional work becomes even more difficult.

10. In Martín Alcoff's view, social identities are relational, contextual, *and* fundamental; this position thus rejects the traditional intrinsic/context-dependent or essential/nonessential dichotomies. Even that which is relational and context-dependent is understood as "fundamental" in the sense that it is essential to the self's experiences (Martín Alcoff 2006, 92). While Martín Alcoff jettisons the intrinsic/extrinsic essential/inessential categories because they "confuse more than they clarify in thinking about the nature of the self" (2006, 92), she holds on to the interior/exterior dichotomy in order to distinguish between public identity and lived subjectivity. Yet, she sees these two categories as "mutually constitutive." The reason why she holds on to what she sees as a "potentially misleading" dichotomy is to explain these cases where our public identities are very different from or don't match our lived subjectivity. She states,

> The philosophical project today, then, is to rearticulate the picture of the "inner" self in such a way as to maintain its correct core intuition—that these disparate aspects of the self are not always perfectly mapped onto each other in our lived experience—while simultaneously critiquing the traditional binary form of the description that ossified the distinction into totally separate and mutually exclusive oppositions between interior/exterior, mind/body, and essential/inessential. Accordingly we need also to explore the ways in which the substantive and particular nature of a given subjectivity is constituted through its publicly recognized identity. (Martín Alcoff 2006, 93)

But how to perform this complicated move? In arguing for the salience of social identity (which is fundamental although relational and contextual), Martín Alcoff runs the risk of overtheorizing public identity. The question is to what extent does the exterior affect or constitute the interior? How fundamental is public identity for the self? While keeping the interior/exterior binary helps Martín Alcoff explain those cases in which one sees oneself differently from one's public identity, it also raises some questions as to the relationship between the interior and exterior. Moreover, given her appeal to realism, does her account assume the subject/object dichotomy? Realism is important in her account because horizons are embodied, material, and historical rather than just discursive. Thus one may have a view of his or her identity and may in fact be wrong about it. From a Heideggerian perspective, an account that rejects or downplays traditional dichotomies would be neither realist nor idealist. In this case the question of realism or idealism would be moot. Martín Alcoff's appeal to realism in the account of self as horizon needs to be understood in a thin sense (commonsense realism) then, given that a strong appeal to realism would commit Martín Alcoff to assume some of the very dichotomies she wishes to move away from so as to show the fundamental aspect of social identity.

11. The killings of black youth and men of color, including Trayvon Martin, Michael Brown, Tamir Rice, and Freddie Gray, as well as the less-discussed killings of black women, such as Tarika Wilson, Aiyana Jones, and Shereese Francis, who were also subject to police brutality, are but a few painful examples of the manner in which the lives of those marked by visible racial identities have become vulnerable and considered disposable.

12. It is distressful to experience various types of racial aggressions and microaggressions—for example, being asked if I have brought tacos; being asked if my partner is my interpreter; being called names of Mexican dishes after my name has been called ("Ortega, chalupa, burrito . . ."). The different ways in which racism is manifested is quite astonishing. Even the seemingly "silly" or "obviously stupid" examples get under one's skin, not to speak of the more injurious ones. And I should add that as a light-skinned Latina, I do not experience racism in the same manner in which darker-skinned Latinas/os do.

13. It is demoralizing to see that feminist theory in general, and contemporary feminist theory in particular, continue either to overlook the theoretical work by women of color or to provide treatments of it that lack depth. As AnaLouise Keating notes, even the now-iconic text *This Bridge Called My Back* (Moraga & Anzaldúa 1983) has really had a minimal impact on white feminist theory (2013, 20). While the collection is constantly used when mentioning diversity and difference among women, engaged white feminist scholarship on the theories proposed by women in *Bridge* is difficult to find. As Keating adds, "Nor do they integrate contributors' most radical lessons into their own lives and intellectual traditions" (2013, 20). For Keating and women of color theorists in general, *Bridge* constitutes a key, transformational text both personally and intellectually. In her view, this anthology not only provided intersectional analyses seven years prior to Crenshaw's use of the term, but also provides a framework that points to the limits of intersectionality by enacting a "politics of interconnectivity" (2013, 30).

14. For Crenshaw's latest assessment of critical race theory, in particular in the current "post-racial" moment, see Crenshaw 2011.

15. Recently, Keating has also offered an account of "transformational identity politics" that attempts to go beyond accounts of oppositional consciousness that she considers overly dichotomous and problematic (Keating 2013, 5–10). I first read Weir's account of transformative identity politics in Weir 2008, which is now chapter 3 of her recently published *Identities and Freedom* (Weir 2013). Here I continue to

use the 2008 article as it was minimally revised in the 2013 version. It is interesting to see the way in which both theorists approach the issue of transformation in identity politics, especially as they work on similar topics while unaware of each other's work. While Weir is in search of a politics that moves away from traditional conceptions of identity as sameness and that allows for global interconnectedness (2008, 126), Keating proposes a transformational identity politics based on a critique of oppositional consciousness and a call for seeing the manner in which we have an "extreme interconnectivity" with each other and the rest of the natural world (2013, 110). It is interesting to note the manner in which both theorists rely on recognition and engagement of difference and also a search for commonalities (not sameness) so as to foment such interconnectedness. I welcome both theorists' move to appeal to a renewed vision of identity that is more inclusive. Keating, however, is much more critical of the notion of identity because she repeatedly sees it as based on oppositional consciousness.

16. For an insightful discussion of the importance of embodied, affective, sensuous knowledge in the context of social movements, in particular the transliberation and genderqueer movements, see (Shotwell 2011, ch. 6). While Weir's identity politics call for a movement away from metaphysics toward political and ethical solidarity, Shotwell engages the connection between the deeper processes within one's body and social and political worlds, or what she describes, following Eli Clare's words in *Exile and Pride: Disability, Queerness, and Liberation*, as "a knowing that resided in my bones" (2011, 135). Shotwell states,

> Sensuous knowledge marks a site where gender norms and their potential reworkings are stitched together and discomfited. Sensuous knowledge for social movement, then, shows up as one site of creating a livable world—a complex home, without guarantees. It is a resource for change, a site of praxis, an unspeakable but deeply political social and ethical mode of being. (2011, 151)

17. I am in agreement with Weir about the importance of our relations with others and that through these relations we can understand each other in our difference and in terms of our position in the web of relations of power. However, I ultimately question her desire for forming "a utopian vision for a future, and a home, that all of us can share," as this desire seems to counter her emphasis on understanding others in their difference (Weir 2008, 126). Weir expands on her notion of "home" as more of a "regulative ideal" rather than a simplistic call for perfect safety or the mother's womb (which excludes those not at home). She notes that given the many people all over the globe that find themselves displaced and without homes, it is a mark of privilege to reject the notion of home for a life of risk as many critics of the notion suggest (Weir 2008, 49). Following Young, she sees home as a site of autonomy and freedom (Weir 2008, 58), and following Frederick Douglass, she sees this freedom as a "home for an extended

family" (2008, 59). While I am in agreement with Weir's move of reinterpreting the notion of home so that it is not just a site of exclusion, I question the use of the notion as a "regulative ideal." While acting "as if" home were a site in which the "spirit will thrive" can be helpful, it may also overemphasize the positive values of home, thus overlooking the particular, material situations in which so many have no possibility of having such a home. In chapter 7, I take up the question of home and introduce the notion of hometactics, an everyday practice that helps the multiplicitous self have some sense of comfort and belonging even when not having a home.

18. An appeal to solidarity is a stronger strategy than an appeal to empathy given influential critiques of empathy. As noted, Heidegger rejects the model of empathy as it already assumes a self that is not connected to others. See Shotwell 2011 for a more recent discussion that provides an important critique of empathy. Shotwell rightly notes that appeals to empathy are problematic for at least three reasons: (1) it is not clear that there can be institutional empathy, empathy between groups of people, or between individuals and groups as the empathic relation seems to be much more complex than relations between individuals; (2) theories of empathy mistakenly assume that there is not an interaction or entanglement with others prior to the empathic relation; and (3) the focus on empathy recenters whiteness and the white experience (107–109). I particularly agree with Shotwell's third point because one of the most problematic issues with appeals to empathy is that the experience of the "other" is always connected to white experience and is thus made secondary; whiteness is further reified as the standard. Nevertheless, it is important to keep in mind that the notion of solidarity is not without problems. For an influential feminist critique of solidarity that argues against conventional and affective solidarity and calls for "reflective solidarity," which relies on ties to others based on dissent, see Dean 1996.

19. It is interesting to note here that Weir criticizes both Mohanty and Reagon for assuming too strict a dichotomy, one in which identity is based on desires of home and nurture whereas coalition is based on action and struggle. Yet I wonder if Weir herself is engaged in too dichotomous a reading of identity.

20. Weir mentions Martín Alcoff's analysis of identity and says that it is a more complex view of positionality than a notion of identity based on the group's opposition to other groups. (Weir 2008,130n4). However, Weir does not provide an analysis of Martín Alcoff's view of self as horizon. This footnote was deleted in Weir 2013. However, in this later text, Weir states that the work on identity by postpositive realists such as Martín Alcoff and Paula Moya is "essential" (2013, 31). She also praises Martín Alcoff for providing a complex philosophical account of relational identities that goes beyond her own argument (2013, 116n5). Nevertheless, we don't find a sustained engagement with Martín Alcoff's realist view of identity (or with Moya's) in her text.

21. I have always been interested in the manner in which some people are immediately certain that they do not understand the words coming out of someone's

mouth, especially when that person has an accent. In my experiences while learning English, as well as now, I continually meet those, if I may invoke Nietzsche, for whom my mouth is not for their ears. Some people are simply not willing to work hard to understand nonnative speakers if they are just learning the language or if they have a strong accent. Others, however, are willing to get past the unfamiliar pronunciation, thick accents, grammatical mistakes. If the way we relate to *other* voices were indicative of a general stance toward difference, we would indeed remain in a tower of Babel.

22. Martín Alcoff describes race contextualism as the view that race is socially constructed and subject to historical and cultural changes. The positive or negative value ascribed to the identity in question is dependent on particular contexts. Contextualism may be objective (concerned with providing general structural features of the identity in question) or subjective (attuned to the everyday, embodied experience of having a particular identity and how it influences our experiences) (Martín Alcoff 2006, 182). Although any discussion of social identities needs to acknowledge both objective and subjective components, I believe that we must be careful not to posit too strict a dichotomy between the two as this would obscure the entanglement between our everyday lived experience and the general structures influencing my experience.

23. It is important to note here that the complications and difficulties that arise because of the multiplicitous aspects of the self might actually prompt some to highlight one identity as the most important so as to feel some sense of comfort. However, as we have seen, understanding one's liminality and in-betweenness is an important source for critical self-understanding. Being a multiplicitous self does not guarantee that one will reject an overly narrow appeal to a central identity, but it does provide conditions for questioning such an approach. Self-identification and collective identification is a complex process that includes various moments of identification, reidentification, negotiation, attunement to difference within and outside groups, as well as understanding oppressive practices and the manner in which they encourage self- and group fragmentation.

24. See Roshanravan 2010 for an important discussion of a specific process of 'becoming" a woman of color. In this instance, Roshanravan offers an account of "passing-as-if" that explains the process when nonwhite women who do not belong to recognized US politically resistant groups that fight racial oppression politically identify as "women of color."

25. See Roshanravan 2014 for a rich discussion on coalitions. Following Lugones's important view about the different ways in which we inhabit a limen and how we come to be politically resistant, Roshanravan analyzes how Chandra Mohanty, M. Jacqui Alexander, and María Lugones herself became resistant to colonialism and global capitalism. She engages these three important theorists in a "plurilogue" that reveals the differences between their resistant strategies. Understanding such differences not only moves us away from resisting what Roshanravan accurately describes as a superficial engagement with women of color theorizing that

sees their work as unified but also allows us to reveal the complexity of the various strategies against oppression that women of color offer. Moreover, it allows for the possibility of "epistemic disobedience," what Mignolo considers as a delinking from the so-called legitimate knowledge fostered by academic disciplines (Roshanravan 2014, 42). See Lebens 2006 for an interesting discussion of the difficulty of white feminism and coalitional anti-racist work.

26. Inspired by Lugones, Hames-García understands the coalitional moment as an understanding that we can expand our political interests through understanding our multiplicity and "opaqueness," or that which is not fully transparent to others, especially those in dominant groups. He states,

> Progressive social struggles and politics can only succeed when straight people of color and white lesbians and gay men come to see the interests of gay, lesbian, bisexual, and transgender people of color as their own. According to this prescription, dominant members of social groups must come to expand their sense of what their own interests are and who their own people are. Coalitions can thereby cease to constitute themselves as coalitions of people with different interests and the fragmentation within them can be healed. For this to happen, everyone must acknowledge opaque interests, reconceiving them as interests shared by all members of both groups (straight people of color on the one hand, and white lesbian, gay, bisexual, and transgender people on the other). In other words, fighting racism and homophobia must become a primary interest of all women and fighting sexism and homophobia must become a primary interest of all people of color within a given coalition. (2011, 27)

In his account, coalition allows us to expand who our "own" people are, and we have to reconceive opaque interests as our interests. I agree with Hames-García's understanding that multiplicity is helpful in expanding political interests and that we have to recognize the opaque interests of others and reconceive them in such a way that they become important to us as well. Yet I think that this is possible only when there is a transformation within me given my relations with others, a becoming-with others that allows me to understand myself as being changed by others through concrete and embodied experiences of struggle with them.

27. Changing our habits of perception, especially as they pertain to visible identities, is indeed difficult given what Martín Alcoff describes as the tacit nature of those habits. I agree with Martín Alcoff that we need to make visible the practices of visibility themselves and thus to understand the manner in which we perceive visible identities. I suspect, however, that there will be tacit practices that have become so transparent that we might not recognize, let alone question, them. I wonder if indeed there might be a future in which color might become less salient as Martín Alcoff suggests (2006, 204).

Chapter 6. Social Location, Knowledge, and Multiplicity

1. See Mohanty 1993, 1997, 2001; Moya & Hames-García 2000; and Moya 2002. See Moya & Hames-García 2000 for a discussion of how various theorists such as Satya P. Mohanty, Michael R. Hames-García, Linda Martín Alcoff, William Wilkerson, and others endorse PPRI. While various theorists hold a postpositivist realist account of identity, I concentrate on Moya's account of PPRI, as she offers the most in-depth explanation and defense of PPRI.

2. For a brief summary of the postpositive realist view of identity and a general review of Moya's attack against postmodernist positions, see Ortega 2007. Moya makes a good point in warning us against some postmodernist positions' overreliance on discursivity. However, Moya groups a number of different positions under the wide umbrella of "postmodernism" and criticizes what she considers are their wrong assumptions. She unfortunately homogenizes these views and misses some of their contributions. Moreover, in emphasizing the way in which postmodernism responds to essentialism, Moya fails to take into consideration other accounts of selfhood and subjectivity that are also engaged in redefining subjectivity so as to separate it from essentialist claims, for example, pragmatist or phenomenological views.

3. Women of color go through various self-identifications or self-understandings when navigating multiple worlds. As we become more political, we realize that previous self-identifications do not accurately represent who we have become in our journey to understanding the manner in which we are situated in these worlds. I distinctly remember the time when I no longer saw myself only as a "Nicaraguan" but also as a "bicultural woman" and a "woman of color." As noted, a woman of color identity arises out of shared political aims. Identifying as woman of color opens coalitional possibilities and, as the members of the Santa Cruz Feminist of Color Collective note, it is a "shift from subjectification to active subjectivity, where collectivized and at times paradoxical identities emerge from coalitional strategies across racial, sexual, class, gender, and generational differences" (Santa Cruz Feminist of Color Collective 2014, 26).

4. Moreover, the pan-ethnic term "Hispanic" is for many Latinos highly problematic given its history as a term coined by the US Census Bureau in the 1970s.

5. It is interesting to note that the term "woman of color" emerged after the circulation of the term "lesbian woman of color" (Santa Cruz Feminist of Color Collective 2014, 29).

6. Cherríe Moraga is of mixed Anglo and Mexican heritage. In her writings she notes that she experienced a great deal of confusion about her lesbian and Chicana identities. See Moraga 1983 for her moving story about her coming of age.

7. Recall Heidegger's explanation of temporality:

Temporalizing does not signify that ecstasies come in a 'succession.' The future is *not later* than having been, and having been is *not earlier* than the Present. Temporality temporalizes itself as a future which makes present in the process of having been. (1962, 401)

8. Moya's concern here is that, given postmodern positions privileging discursivity and undermining the material conditions of our location, such positions allow for selves making claims about their identities that are not based on actual conditions and that relegate all identity claims to the same status. As noted, Moya worries about the way in which individuals can claim marginal identities when, in reality, some individuals are more marginalized than others given specific material conditions. I am very sympathetic to Moya's concern, as it is easy to see how claims of oppression and marginality are wrongly taken up by members of dominant groups. Yet I worry that in an effort to avoid problematic appropriation of identities and conditions of oppression, PPRI as conceived by Moya misses the fluid character of the processes of our self-understanding and self-identification. This does not mean that this process does not have any connection to material conditions and that individuals can willy-nilly claim identities or conditions of oppression, but rather that this process does not always reveal the kind of temporal path of self-understanding that Moya emphasizes.

9. I thank an anonymous reviewer for this point.

10. While Moya is in no way advocating "absolute sameness or constancy," she is more interested in a model that privileges a search for a truer identity. Here, we can appreciate how Hames-García's addition of Lugones's view enhances a postpositivist realist position and allows that theory to deal more productively with the issue of multiplicity within the self. Whether Lugones's view is ultimately compatible with a postpositive realist theory of identity characterized by the search for more epistemically accurate claims, for objectivity, and for justifying normative claims against dominant social relations is another matter.

Chapter 7. Hometactics

1. My notion of self-mapping pertains the way in which one attempts to understand one's position in different worlds. Such a position is not to be understood as merely spatial—as related to establishing borders and engaging in an exercise that leads to fixity, as a cartographer might wish to do. Rather, I use self-mapping as indicative of a process of being attuned to who one is and where one fits and does not fit, how one fares in the different worlds traveled, and why one feels the way one does while being in different worlds. Self-mapping, then, is not about naming one's country and differentiating its borders but about being attuned to feelings of *be-longing*, of being and longing, in the different worlds we traverse.

2. Adrienne Rich coined the notion "politics of location" in her analysis of her own positionality as a white, Jewish, lesbian, privileged woman (Rich 1986, 210–231). It has become a crucial idea in feminism, as feminists carry out

investigations about their own spatial and social positionality and how this positionality informs their political responsibilities.

3. Such "nurturing" spaces might not always become unsafe for those inhabiting them. However, given the heterogeneity of groups, it is likely that questions about who really belongs in them might arise.

4. I must be clear here and add that by appealing to a "will to belong" I am not appealing to some metaphysical or psychological aspect or drive that we all must have by virtue of being human. It would be incredibly pretentious for me to make such a claim. Perhaps Schopenhauer and Nietzsche knew more when they made their appeals to the "will to live" and the "will to truth" and "the will to power," respectively. I am simply naming a feeling, perhaps an attitude that I find in myself as well as many other people, whether they are immigrants or exiles or not, although many exiles certainly discuss it more. I am making explicit something that is already there in my lived experience as well as in the experience of others. It is not my wish to reify, naturalize, or generalize from such an experience, but I do wish to engage this feeling in light of questions of home, location, and multiplicitous selfhood.

5. I thank Kyoo Lee for her comments regarding the possibility of being without longing, or as she puts it, "without being forced to choose sites/sides of be-longing." I realize that I am still invested in being "with longing" even when the sites of belonging and belonging itself are being problematized.

6. Sometimes I wonder whether my use of hometactics can become, as Sartre would say, a project of "bad faith," what he describes as a certain lying to oneself, another way of denying one's transcendence or freedom to make choices in order to become a facticity—in this instance, a sense of having a"home" when in fact we have the freedom to move, to be nomads, if we so desire (Sartre, 1966, I, ch. 2).

7. I thank Ada Demaj for pressing me to think more about this question regarding the use of hometactics in the context of the colonizer. It is important to remember that even practices such as world-traveling and hometactics can be used by those in dominant positions inappropriately, thus undermining their positive elements and the practices themselves.

Bibliography

Adell, Sandra. 1994. *Double Consciousness/Double Bind: Theoretical Issues in Twentieth-Century Black Literature*. Urbana: University of Illinois Press.

Ahmed, Sara. 2006. *Queer Phenomenology: Orientations, Objects, Others*. Durham, NC: Duke University Press.

Aho, Kevin. 2010. *Heidegger's Neglect of the Body*. Albany, NY: State University of New York Press.

Alarcón, Norma. 1983. "Chicana's Feminist Literature: A Re-vision through Malintzín/or Malintzín: Putting Flesh Back on the Object." In *This Bridge Called My Back: Writings by Radical Women of Color*, eds. Cherríe Moraga and Gloria Anzaldúa, 182–188. New York: Kitchen Table/Women of Color Press.

———. 1991. "The Theoretical Subject(s) of *This Bridge Called My Back* and Anglo-American Feminism." In *Criticism in the Borderlands: Studies in Chicano Literature, Culture, and Ideology*, eds. Héctor Calderón and José David Saldívar, 28–42. Durham, NC: Duke University Press.

———. 1994. "Conjugating Subjects: The Heteroglossia of Essence and Resistance." In *An Other Tongue: Nation and Ethnicity in the Linguistic Borderlands*, ed. Alfred Arteaga, 125–138. Durham, NC: Duke University Press.

Alcoff, Linda. 2001. "Phenomenology, Poststructuralism, and Feminist Theory on the Concept of Experience." In *Feminist Phenomenology*, eds. Linda Fisher and Lester Embree, 39–56. Dordrecht: Kluwer Academic.

Alexander, M. Jacqui. 2005. *Pedagogies of Crossing: Meditations on Feminism, Sexual Politics, Memory, and the Sacred*. Durham, NC: Duke University Press.

Alexander, M. Jacqui, and Chandra Talpade Mohanty. 1997. "Introduction: Genealogies, Legacies, Movements." In *Feminist Genealogies, Colonial Legacies, Democratic Futures*, eds. M. Jacqui Alexander and Chandra Talpade Mohanty, xiii–xlii. New York: Routledge.

Allen, Ernest. 2002. "Du Boisian Double Consciousness: The Unsustainable Argument." *Massachusetts Review* 43(2) (Summer): 217–253.

Al Saji, Alia. 2014. "A Phenomenology of Hesitation: Interrupting Racializing Habits of Seeing." In *Living Alterities: Phenomenology, Embodiment, and Race*, ed. Emily Lee, 133–172. Albany, NY: State University of New York Press.

American Psychiatric Association. 2013. *Diagnostic and Statistical Manual of Mental Disorders (Fifth ed.)*. Arlington, VA: American Psychiatric Publishing.

Anzaldúa, Gloria E. 1987. *Borderlands/La Frontera: The New Mestiza*. San Francisco: Aunt Lute.

———, ed. 1990. *Making Face, Making Soul/Haciendo Caras: Creative and Critical Perspectives by Feminists of Color*. San Francisco: Aunt Lute.

———. 1998. "To(o) Queer the Writer." In *Living Chicana Theory*, ed. Carla Trujillo, 263–276. Berkeley, CA: Third Woman Press.

———. 2000. *Interviews/Entrevistas*, ed. AnaLouise Keating. New York: Routledge.

———. 2005. "Let Us Be the Healing of the Wound: The Coyolxauhqui Imperative—la sombra y el sueño." In *One Wound for Another: Una Herida por otra, Testimonios de Latinas in the U.S. through Cyberspace (11 de septiembre de 2001–1 de marzo de 2002)*, eds. Claire Joysmith and Clara Lomas, 92–103. Mexico City: UNAM-CISAN.

———. 2009. *The Gloria Anzaldúa Reader*. Ed. AnaLouise Keating. Durham, NC: Duke University Press.

Anzaldúa, Gloria E., and AnaLouise Keating, eds. 2002. *This Bridge We Call Home: Radical Visions for Transformation*. New York: Routledge.

Arrizón, Alicia. 2006. *Queering Mestizaje: Transculturation and Performance*. Ann Arbor: University of Michigan Press.

Bailey, Alison. 2007. "Strategic Ignorance." In *Race and Epistemologies of Ignorance*, eds. Shannon Sullivan and Nancy Tuana, 77–94. Albany, NY: State University of New York Press.

Bambara, Toni Cade. 2005. *The Black Woman: An Anthology*. New York: Washington Square Press.

Barnard, Ian. 2004. *Queer Race, Cultural Interventions in the Racial Politics of Queer Theory*. New York: Peter Lang.

Bartky, Sandra. 1998. "Pitfalls and Politics of 'World-Traveling,' a Comment on Linda LeMoncheck's *Loose Women, Lecherous Men: A Feminist Philosophy of Sex*." *Philosophical Studies* 89: 387–393.

Barvosa, Edwina. 2008. *Wealth of Selves: Multiple Identities, Mestiza Consciousness, and the Subject of Politics*. College Station: Texas A&M Press.

Beale, Frances. 1995. "Double Jeopardy: To Be Black and Female." In *Words of Fire: An Anthology of African-American Feminist Thought*, ed. Beverly Guy-Sheftall, 146–155. New York: The New Press.

Bell, Bernard W. 1996. "Genealogical Shifts in Du Bois's Discourse on Double Consciousness as the Sign of the African American Difference." In *W.E.B Du Bois on Race and Culture*, eds. Bernard W. Bell, Emily R. Grosholz, and James B. Stewart, 87–108. New York: Routledge.

Beltrán, Cristina. 2010. *The Trouble with Unity: Latino Politics and the Creation of Identity*. Oxford: Oxford University Press.

———. 2004. "Patrolling Borders: Hybrids, Hierarchies and the Challenge of Mestizaje." *Political Research Quarterly* 57(4) (December): 595–607.

Benhabib, Seyla, Judith Butler, Drucilla Cornell, and Nancy Fraser. 1994. *Feminist Contentions: A Philosophical Exchange*. New York: Routledge.

Bernasconi, Robert, and Sybil Cook, eds. 2003. *Race and Racism in Continental Philosophy*. Bloomington: Indiana University Press.

Bettcher, Talia Mae. 2013. "Trapped in the Wrong Theory: Rethinking Trans Oppression and Resistance." *Signs: Journal of Women in Culture and Society* 39(2): 383–406.

Bhabha, Homi K. 1994. *Location of Culture*. London: Routledge.

———. 1996. "Cultures in Between." In *Questions of Cultural Identity*, eds. Stuart Hall and Paul Du Gay. London: Sage Publications.

Bird-Soto, Nancy. 2014. "Theory/Latin-aTheory/Atheory." *Letras Salvajes: Revista de Literatura, Arte y Pensamiento de Alta Velocidad* (15): 91–98.

Blackwell, Maylei. 2011. *¡Chicana Power! Contested Histories of Feminism in the Chicano Movement*. Austin: University of Texas Press.

Bloodsworth-Lugo, Mary K. 2007. *In-between Bodies: Sexual Difference, Race and Sexuality*. Albany, NY: State University of New York Press.

Brown, Wendy. 1995. *States of Injury: Power and Freedom in Late Modernity*. Princeton, NJ: Princeton University Press.

Bruce, Dickson D., Jr. 1992. "W.E.B Du Bois and the Idea of Double Consciousness." *American Literature* 64(2) (June): 299–309.

Butler, Judith. 1988. "Performative Acts and Gender Constitution: An Essay in Phenomenology and Feminist Theory." *Theatre Journal* 40(4): 519–531.

———. 1990. *Gender Trouble: Feminism and the Subversion of Identity*. London: Routledge.

———. 1997. *The Psychic Life of Power: Theories in Subjection*. Stanford, CA: Stanford University Press.

Calvino, Italo. 1986. *The Uses of Literature*. New York: Harcourt Brace.

Campbell, Sue, and Susan E. Babbit, eds. 1999. *Dominant Identities and Settled Expectations in Racism and Philosophy*. Ithaca, NY: Cornell University Press.

Carastathis, Anna. 2013. "Identity Categories as Potential Coalitions." *Signs: Journal of Women in Culture and Society* 38(4): 941–965.

Carman, Taylor. 1994. "On Being Social: A Reply to Olafson." *Inquiry* 37(2): 203–223.

Carrillo Rowe, Aimee. 2008. *Power Lines: On the Subject of Feminist Alliances*. Durham, NC: Duke University Press.

Castillo Debra A. 2006. "Anzaldúa and Transnational American Studies." *PMLA* 121(1): 260–265.

Castillo, Debra A., and María Socorro Tabuenca Córdoba, eds. 2002. *Border Women: Writing from La Frontera*. Minneapolis: University of Minnesota Press.

Clack, Beverley. 1999. *Misogyny in the Western Philosophical Tradition: A Reader*. New York: Routledge.

Clare, Eli. 1999. *Exile and Pride: Disability, Queerness, and Liberation*. Cambridge, MA: South End Press.

Collins, Patricia Hill. 1998. *Fighting Words: Black Women and the Search for Justice*. Minneapolis: University of Minnesota Press.

————. 2008. *Black Feminist Thought: Knowledge, Consciousness, and the Politics of Empowerment.* New York: Routledge.

Combahee River Collective. 1979. "A Black Feminist Statement." In *Capitalist Patriarchy and the Case for Socialist Feminism,* ed. Zillah R. Eisenstein, 362–372. New York: Monthly Review Press.

Crenshaw, Kimberlé. 1989. "Demarginalizing the Intersection of Race and Sex: A Black Feminist Critique of Antidiscrimination Doctrine, Feminist Theory, and Antiracist Politics." *The University of Chicago Legal Forum* 139 (1989): 138–167.

————. 1995. "Mapping the Margins: Intersectionality, Identity Politics, and Violence against Women of Color." In *Critical Race Theory: The Key Writings That Formed the Movement,* eds. Kimberlé Crenshaw, Neil Gotanda, Gary Peller, and Kendal Thomas, 357–383. New York: The New Press.

————. 2006. "On Gendered Violence and Racialized Prisons: An Intersectional Tale of Two Movements." Talk at the University of California Santa Barbara. Available at http://www.youtube.com/watch?v=d1v9E83yTNA. Accessed May 22, 2015.

————. 2011. "Twenty Years of Critical Race Theory: Looking Back to Move Forward." *Connecticut Law Review* 43(5): 1253–1352.

————. 2012. "From Private Violence to Mass Incarceration: Thinking Intersectionally about Women, Race, and Social Control." *UCLA Law Review* 59 (2012): 1418.

Davis, Angela. 1983. *Women, Race, and Class.* New York: Vintage Books.

de Beauvoir, Simone. 2000. *The Ethics of Ambiguity.* New York: Citadel Press.

de Beistegui, Miguel. 1998. *Heidegger and the Political: Dystopias.* New York: Routledge.

de Certeau, Michel. 1984. *The Practice of Everyday Life.* Berkeley: University of California Press.

de Laurentis, Teresa. 1990. "Eccentric Subjects: Feminist Theory and Historical Consciousness." *Feminist Studies* 16(1): 115–150.

Dean, Jodi. 1996. *Solidarity of Strangers: Feminism after Identity Politics.* Berkeley: University of California Press.

Delgadillo, Theresa. 2011. *Spiritual Mestizaje: Religion, Gender, Race, and Nation in Contemporary Chicana Narrative.* Durham, NC: Duke University Press.

Dotson, Kristie, ed. 2014. *Interstices: Inheriting Women of Color Feminist Philosophy.* *Hypatia* 29(1). Special issue.

————. 2011. "Tracking Epistemic Violence: Tracking Practices of Silencing." *Hypatia* 26(2) (Spring): 236–257.

————. "Knowing in Space: Three Lessons from Black Women's Social Theory." Unpublished manuscript.

Drabinski, John E. 2014. "Heidegger, Racism and Scholarship." Available at http://jdrabinski.com/heidegger-racism-and-scholarship/?utm_content= buffer7950e&utm_medium=social&utm_source=facebook.com&utm_campaign=buffer. Accessed July 26, 2014.

Dreyfus, Hubert. 1991. *Being-in-the-World: A Commentary on Heidegger's "Being and Time, division I."* Cambridge: MIT Press.

Du Bois, W.E.B. 1897. "Strivings of the Negro People." *Atlantic* 80 (August).

———. 1999. *The Souls of Black Folk.* New York: W.W. Norton.

Dussel, Enrique. 2009. "'Being-in-the-World-Hispanically': A World on the 'Border' of Many Worlds." Trans. Alexander Stehn. *Comparative Literature* 61(3): 256–273.

———. 1995. *The Invention of the Americas: Eclipse of "the Other" and the Myth of Modernity.* Trans. Michael D. Barber. New York: Continuum.

Egan, David. 2012. "*Das Man* and Distantiality in *Being and Time.*" Inquiry 55(3): 289–306.

Eze, Emmanuel Chukwudi. 1997. *Race and the Enlightenment: A Reader.* Malden, MA: Blackwell.

Farías, Victor. 1991. *Heidegger and Nazism.* Philadelphia, PA: Temple University Press.

Faye, Emmanuel. 2009. *Heidegger: The Introduction of Nazism into Philosophy in Light of the Unpublished Seminars of 1933–1935.* New Haven, CT: Yale University Press.

Feder, Ellen. 2007. *Family Bonds: Genealogies of Race and Gender.* Oxford: Oxford University Press.

Fielding, Helen A. 2012. "Feminism." In *The Routledge Companion to Phenomenology*, eds. Sebastian Luft and Søren Overgaard, 518–527. New York: Routledge.

Fisher, Linda. 2000. "Phenomenology and Feminism: Perspectives on Their Relation." In *Feminist Phenomenology*, eds. Linda Fisher and Lester Embree, 17–38. Dordrecht: Kluwer Academic.

Fisher, Linda, and Lester Embree, eds. 2000. *Feminist Phenomenology.* Dordrecht: Kluwer Academic.

Freire, Paulo. 2000. *The Pedagogy of the Oppressed.* New York: Continuum International.

Garber, Linda. 2001. *Identity Poetics: Race, Class, and the Lesbian-Feminist Roots of Queer Theory.* New York: Columbia University Press.

García, Alma. 1997. *Chicana Feminist Thought: The Basic Historical Writings.* New York: Routledge.

Geertz, Clifford. 1986. "Making Experiences, Authoring Selves." In *The Anthropology of Experience*, eds. Victor W. Turner and Edward M. Bruner, 373–380. Urbana: University of Illinois Press.

Gilroy, Paul. 2000. *Against Race: Imagining Political Culture Beyond the Color Line.* Cambridge, MA: The Belknap Press of Harvard University Press.

Gines, Kathryn T. 2011. "Black Feminism and Intersectional Analyses: A Defense of Intersectionality." *Philosophy Today* 55: 275–284. SPEP supplement.

———. 2014. "Race Women, Race Men and Early Expressions of Proto-Intersectionality, 1830s–1930s." In *Why Race and Gender Still Matter*, eds. Namita Goswami, Maeve M. O'Donovan, and Lisa Yount, 13–25. London: Pickering & Chatto.

Gooding-Williams, Robert. 2009. *In the Shadow of Du Bois: Afro-Modern Political Thought in America*. Cambridge, MA: Harvard University Press.

Gordon, Lewis. 1995. *Bad Faith and Antiblack Racism*. Atlantic Highlands, NJ: Humanities Books.

Grewal, Inderpal. 1994. "Autobiographic Subjects and Diasporic Locations: Meatless Days." In *Scattered Hegemonies*, eds. Inderpal Grewal and Karen Kaplan. Minneapolis: University of Minnesota Press.

Gutierrez y Muhs, Gabriella, Yolanda Flores Niemann, Carmen G. Gonzalez, and Angela P. Harris, eds. 2012. *Presumed Incompetent: The Intersections of Race and Class for Women in Academia*. Boulder: University Press of Colorado.

Guy-Sheftall, Beverly. 1995. *Words of Fire: An Anthology of African-American Feminist Thought*. New York: The New Press.

Hames-García, Michael. 2011. *Identity Complex: Making the Case for Multiplicity*. Minneapolis: University of Minnesota Press.

Haraway, Donna. 1990. "A Manifesto for Cyborgs: Science, Technology, and Socialist Feminism in the 1980s." In *Feminism/Postmodernism*, ed. Linda J. Nicholson, 190–233. New York: Routledge.

———. 1991. *Simians, Cyborgs, and Women: The Reinvention of Nature*. New York: Routledge.

Harding, Sandra. 1991. *Whose Science? Whose Knowledge? Thinking from Women's Lives*. Ithaca, NY: Cornell University Press.

Harding, Sandra, ed. 2004. *The Feminist Standpoint Theory Reader*. New York and London: Routledge.

Hart, Mechthild. 2013. "Laboring and Hanging Out in the Embodied In-Between." *Hypatia* 28(1) (Winter): 49–68.

Hatab, Lawrence J. 2000. *Ethics and Finitude: Heideggerian Contributions to Moral Philosophy*. Lanham, MD: Rowman & Littlefield.

Heidegger, Martin. 1962. *Being and Time*. Trans. John Macquarrie and Edward Robinson. New York: Harper and Row.

———. 1969. *Identity and Difference*. Trans. Joan Stambaugh. New York: Harper and Row.

———. 1977. *The Question concerning Technology*. Trans. W. Lovitt. New York: Harper and Row.

———. 1982. *The Basic Problems of Phenomenology*. Trans. Albert Hofstadter. Bloomington: Indiana University Press.

———. 1992. The Concept of Time. Trans. William McNeill. Oxford: Blackwell.

———. 1995. *The Fundamental Concepts of Metaphysics: World, Finitude, Solitude*. Trans. William McBride and Nicholas Walker. Bloomington: Indiana University Press.

———. 2000. *Introduction to Metaphysics*. Trans. Gregory Fried and Richard Polt. New Haven, CT: Yale University Press.

Heinämaa, Sara. 1995. *Toward a Phenomenology of Sexual Difference: Husserl, Merleau-Ponty, Beauvoir*. Lanham, MD: Rowman & Littlefield.

Heinämaa, Sara, and Lanei Rodemeyer, eds. 2010. *Continental Philosophy Review* 43(1), Special issue on Phenomenology and Feminism.

Hekman, Susan. 1999. "Identity Crises: Identity, Identity Politics, and Beyond." In *Feminism, Identity and Difference*, ed. Susan Hekman, 3–26. London: Frank Cass.

———. 2000. "Beyond Identity: Feminism, Identity, and Identity Politics." *Feminist Theory* 1(3): 289–308.

Heyes, Cressida J. 2011. "Identity Politics." *Stanford Encyclopedia of Philosophy.* Available at http://plato.stanford.edu/cgi-bin/encyclopedia/archinfo.cgi?entry= identity-politics.

Holland, Nancy J., and Patricia Huntington, eds. 2001. *Feminist Interpretations of Martin Heidegger*. University Park: Pennsylvania State University Press.

hooks, bell. 1981. *Ain't I a Woman? Black Women and Feminism*. Boston: South End Press.

———. 1984. *Feminist Theory: From Margin to Center*. Boston: South End Press.

———. 2009. *Belonging: A Culture of Place*. New York: Routledge.

Hoy, David. 1993. "Heidegger and the Hermeneutic Turn." In *The Cambridge Companion to Heidegger*, ed. Charles Guignon, 170–194. Cambridge: Cambridge University Press.

Hull, Gloria. T., Patricia Bell Scott, and Barbara Smith, eds. 1982. *All the Women Are White, All the Blacks Are Men, but Some of Us Are Brave: Black Women's Studies*. Old Westbury, NY: Feminist Press.

Huntington, Patricia. 2001. "Introduction I—General Background: History of the Feminist Reception of Heidegger and a Guide to Heidegger's Thought." In *Feminist Interpretations of Martin Heidegger*, eds. Nancy J. Holland and Patricia Huntington, 1–42. University Park: Pennsylvania State University Press.

Hurtado, Aída. 1998. "Sitios y Lenguas: Chicanas Theorize Feminisms." *Hypatia* 13(2) (Spring): 134–161.

Husserl, Edmund. 1982. *Ideas Pertaining to a Pure Phenomenology and to a Phenomenological Philosophy—First Book: General Introduction to a Pure Phenomenology*. Trans. F. Kersten. The Hague: Martinus Nijhoff.

———. 1993. *Cartesian Meditations*. Trans. Dorian Cairns. Dordrecht: Kluwer Academic.

James, William. 1981. *Principles of Psychology*. Cambridge: Harvard University Press.

———. 1987. *William James: Selected Writings*. New York: Book-of-the-Month Club.

Jay, Martin. 2005. *Songs of Experience: Modern American and European Variations on a Universal Theme*. Berkeley: University of California Press.

Kaplan, Caren. 1994. "The Politics of Location as Transnational Feminist Critical Practice." In *Scattered Hegemonies: Postmodernity and Transnational Feminist Practices*, eds. Inderpal Grewal and Caren Kaplan, 137–152. Minneapolis: University of Minnesota Press.

———. 1996. *Questions of Travel: Postmodern Discourses of Displacement.* Durham, NC: Duke University Press.

Keating, AnaLouise, ed. 2005. *EntreMundos/AmongWorlds: New Perspectives on Gloria Anzaldúa.* New York: Palgrave Macmillan.

———. 2006. "From Borderlands and New Mestizas to Nepantlas and Nepantleras: Anzaldúan Theories for Social Change." *Human Architecture: Journal of the Sociology of Self-Knowledge* 6 (Summer): 5–16. Special issue.

———. 2013. *Transformation Now! Toward a Post-Oppositional Politics of Change.* Urbana: University of Illinois Press.

Keating, AnaLouise, and Gloria González-López, eds. 2002. *Bridging: How Gloria Anzaldúa's Life and Work Transformed Our Own.* Austin: University of Texas Press.

Kincaid, Jamaica. 1988. *A Small Place.* New York: A Plume Book.

King, Deborah K. 1995. "Multiple Jeopardy, Multiple Consciousness: The Context of Black Feminist Ideology." In *Words of Fire: An Anthology of African-American Feminist Thought*, ed. Beverly Guy-Sheftall, 294–318. New York: The New Press.

Kisiel, Theodore. 1993. *The Genesis of Heidegger's "Being and Time."* Berkeley: University of California Press.

Koegeler-Abdi, Martina. 2013. "Shifting Subjectivities: Mestizas, Nepantleras, and Gloria Anzaldúa's Legacy." *MELUS* 38(2) (Summer): 71–88.

Kruks, Sonia. 1995. "Identity Politics and Dialectical Reason: Beyond and Epistemology of Provenance." *Hypatia* 10(2): 1–22.

———. 2001. *Retrieving Experience: Subjectivity and Recognition in Feminist Politics.* Ithaca, NY: Cornell University Press.

Lacoue-Labarthe, Philippe. 1990. *Heidegger, Art, and Politics: The Fiction of the Political.* Malden: Blackwell.

Lebens, Crista. 2006. "White Feminism and Antiracism: Connecting Within/Across Communities." *International Studies in Philosophy*, 38(1): 73–84.

Lloyd, Moya. 2005. *Beyond Identity Politics: Feminism, Power and Politics.* London: SAGE Publications Ltd.

Lorde, Audre. 1984. *Sister Outsider: Essays and Speeches.* Freedom, MN: Crossings Press.

Lott, Tommy. 1995. "Review of Paul Gilroy's *Black Atlantic: Modernity and Double-Consciousness.*" *Social Identities* 1(1) (February): 200–221.

Lowe, Lisa. 1996. *Immigrant Acts: On Asian American Cultural Politics.* Durham, NC: Duke University Press.

Lowe, Lisa, and David Lloyd, eds. 1997. *The Politics of Culture in the Shadow of Capital.* Durham, NC: Duke University Press.

Lugo-Lugo, Carmen R. 2008. " 'So you are a mestiza': Exploring the Consequences of Ethnic and Racial Clumping in the US Academy." *Ethnic and Racial Studies* 31(3): 611–628.

Lugones, María. 1987. "Playfulness, 'World'-Traveling, and Loving Perception." *Hypatia* 2(4) (Summer): 3–19.

———. 1990. "Hispaneando y Lesbiando: On Sarah Hoagland's Lesbian Ethics." *Hypatia* 5(3) (Fall): 138–147.

———. 1992. "On *Borderlands/La Frontera*: An Interpretative Essay." *Hypatia* 7(4) (Fall): 31–37.

———. 1994. "Purity, Impurity, Separation." *Signs* (Winter): 458–479.

———. 1999. "Tenuous Connections in Impure Communities." *Ethics and the Environment* 4(1): 85–90.

———. 2002. "Impure Communities." In *Diversity and Community: An Interdisciplinary Reader*, ed. Philip Alperson, 58–64. Malden, MA: Blackwell.

———. 2003. *Pilgrimages/Peregrinajes: Theorizing Coalition against Multiple Oppressions*. New York: Rowman & Littlefield.

———. 2005. "From within Germinative Stasis: Creating Active Subjectivity, Resistant Agency." In *EntreMundos/AmongWorlds: New Perspectives on Gloria Anzaldúa*, ed. AnaLouise Keating, 84–99. New York: Palgrave Macmillan.

———. 2006. "On Complex Communication." *Hypatia* 21(3) (Summer): 75–85.

———. 2007. "Heterosexualism and the Colonial/Modern Gender System." *Hypatia* 22(1): 186–219.

———. 2010. "Toward a Decolonial Feminism." *Hypatia* 25(3): 742–759.

———. 2014. "Radical Multiculturalism and Women of Color Feminisms." *Journal for Cultural and Religious Theory* 13(1) (Winter): 68–80.

Lugones, María and Joshua M. Price. 2009. "Faith in Unity: The Nationalist Erasure of Multiplicity." In *Constructing the Nation: A Race and Nationalism Reader*, eds. Mariana Ortega and Linda Martín Alcoff, 91–102. Albany, NY: State University of New York Press.

Maldonado-Torres, Nelson. 2011. "Thinking through the Decolonial Turn: Post-Continental Interventions in Theory, Philosophy, and Critique." *Transmodernity: Journal of Peripheral Cultural Production of the Luso-Hispanic World* 1(2): 1–15.

Marcano, Donna-Dale. 2012. "Re-reading Plato's Symposium through the Lens of a Black Woman" in *Reframing the Practice of Philosophy: Bodies of Color, Bodies of Knowledge,* ed. George Yancy, 225–233. Albany, NY: State University of New York Press.

Marder, Michael. 2014. "A Fight for the Right to Read Heidegger." Available at http://opinionator.blogs.nytimes.com/2014/07/20/a-fight-for-the-right-to-read-heidegger/?_php=true&_type=blogs&_php=true&_type=blogs&smid=fb-share&_r=1. Accessed July 26 2014.

Márquez, Gabriel García. 2006. *One Hundred Years of Solitude*. New York: Harper Perennial Modern Classics.

Martín Alcoff, Linda. 2006. *Visible Identities: Race, Gender, and the Self.* Oxford: Oxford University Press.

———. 2012. "Enrique Dussel's Transmodernism." *Transmodernity: Journal of Peripheral Cultural Production of the Luso-Hispanic World* 1(3): 60–68.

Martinez, Jacqueline. 2000. *Phenomenology of Chicana Experience and Identity: Communication and Transformation in Praxis*. Boston: Rowman & Littlefield.

————. 2011. *Communicative Sexualities: A Communicology of Sexual Experience.* Lanham, MD: Lexington Books.

————. 2014. "Culture, Communication, and Latina Feminist Philosophy: Toward a Critical Phenomenology of Culture." *Hypatia* 29(1): 221–236. Special issue *Interstices: Inheriting Women of Color Feminist Philosophy*, ed. Kristie Dotson.

Matsuda, Mari J. 1996. *Where Is Your Body? and Other Essays of Race, Gender, and the Law.* Boston: Beacon Press.

————. 2003. *Feminism without Borders: Decolonizing Theory, Practicing Solidarity.* Durham, NC: Duke University Press.

McWeeny, Jen. 2010. "Liberating Anger, Embodying Knowledge: A Comparative Study of María Lugones and Zen Master Hakuin." *Hypatia* 25(2) (Spring): 206–315.

Medina, José. 2013. *The Epistemology of Resistance: Gender and Racial Oppression, Epistemic Injustice, and Resistant Imagination.* Oxford: Oxford University Press.

Merleau-Ponty, Maurice. 2003. *The Phenomenology of Perception.* Trans. Colin Smith. London: Routledge.

Meyers, Diana T. 1994. *Subjection and Subjectivity: Psychoanalytic Feminism and Moral Philosophy.* New York: Routledge.

————. 2004. *Being Yourself: Essays on Identity, Action, and Social Life* (A Selection of New and Previously Published Essays with an Introduction by the Author). New York: Rowman and Littlefield.

Mignolo, Walter. 2000. *Global Histories/Global Designs: Coloniality, Subaltern Knowledges, and Border Thinking.* Princeton, NJ: Princeton University Press.

————. 2007. "DELINKING: The Rhetoric of Modernity, the Logic of Coloniality, and the Grammar of Decoloniality." *Cultural Studies* 21(2): 449–514.

————. 2011. "Geopolitics of Sensing and Knowing: On (De)Coloniality, Border Thinking, and Epistemic Disobedience." Available at http://eipcp.net/transversal/0112/mignolo/en.

Mills, Charles. 1997. *The Racial Contract.* Ithaca: Cornell University Press.

Minh-Ha, Trinh. 1989. *Woman, Native, Other: Writing Postcoloniality and Feminism.* Bloomington: Indiana University Press.

Mohanty, Chandra Talpade. 1991. "Cartographies of Struggle: Third World Women and the Politics of Feminism." In *Third World Women and the Politics of Feminism,* eds. Chandra Talpade Mohanty, Ann Russo, and Lourdes Torres, 1–47. Bloomington: Indiana University Press.

————. 2003. *Feminism without Borders: Decolonizing Theory, Practicing Solidarity.* Durham, NC: Duke University Press.

Mohanty, Chandra Talpade, Ann Russo, and Lourdes Torres, eds. 1991. *Third World Women and the Politics of Feminism.* Bloomington: Indiana University Press.

Mohanty, Satya. 1993. "The Epistemic Status of Cultural Identity: On Beloved and the Postcolonial Condition." *Cultural Critique* 24: 41–80.

————. 1997. *Literary Theory and the Claims of History: Postmodernism, Objectivity, Multicultural Politics.* Ithaca, NY: Cornell University Press.

———. 2001. "Can Our Values Be Objective? On Ethics, Aesthetics, and Progressive Politics." *New Literary History* 32(4) (2001): 803–833.

Moraga, Cherríe. 1983. *Loving in the War Years: Lo que nunca pasó sus labios.* Boston: South End Press.

Moraga, Cherríe, and Gloria Anzaldúa, eds. 1983. *This Bridge Called My Back: Writings by Radical Women of Color.* New York: Kitchen Table/Women of Color Press.

Moya, Paula. 2002. *Learning from Experience: Minority Identities, Multicultural Struggles.* Berkeley: University of California Press.

Moya, Paula, and Hames García, Michael, eds. 2000. *Reclaiming Identity: Realist Theory and the Predicament of Postmodernism.* Berkeley: University of California Press.

Muñoz, José Esteban. 1999. *Disidentifications: Queers of Color and the Performance of Politics.* Minneapolis: University of Minnesota Press.

Nagel, Mechthild. 2001. "Throwness, Playing-in-the-World, and the Question of Authenticity." In *Feminist Interpretations of Heidegger*, eds. Patricia Huntington and Nancy Holland, 289–306. University Park: Pennsylvania State University Press.

Narayan, Uma. 1997. *Dislocating Cultures: Identities, Traditions, and Third World Feminism.* New York: Routledge.

Nash, Jennifer C. 2008. "Rethinking Intersectionality." *Feminist Review* 89: 1–15.

Olafson, Frederick. 1987. *Heidegger and the Philosophy of Mind.* New Haven, CT: Yale University Press.

———. 1994. "Heidegger à la Wittgenstein or 'Coping' with Professor Dreyfus." *Inquiry* 37(1): 45–64.

Ortega, Mariana. 2000. "Dasein Comes after the Epistemic Subject, but Who Is Dasein?" *International Philosophical Quarterly* 40(1): 51–67.

———. 2001. " 'New Mestizas,' 'World-Travelers,' and Dasein: Phenomenology and the Multivoiced Multicultural Self." *Hypatia* 16(3) (Summer): 1–29.

———. 2004. "Exiled Space, In-Between Space: Existential Spatiality in Ana Mendieta's Siluetas Series." *Philosophy and Geography* 7(1) (February): 25–41.

———. 2005. "When Conscience Calls, Will Dasein Answer? Heideggerian Authenticity and the Possibility of Ethical Life." *International Journal of Philosophic Studies* 13(1): 15–34.

———. 2006a. "Being Lovingly, Knowingly Ignorant: White Feminism and Women of Color." *Hypatia* 21(3) (Summer): 56–74.

———. 2006b. "Phenomenological Encuentros: Existential Phenomenology and Latin American & U.S. Latina Feminism." *Radical Philosophy Review* 9(1) (2006): 45–64.

———. 2007. "The Epistemic Importance of Social Location: Review of Paula Moya, *Learning from Experience.*" *Radical Philosophy Review* 10(1): 79–90.

———. 2008. "Wounds of Self: Experience, Word, Image, and Identity." *Journal of Speculative Philosophy* 22(4): 235–247.

———. 2009. "Othering the Other: The Spectacle of Katrina." *Contemporary Aesthetics* 2, Special volume. Available at http://www.contempaesthetics.org/ newvolume/pages/article.php?articleID=531. Accessed February 1, 2015.

———. 2013. "Photographic Representations of Racialized Bodies: Afro-Mexicans, the Visible, and the Invisible." *Critical Philosophy of Race* 1(2): 163–189.

Park, Peter K. J., 2013. *Africa, Asia, and the History of Philosophy: Racism in the Formation of the Philosophical Canon, 1780–1830.* Albany, NY: State University of New York Press.

Pérez, Emma. 1999. *The Decolonial Imaginary: Writing Chicanas into History.* Bloomington: Indiana University Press.

———. 2005. "Gloria Anzaldúa: La Gran Nueva Mestiza, Theorist, Writer, Activist-Scholar." *NWSA Journal* 17(2): 1–10.

Pérez, Laura. 2007. *Chicana Art: The Politics of Spiritual and Aesthetic Alterities.* Durham, NC: Duke University Press.

———. 2010. "Enrique Dussel's Etica de la liberación, U.S. Women of Color Decolonizing Practices, and Coalitionary Politics amidst Difference." *Qui Parle: Critical Humanities and Social Sciences* 18(2): 121–146.

Pérez-Torres, Rafael. 2006. *Mestizaje: Critical Uses of Race in Chicano Culture.* Minneapolis: University of Minnesota Press.

Perpich, Diane. 2010. "Black Feminism, Poststructuralism, and the Contested Character of Experience." In *Convergences: Black Feminism and Continental Philosophy*, eds. Maria Guadalupe Davidson, Kathryn T. Gines, and Donna-Dale I. Marcano, 13–34. Albany, NY: State University of New York Press.

Perry, John. 1975. *On Personal Identity.* Berkeley: University of California Press.

———. 2002. *Identity, Personal Identity, and the Self.* Indianapolis, IN: Hackett.

Phelan, Shane. 1989. *Identity Politics.* Philadelphia, PA: Temple University Press.

———. 1994. *Getting Specific: Postmodern Lesbian Politics.* Minneapolis: University of Minnesota Press.

Pitts, Andrea J. 2014. "Toward an Aesthetics of Race: Bridging the Writings of Gloria Anzaldúa and José Vasconcelos." *Inter-American Journal of Philosophy* 5(1): 80–100.

Quijano, Anibal. 2000. "Coloniality of Power: Eurocentrism and Latin America." *Nepantla* 1(3): 533–580.

Radloff, Bernhard. 2007. *Heidegger and the Question of National Socialism: Disclosure and Gestalt.* Toronto: University of Toronto Press.

Reagon, Bernice Johnson. 1983. "Coalitional Politics: Turning the Century." In *Home Girls: A Black Feminist Anthology*, ed. Barbara Smith, 356–368. New York: Kitchen Table/ Women of Color Press.

Rich, Adrienne. 1986. *Blood, Bread, and Poetry: Selected Prose, 1979–1985.* New York: Norton.

Rieff, David. 1991. "Professional Aztecs and Popular Culture." *New Perspectives Quarterly* 8 (Winter): 42–46.

Rivera Berruz, Stephanie. 2014. "Extending into Space: The Materiality of Language and the Arrival of Latina/o Bodies." *Inter-American Journal of Philosophy* 5(1): 23–41.

Rockmore, Tom, and Joseph Margolis. 1992. *The Heidegger Case: On Philosophy and Politics*. Philadelphia: Temple University Press.

Rodriguez, Juana María. 2003. *Queer Latinidad: Identity Practices, Discursive Spaces*. New York: New York University Press.

Roof, María. 1996. "W.E.B. Du Bois, Isabel Allende, and the Empowerment of Third World Women." *CLA Journal* 39(4) (June): 401–417.

Román-Odio, Clara. 2013. *Sacred Iconographies in Chicana Cultural Productions*. New York: Palgrave Macmillan.

Roshanravan, Shireen. 2010. "Passing-as-if: Model Minority Subjectivity and Women of Color Identification." *Meridians: feminism, race, transnationalism* 10(1): 1–31.

———. 2014. "Motivating Coalition: Women of Color and Epistemic Disobedience." *Hypatia* 29(1) (Winter): 41–58.

Ruiz-Aho, Elena. 2011. "Feminist Border Theory." In *The Routledge International Handbook of Contemporary Social and Political Theory*, eds. Gerard Delanty and Stephen Turner, 350–361. New York: Routledge.

Ryan, Barbara, ed. 2001. *Identity Politics in the Women's Movement*. New York: New York University Press.

Sáenz, Benjamin Alire. 1997. "In the Borderlands of Chicano Identity, There Are Only Fragments." In *Border Theory: The Limits of Cultural Politics*, eds. Scott Michaelsen and David E. Johnson, 68–96. Minneapolis: University of Minnesota Press.

Saldaña-Portillo, María Josefina. 2001. "Who's the Indian in Aztlán? Re-Writing Mestizaje, Indianism, and Chicanismo from the Lacadón." In *The Latin American Subaltern Studies Reader*, ed. Ileana Rodríguez. Durham, NC: Duke University Press.

Saldívar, José David. 1991. *The Dialectics of Our America: Genealogy, Cultural Critique, and Literature*. Durham, NC: Duke University Press.

Saldivar-Hull, Sonia. 1991. "Feminism on the Border: From Gender Politics to Geopolitics." In *Criticism in the Borderlands: Studies in Chicano Literature, Culture and Ideology*, eds. Hector Calderón and José David Saldívar, 203–220. Durham, NC: Duke University Press.

———. 2000. *Feminism on the Border: Chicana Gender Politics and Literature*. Berkeley: University of California Press.

Sandoval, Chela. 1995. "Feminist Forms of Agency and Oppositional Consciousness: U.S. Third World Feminist Criticism." In *Provoking Agents: Gender and Agency in Theory and Practice*, ed. Judith Kegan Gardiner, 208–226. Urbana: University of Illinois Press.

———. 1998. "Mestizaje as Method: Feminists-of-Color Challenge the Canon." In *Living Chicana Theory*, ed. Carla Trujillo, 352–370. Berkeley, CA: Third Woman Press.

———. 2000. *The Methodology of the Oppressed*. Minneapolis: University of Minnesota Press.

Santa Cruz Feminist of Color Collective. 2014. "Building on the Edge of Each Other's Battles": A Feminist of Color Multidimensional Lens." *Hypatia* 29(1) (Winter): 23–40.

Sartre, Jean-Paul. 1966. *Being and Nothingness: An Essay on Phenomenological Ontology*. Trans. Hazel E. Barnes. New York: Philosophical Library.

Saucedo Dominic. 1996. "Chicanismo, Du Bois, and Double-Consciousness." *Latino Studies Journal* 7(3) (Fall): 90–101.

Schües, Christina, Dorothea E. Olkowski, and Helen A. Fielding, eds. 2011. *Time in Feminist Phenomenology*. Bloomington: Indiana University Press.

Schutte, Ofelia. 1993. *Cultural Identity and Social Liberation in Latin American Thought*. Albany, NY: State University of New York Press.

———. 1998. "Cultural Alterity: Cross-Cultural Communication and Feminist Theory in North-South Contexts." *Hypatia* 13(2) (Spring): 53–72.

———. 2009. "Theorizing Identities, Reflections on Alcoff." *Philosophy Today* 53, 28–34. SPEP supplement.

Scott, Joan Wallach. 1991. "The Evidence of Experience." *Critical Inquiry* 17: 773–797.

Sheth, Falguni A. 2009. *Toward a Political Philosophy of Race*. Albany, NY: State University of New York Press.

Shotwell, Alexis. 2011. *Knowing Otherwise: Race, Gender, and Implicit Understanding*. University Park: Pennsylvania State University Press.

Simms, Eva-Maria, and Beata Stawarska, eds. 2013. *Janus Head* 13(1). Special issue: Feminist Phenomenology.

Smith, Andrea. 2005. *Conquest: Sexual Violence and American Indian Genocide*. Cambridge, MA: South End Press.

Spelman, Elizabeth V. 1988. *Inessential Woman: Problems of Exclusion in Feminist Thought*. Boston: Beacon Press.

Spiegelberg, Herbert. 1984. *The Phenomenological Movement: A Historical Introduction*. The Hague: Martinus Nijhoff.

Spivak, Gayatri Chakravorty. 1987. *In Other Worlds: Essays in Cultural Politics*. New York: Routledge.

———. 1990. *The Post-Colonial Critic: Interviews, Strategies, Dialogues*. Ed. Sara Harasym. New York: Routledge.

Stoller, Silvia, Veronica Vasterling, and Linda Fisher, eds. 2005. *Feministische Phanomenologie und Hermeneutik*. Wurzburg: Konigshausen & Neumann.

Stone-Mediatore, Shari. 2003. *Reading Across Borders: Storytelling and Knowledges of Resistance*. New York: Palgrave Macmillan.

Sullivan, Shannon. 2001. "The Racialization of Space: Toward a Phenomenological Account of Raced and Anti-Racist Spatiality." In *The Problems of Resistance: Studies in Alternate Political Cultures*, ed. Steve Martinot. Atlantic Highlands, NJ: Prometheus/Humanity Books.

———. 2003a. "Enigma Variations: Laplanchean Psychoanalysis and the Formation of the Raced Unconscious." *Radical Philosophy* 122 (November/December): 20–33.

———. 2003b. "Remembering the Gift: Du Bois on the Unconscious and Economic Operations of Racism." *Transactions of the C. S. Peirce Society* 39(2): 205–225.

————. 2004. "White World-Traveling." *Journal of Speculative Philosophy* 18(4): 300–304.

————. 2006. *Revealing Whiteness: The Unconscious Habits of Racial Privilege.* Bloomington: Indiana University Press.

Sushytska, Julia. 2012. "What is Eastern Europe? A Philosophical Approach. *Angelaki* 15(3): 53–65.

Sylvester, Christine. 1995. "African and Western Feminism: World-Traveling the Tendencies and Possibilities." *Signs* 20 (Summer): 941–969.

Tabuenca Córdoba, María Socorro. 1995–1996. "Viewing the Border: Perspectives from 'The Open Wound.'" *Discourse* 18(1–2): 146–168.

Trujillo, Carla, ed. 1998. *Living Chicana Theory.* Berkeley, CA: Third Woman Press.

Vallega, Alejandro. 2013. "Heidegger and Latin American Philosophy." In *The Bloomsbury Companion to Martin Heidegger*, eds. François Raffoul and Eric S. Nelson, 473–482. London: Bloomsbury.

Velazco y Trianosky, Gregory. 2010. "Mestizaje and Hispanic Identity." In *A Companion to Latin American Philosophy*, eds. Susana Nuccetelli, Ofelia Schutte, and Oávio Bueno, 283–296. Malden, MA: Blackwell.

Weir, Allison. 1996. *Sacrificial Logics: Feminist Theory and the Critique of Identity.* New York: Routledge.

————. 2008. "Global Feminism and Transformative Identity Politics." *Hypatia* 23(4) (October–December): 110–132.

————. 2013. *Identities and Freedom: Feminist Theory between Power and Connection.* Oxford: Oxford University Press.

Weiss, Gail. 2008. *Refiguring the Ordinary.* Bloomington: Indiana University Press.

————. 2011. "Sharing Time Across Unshared Horizons." In *Time in Feminist Phenomenology*, eds. Christina Schües, Dorothea E. Olkowski, and Helen A. Fielding, 171–188. Bloomington: Indiana University Press.

Wilkerson, William. "The Continuity of Consciousness and the Freedom of the Will." Unpublished manuscript.

Wolff, Janet. 1992. "On the Road Again: Metaphors of Travel in Cultural Criticism." *Cultural Studies* 7(2): 224–239.

Wolin, Richard, ed. 1993. *The Heidegger Controversy: A Critical Reader.* Cambridge, MA: MIT Press.

Yabro-Bejarano, Yvonne. 1994. "Gloria Anzaldúa's *Borderlands/La Frontera*: Cultural Studies, 'Difference,' and the Non-Unitary Subject." *Cultural Critique* 28 (Autumn): 5–28.

Young, Iris Marion. 1997. *Intersecting Voices: Dilemmas of Gender, Political Philosophy, and Policy.* Princeton, NJ: Princeton University Press.

————. 2005. *On Female Body Experience: "Throwing Like a Girl" and Other Essays.* Oxford: Oxford University Press.

Young, Julian. 1998. *Heidegger, Philosophy, Nazism.* Cambridge: Cambridge University Press.

Zeiler, Kristin, and Lisa Folkmarson Käll. 2014. *Feminist Phenomenology and Medicine.* Albany, NY: State University of New York Press.

Zamir, Shamoon. 1995. *Dark Voices: W.E.B. Du Bois and American Thought, 1888–1903*. Chicago: University of Chicago Press.

Zaytoun, Kelli. 2013. "A Case for the Self-in-Coalition: Exploring Anzaldúa's Legacy of La Naguala with Lugones' Complex Communication." In *El Mundo Zurdo 3*, eds. Larissa M. Mercado-López, Sonia Saldivar-Hull, and Antonia Castañeda, 209–224. San Francisco: Aunt Lute.

———. forthcoming. "Theorizing the Self-in-Coalition with the Work of María Lugones." In *Speaking Face to Face/Hablando Cara a Cara: The Visionary Philosophy of María Lugones*, eds. Pedro DiPietro, Shireen Roshanravan, and Jen McWeeny.

Zerilli, Linda. 2005. *Feminism and the Abyss of Freedom*. Chicago: University of Chicago Press.

Index

active subjectivity, 89, 97, 102–103,
106–114, 228, 232, 236
Adell, Sandra, 242
Ahmed, Sara, 2, 9, 225
Aho, Kevin, 222
Alarcón, Norma, 7, 75, 211, 222, 244
Alcoff, Linda. *See* Martín Alcoff, Linda
Alexander, M. Jacqui, 164, 222, 250
Allen, Ernest, 243
Al-Saji, Alia, 222
American Psychiatric Association, 237
angst. *See* anxiety
anxiety, 53, 61–62, 216
Anzaldúa, Gloria E. (see also *los
atravesados, autohistoria; El Mundo
Zurdo;* intimate terrorism; *mestiza*
consciousness; new *mestiza;
nepantla; la nepantlera;* spiritual
activism)
and *amasamiento*, 47, 49
and border and borderland,
distinctions
between, 3–4, 18, 24–25, 230
and the *Coatlicue* state, 3, 26–27,
41, 45, 54
and the Coyolxauhqui Imperative, 46
and *conocimiento*, 34, 36, 38, 230
and *de las otras*, 49, 63–64
and *la facultad*, 34, 37–38, 59, 62,
178, 186, 232
compared to Heidegger, 52–54, 61,
69–70, 225, 232, 244

and hermeneutics, 57–58
and intersectionality, 74, 77,
225–226
and Latina feminist phenomenology,
7–10
and metaphor, use of, 29–32
and multiplicity, 89, 105, 146, 152,
162, 168, 174
and *El Mundo Zurdo*, 3, 23–24
and *La naguala*, 19, 32, 37–38, 45,
239
and new tribalism, 19–24, 228, 230
and *Nos/otras*, 19, 21–24, 228
and rationalism, 43
and subject-object distinction, 55–56
and world-traveling, 66, 76, 96, 98,
116, 134–135, 180, 183
and writing, 4, 57, 88, 211,
226–226
Arendt, Hannah, 51, 219, 232, 240
Aristotle, 79
Arrizón, Alicia, 229
los atravesados, 3, 38, 50–51, 62, 106,
126, 153, 209, 216, 230
authenticity, 14, 53–54, 62, 129–131,
194, 196–197, 244
autohistoria, 6, 17, 226
Aztec culture and mythology, 33–34,
46, 56–57
Aztlán, 33

Babbit, Susan E., 139

271

bad faith, 254
Bailey, Alison, 239
Bambara, Toni Cade, 222
Barnard, Ian, 229
Barthes, Roland, 9
Bartky, Sandra, 136–138, 224
Barvosa, Edwina, 7, 28, 74, 76, 135, 152, 198–201, 231, 234–235
Beale, Frances, 72, 225
becoming-with, 3, 10, 13, 146, 155, 163, 168–169
being-at-ease (*see also* not being-at-ease), 10, 56, 59–60, 62, 99, 153, 196, 232–233
being-between-worlds
    and communication, 167
    and decolonial theory, 114
    and Heidegger, 10–12, 64, 77
    and identity, 145, 152–54, 183, 202, 244
    and Latina feminist phenomenology, 3, 64, 66–68, 71, 74, 76–77, 81–82, 115–116, 189
    and multiplicitous selfhood, 50
    and ontological pluralism, 238
    and world-traveling, 87, 100, 115–116, 123, 134–135, 169
being-in-worlds
    and Dussel, 233
    and Heidegger, 10–12, 49, 50–51, 62, 64, 67–71
    and identity, 18–19, 74, 76–77, 83, 145, 152, 154, 183, 202, 237, 244
    and intersectionality, 76–77
    and Latina feminist phenomenology, 3, 50, 64–68, 71, 81, 198, 232
    and ontological pluralism, 93, 116
    and social location, 18–19
    and world-traveling, 82, 87, 123, 169
being-with (*Mitsein*), 56, 148–150, 163
Bell, Bernard W., 122

Bell Scott, Patricia, 222
Belonging. *See* being-at-ease; not being-at-ease; hometactics
Beltrán, Cristina, 7, 33–34, 157
Benhabib, Seyla, 187
Bergson, Henri, 79
Bernasconi, Robert, 216
Bettcher, Talia Mae, 238
Bhabha, Homi K., 229
Bird-Soto, Nancy, 230
Black feminist theory, 7, 20, 157, 163, 225
Blackwell, Maylei, 157
Bloodsworth-Lugo, Mary K., 230
Brown, Michael, 247
Brison, Susan, 245
Brown, Wendy, 156, 244
Bruce, Dickson D., Jr., 242
Butler, Judith, 7, 146–147, 156, 187, 244–245

Calvino, Italo, 2, 216
Campbell, Sue, 139
Carastathis, Anna, 165
Carillo-Rowe, Aimee, 7, 157, 194–195, 201
Carman, Taylor, 232
Cartesian subjectivity, 40, 51, 80, 147, 221, 227, 231
Castillo, Debra A., 29–31, 226
Chicana identity (*see also* Latina identity)
    and Anzaldúa, 4, 20, 24–25, 31, 33–35, 40–41, 44, 198, 229, 230–231
    relationship to Latina identity, 9
    and Moraga
    and Moya, 13, 174, 178–181, 188
    and intersectionality, 72
    and Sandoval, 40–41, 184
    and white feminism, 224
Chicano nationalism, 33
Cisneros, Natalie, 231
Clack, Beverly, 216

Clare, Eli, 248
coalitional politics (*see also* deep
  coalition)
  and Anzaldúa, 23, 239
  and becoming, 13, 155, 161–162,
    167–169, 173, 201, 206
  and Crenshaw, 219
  elements of, 163–165
  and Hames-García, 251
  and Heidegger, 125
  and Lebens, 251
  and Lugones, 102, 104, 106, 146,
    165–169, 190, 220, 238
  and Roshanravan, 250
  and Reagon, 194–195, 249
  and Santa Cruz Feminist of Color
    Collective, 252
  and world-traveling, 100, 134, 137,
    162, 246
Code, Lorraine, 245
Collins, Patricia Hill
  and coalitional politics, 163–165
  and epistemology, 233
  and feminism, 222
  and identity politics, 244
  and intersectionality, 7, 71–72, 157–
    159, 164, 218, 220, 226, 234
colonialism, 87, 209, 229–230, 241,
  254
colorblindness, 23
Combahee River Collective, 20, 157,
  244
consciousness, differential (*see also*
  Sandoval), 75, 83, 98, 184–186,
  201
consciousness, *mestiza* (*see also*
  mestizaje; new *mestiza*)
  in Anzaldúa scholarship, 227
  and differential consciousness, 75,
    83–84
  and dualisms, 55
  and lesbian subjectivity, 229
  and transformation, 26–27, 32, 35,
    41, 201, 230–231

contextualism, 162, 250
contradiction
  in Anzaldúa, 27–29, 32–33, 83
  and existential continuity, 81–83
  and pathology, 237
  and political activism, 199–200,
    234
  and world-traveling, 88, 91, 97–99
Cook, Sybil, 216
Cooper, Anna Julia, 72, 225
Crenshaw, Kimberlé, 7, 23, 71–72,
  157–158, 219, 222, 234, 247
critical race theory, 217–218, 247
curdling, 89–90, 100, 102–106, 108,
  112–114, 239

Danto, Arthur, 111, 233
Dasein, 3, 5, 12, 49–51, 53, 56, 59,
  62–65, 68, 77, 80, 125, 127,
  131, 148–149, 217, 223–225,
  244
Davis, Angela, 163, 222
de Beauvoir, Simone, 103, 219, 221,
  224, 233, 237
de Beistegui, Miguel, 222
decenteredness, 74, 76, 83, 111, 182,
  201, 203
de Certeau, Michel, 14, 194, 202–204,
  240
decolonial feminism, 114–116,
  250–252
deep coalition (*see also* coalitional
  politics), 146, 155, 163, 165–166,
  168, 220, 238
de Laurentis, Teresa, 244
Delgadillo, Theresa, 42
Demaj, Ada, 254
Derrida, Jacques, 51, 232
dichotomy, rejection of (*see also*
  Anzaldúa; Heidegger)
  and Anzaldúa, 33–34
  and Freire, 240
  and identity politics, 161, 164, 189,
    246–247, 250

dichotomy, rejection of *(continued)*
   and Lugones, 51, 55, 106, 124,
      133, 140, 146, 203–205, 208,
      232, 236, 239–240
   and Merleau-Ponty, 113
   and philosophy, 2
   and Weir, 249
Dickens, Charles, 191, 193–194
disability studies, 246, 248
double-consciousness, 12, 242–243
Douglass, Frederick, 248–249
Dotson, Kristie, 219, 222
Drabinski, John E., 222–223
Dreyfus, Hubert, 232
Du Bois, W.E.B. *(see also* double-
   consciousness; world-travelling
   and double-consciousness), 12,
   119–123, 128–129, 198, 242–243
Dussel, Enrique, 115, 233, 241–242

Egan, David, 232
embodiment, 1, 58, 75, 77, 96, 108,
   168, 222, 233
Embree, Lester, 224
empathy, 148–149, 249
empiricism, 8, 175
essentialism, 24–25, 34, 38, 43, 145–
   147, 155, 178, 182, 229, 235
everydayness, 53, 63, 70, 127,
   129–130, 202, 205–206
exile, 193, 254
existential pluralism, 12, 89, 102, 114,
   116
Eze, Emmanuel Chukwudi, 216

facticity, 68, 73, 254
Fanon, Frantz, 85, 219
Farías, Victor, 222
Faye, Emmanuel, 222
fearing the other, 145, 147–150, 155,
   168–169, 218
Feder, Ellen, 234
Ferguson, Ann, 159
Fielding, Helen, 224

Fisher, Linda, 224
flexibility of self, 32, 64, 71, 74–77,
   186
Folkmarson Käll, Lisa, 224
Foucault, Michel, 66, 147, 191
Francis, Shereese, 247
Freire, Paulo, 129, 239–240
Frye, Marilyn, 136

Gadamer, Hans-Georg, 58, 154–155
Garber, Linda, 229
García, Alma, 72, 157, 222
Geertz, Clifford, 7
Gilroy, Paul, 244
Gines, Kathryn, 7, 71, 73
González López, Gloria, 23, 226
Gooding-Williams, Robert, 122,
   242–243
Gordon, Lewis, 233
Gray, Freddie, 247
Grewal, Inderpal, 105, 181
Gutierrez y Muhs, Gabriella, 153–154
Guy-Sheftall, Beverley, 222

Hames-García, Michael, 72–73, 173,
   188, 226, 251–253
Harding, Sandra, 7, 34, 230, 233
Hart, Mechthild, 240
Hatab, Lawrence, 80
Hegel, G.W.F., 121, 168, 210,
   217–219
Heidegger, Martin *(see also* anxiety,
   being-with; *Dasein;* everydayness;
   mineness; ontic-ontological
   distinction)
   and being-at-ease, 60–62, 129
   and being-in-the-world, 65, 68–70,
      149, 233, 240
   and embodiment, 222
   and Eurocentrism, 115
   and feminism, 5–6, 12, 224
   and hermeneutics, 57, 154, 236
   and intentionality, 107, 111
   and Nazism, 4–5, 217, 222–223

and phenomenology, 221
and publicness, 120, 125–129, 136,
    232, 244
and the subject-object distinction,
    55–56, 62, 240
and temporality, 52, 79–80, 182,
    252–253
and the They (*das Man*), 13, 53–54,
    56, 62, 70, 120, 125–127,
    129–130, 149, 232–233, 245
and thrownness, 53–54, 62, 208
and worldhood, 68, 234
Heinämaa, Sara, 224
Hekman, Susan, 146, 156, 244–245
Heraclitus, 231
Hermeneutics (*see also* identity as
    horizon), 57–58, 150–151, 155
Hoagland, Sarah, 197
hometactics, 1, 14, 194, 201–210,
    215, 249, 254
hooks, bell, 193, 222, 244
Hurtado, Aída, 224–225
Hull, Gloria T., 222
Hume, David, 216
Huntington, Patricia, 224
Husserl, Edmund, 7, 148, 221, 230

identity as horizon
    and embodiment, 151, 168–169,
        247
    and perspective, 31, 151, 153–154,
        161, 176, 216, 245–246, 249
    and resistance, 166
    and self-other distinction, 13, 145,
        147, 150, 152–153, 160, 249
identity politics (*see also* Martín Alcoff;
    Moya; Weir)
    and Anzaldúa, 19–20, 34
    and Lugones, 104
    as discussed in Martín Alcoff,
        145–148, 155–158, 161–162, 245
    as discussed in Moya, 190
    as discussed in Weir, 159–163, 168,
        248

immigration, 1, 3, 8, 89, 128, 198,
    207, 240, 254
in-betweenness. *See* being-between-
    worlds existential pluralism;
    nepantla; la nepantlera;
    multiplicitous selfhood; world-
    traveling
indigenous identity and peoples, 8, 25,
    28, 33–34
integration of self (*see also* existential
    pluralism; multiplicitous selfhood)
    and Barvosa, 199–202, 231, 234
    and double-consciousness, 243
    and Lugones, 75–76, 123, 231
    and Moya, 174, 184, 188–189, 231
    and new *mestiza*, 41–42, 46
intergenerational dialogue, 22
intermeshedness
    and Anzaldúa, 17, 30
    and coalitional politics, 155,
        162–164
    and Heidegger, 69
    compared to intersectionality, 72–74,
        226
    and Latina feminist phenomenology,
        10
    and Lugones, 69, 93, 100, 104–105,
        113–114, 122, 237, 239
    and multiplicitous selfhood, 71, 76,
        104–105, 163–164, 169, 183,
        188, 216
    and philosophy, 218
intersectionality (*see also* Collins,
    Patricia Hill; Crenshaw, Kimberlé;
    intermeshedness)
    and Anzaldúa, 17, 30, 46, 135, 181,
        226, 247
    and coalitional politics, 162–164,
        165, 168
    and identity politics, 155, 157
    compared to intermeshedness,
        72–74, 226
    and Latina feminist phenomenology,
        10, 62, 181

intersectionality *(continued)*
  and Lugones, 69, 72–73, 88, 92–93,
    96, 105, 111, 146, 239
  and multiplicitous selfhood, 12, 50,
    71, 74, 76–77, 154, 181, 183,
    188, 234
  and the new *mestiza*, 28
  and philosophy, 14, 218–219
  and women of color feminisms, 7,
    71–73, 225, 234, 247
intentionality, 89, 107–111
intimate terrorism, 20, 50, 58, 71, 83,
  129, 198, 210
Irigaray, Luce, 219

James, William, 121, 123, 242–243
Jones, Aiyana, 247

Kant, Immanuel, 217–219
Kant and Kantianism, 40, 78–79, 147,
  217–219, 221
Kaplan, Caren, 90, 193
Keating, AnaLouise, 19–23, 26, 34, 36,
  39–40, 42, 226–230, 247–248
Kierkegaard, Søren, 53
King, Deborah, 72, 225
Kisiel, Theodore, 236
Koegeler-Abdi, Martina, 227, 230–231
Kristeva, Julia, 219
Kruks, Sonia, 139–140, 146, 156,
  161, 244

Lacoue-Labarthe, Phillippe, 222
Latina feminist theory *(see also*
  phenomenology, Latina feminist),
  4–5, 12, 224–225
Latina identity *(see also* Chicana
  identity; Nicaraguan identity)
  and belonging, 200–201
  heterogeneity of, 8, 233–234, 252
  and double-consciousness, 123–124
  and identity as horizon, 151–154
  and hometactics, 206–207

  and multiplicitous selfhood, 66, 76,
    123–125, 196, 209
  and playfulness, 81, 101
  and queer identity, 229, 240
  and postpositive realist theory of
    identity, 173–174, 179–181, 184,
    188
  and racism, 247
  and social locations, 161
  and world-traveling, 128, 133,
    197–199, 235
Latin America, 8, 10, 33, 67, 196,
  224, 239–240
Lebens, Crista, 251
Lee, Kyoo, 254
LeMoncheck, Linda, 136
lesbian identity *(see also* Anzaldúa and
    de las otras; queer identity), 15,
    66, 74, 108, 124, 128, 153, 157,
    180, 184, 195–199, 201, 229,
    240, 251–253
lesbian separatism, 197
Lin, Maya, 117
lived experience. *See* authenticity;
    Black feminist theory; double-
    consciousness; consciousness,
    mestiza; consciousness, differential;
    intermeshedness; intersectionality;
    multiplicitous selfhood, existential
    continuity of; phenomenology
Lloyd, David, 163
Lloyd, Moya, 244
Locke, John, 221
logic of purity, 75, 89–90, 192–104,
  108, 239
Lorde, Audre, 2, 143, 171, 198, 222
Lott, Tommy, 122
Lugo-Lugo, Carmen R., 8–9
Lugones, María *(see also* active
    subjectivity; coalitional politics;
    deep coalition; curdling;
    decolonial feminism; logic of
    purity; ontological pluralism;

streetwalker theorizing; tactical strategies; world-traveling)
and Anzaldúa, 27–28
and being-at-ease, 60–62, 99
and complex communication, 146, 155, 163, 165–168, 220
Du Bois, compared to, 242
and fragmentation, 104–106, 108, 112–113, 124–125, 231, 239
and hangouts, 112, 240
and Heidegger, 2–3, 5–6, 51, 236
and hermeneutics, 57–58, 154, 236
and intersectionality, 72, 74, 188, 199, 226
and intersubjectivity, 152, 201
and Latina feminist phenomenology, 7–10, 222
and lesbian separatism, 197
and *mestizo* self, 102–105
and subject-object distinction, 55, 181
and *tantear*, 122, 236, 242
and trespassing, 102, 114, 239
and worlds, 12, 65–67, 69–70, 76, 81, 85, 92, 117, 138–139, 174, 180, 208–209, 233, 235–236
Lowe, Lisa, 163, 222

Maldonado-Torres, Nelson, 241
Mamardashvili, Merab, 231
Marcano, Donna-Dale, 216
Marder, Michael, 222
Margolis, Joseph, 222
Martín Alcoff, Linda (*see also* identity as horizon)
and contexualism, 250
and decolonial theory, 241–242
and embodiment, 222, 244, 251
and identity as horizon, 13, 58, 234
and identity politics, 20, 145, 147–148, 153–155, 159–162, 168, 173, 227, 245, 249, 252
and Latina feminist theory, 7, 222, 224

and self/Other relationship, 149–150, 246–247
Martinez, Jacqueline, 4, 7, 30, 230
Martin, Trayvon, 247
Márquez, Gabriel García, 244
Matsuda, Mary, 143, 155, 158
Maturana, Humberto, 220
McWeeny, Jen, 96–97, 237–238
Mendieta, Ana, 193
Medina, José, 243
Merleau-Ponty, Maurice
and European phenomenological traditions, 1, 50–51, 58, 103, 129, 221–222, 232–233
and Latina feminist phenomenology, 59, 62, 151, 221–222, 224
and multiplicitous selfhood, 77
and spatiality, 113
mestizaje
and Anzaldúa, 3, 11, 12, 18, 21, 45, 220, 228–229
critical mestizaje, 25
criticism of, 29–30, 32–34
and decolonial theory, 115
and Latina feminist phenomenology, 6, 10, 12, 216
in Latin America, 25
and Lugones, 102–103
and multiplicity and oneness, 40, 46, 49, 64, 84, 162
and philosophy, 219
and spiritual mestizaje, 227
Mexican American identity, 21, 31, 39, 57
Mexican literature, 31
Mexico-U.S. relations, 11, 21, 25–26, 28–29, 31, 40, 53, 56, 58
Meyers, Diana T., 244
Mignolo, Walter, 115, 241, 251
Mills, Charles, 216
mineness (*Jemeinigkeit*), 12, 50, 78, 80–81, 84, 98, 146, 235
Minh-Ha, Trinh, 222

Mohanty, Chandra Talpade, 8, 38,
    164, 194–195, 201, 222, 244,
    249–250, 252
Mohanty, Satya P., 173, 175, 252
Moraga, Cherríe, 4, 7, 15, 23, 30, 59,
    72, 174, 180–181, 222, 252
Moya, Paula (*see also* postpositive
    realist theory of identity), 7, 13,
    75, 173–190, 199, 231, 249,
    252–253
mulataje, 3, 8, 25
multiplicitous selfhood (*see also* being-
    between-worlds; being-in-worlds;
    existential pluralism; unity and
    plurality)
  and Anzaldúa, 7, 9, 24–25, 39–45
  and being-at-ease, 14, 63, 68,
    196–197, 205–206, 208
  and being-between-worlds, 67–68,
    74, 81–82, 84, 93, 115, 135,
    152, 155, 169, 198, 202
  epistemic aspects, 89, 123, 153, 243
  existential continuity of, 75–80, 83,
    180–183, 187, 189–190, 200,
    204
  and Heidegger, 5, 10–12, 49–50,
    59–60, 65, 70, 127, 131, 150
  and identity politics, 13, 145–146,
    162–163
  and intersectionality, 50, 71, 76–77,
    216
  and world-traveling, 88, 91, 98,
    100–101, 114–116, 119–121,
    124–126, 129, 132, 134, 136,
    140, 154, 166, 209
Muñoz, José Esteban, 244
Murphy, Robert, 246

Nagel, Mechthild, 244
Náhuatl language, 27, 32, 45, 228
Narayan, Uma, 222
Nash, Jennifer C., 73
National Socialism. *See* Nazism

nepantla, 3, 11, 19, 26–29, 35–36, 46,
    135, 229–230
la nepantlera, 17, 19, 21, 24–26,
    35–40, 162, 227, 230
new *mestiza* (*see also* Anzaldúa,
    Gloria E.; mestiza consciousness;
    mestizaje; *nepantla*; *nepantlera*)
  and authenticity, 130, 196
  and border-crossing, 32–36, 38–41,
    45–46
  and collective transformation, 19,
    26–28, 107, 162–163
  compared to *Dasein*, 50, 53, 54,
    59–60, 70, 127
  and embodiment, 11, 77–78
  and hermeneutics, 57–58, 230
  and not being-at-ease, 63, 128
  and rationality, 74–75
  and standpoint theory, 230–231
  and world-traveling, 3, 81, 83–84,
    89, 98, 125, 131, 180–181, 183
Nicaraguan identity (*see also* Latina
    identity), 17–18, 60, 66–67, 98,
    101, 123–124, 128, 161, 196,
    207, 233, 235, 252
Nietzsche, Friedrich, 33, 197, 250, 254
not being-at-ease, 61, 129
  thick and thin senses of, 61, 63, 70,
    82–83, 101, 153, 198, 203

Obama, Barack, 23
Olafson, Frederick, 223, 232, 240
Olkowski, Dorothea, 222, 224
ontic-ontological distinction, 10–11, 53,
    58–59, 67, 225, 233–234, 245
ontological pluralism (*see also*
    existential pluralism; Lugones),
    81–82, 88–89, 91–97, 100–102,
    108, 114, 116, 122, 200, 238
ontology, 53, 190, 225, 236
Ortega, Mariana, 9, 52, 80, 93, 97,
    193, 218–219, 223–224, 235
Ortega y Gasset, José, 51, 232

Park, Peter K. J., 216
Pérez, Emma, 222
Pérez, Laura, 226–227, 229, 241
Pérez-Torres, Rafael, 25
Perpich, Diane, 8
Perry, John, 221
Phelan, Shane, 229, 244
phenomenology (see also Anzaldúa;
    Heidegger; Lugones; Merleau-
    Ponty; Ortega)
  European existential, 2–6, 9–10, 49,
    51–52, 58, 65, 68, 78, 115, 130,
    182, 221–222, 224, 236
  Latina feminist, 3–5, 9–10, 29, 39,
    49, 51–52, 65, 78, 90–91, 116,
    206, 216, 224
philosophy
  as academic discipline, 1–6, 9–10,
    14, 91, 106, 152, 154, 210,
    217–218, 220, 225, 227, 231
  feminist philosophy, 4, 136, 210
  and literature, 2
Pitts, Andrea, 231
playfulness, 94, 98, 101, 119, 122,
    132–134, 139, 141, 242, 244
pluralism. See existential pluralism;
    ontological pluralism
politics of location, 14, 161, 164,
    194–195, 201, 253
postmodernism, 104, 175–176, 184,
    186–187, 252–253
postpositive realist theory of identity,
    13, 173–179, 182–184, 186–190,
    249, 252–253
postracialism, 23
poststructuralism, 7–8
pragmatism, 40
Price, Joshua M., 123

queer identity (see also lesbian
    identity), 3–4, 20–23, 40–41, 50,
    63, 225, 229, 248
queer studies, 17, 229

Quijano, Aníbal, 114, 241

racism, 121, 123, 134, 139, 233,
    242–244, 247
Radloff, Bernhard, 222
Reagon, Bernice Johnson, 191,
    194–195, 249
resistance. See active subjectivity;
    hometactics; coalitional politics;
    deep coalition; consciousness,
    differential; consciousness, mestiza;
    nepantla; la nepantlera; spiritual
    activism; streetwalker theorizing;
    tactical strategies; world-traveling
Rice, Tamir, 247
Rich, Adrienne, 253–254
Ricoeur, Paul, 245
Rieff, David, 228
Rivera Berruz, Stephanie, 231
Rockmore, Tom, 222
Rodemeyer, Lanei, 224
Rodriguez, Juana María, 7, 157
Rodriguez, Richard, 175
Román-Odio, Clara, 229
Roshanravan, Shireen, 250–251
Roof, María, 243
Ruiz-Aho, Elena, 24
Russo, Ann, 222
Ryan, Barbara, 244

Sáenz, Benjamin, 35
Saldaña-Portillo, María Josefina, 33–34
Saldivar-Hull, Sonia, 224–225
Saldívar, José David, 25
Sandoval, Chela (see also consciousness,
    differential), 7, 40, 45, 75–76, 83,
    174, 179, 184–187, 222, 231
Santa Cruz Feminist of Color
    Collective, 252
Sartre, Jean-Paul, 50–51, 59, 62, 103,
    129, 221, 232–233, 254
Saucedo, Dominic, 243
Schleiermacher, Friedrich, 57

Schopenhauer, Arthur, 254
Schües, Christina, 224
Schutte, Ofelia, 2, 7, 67, 75, 167, 190, 222
Scott, Joan, 8
Seidel, Michael, 193
Sheth, Falguni, 216
Shotwell, Alexis, 169, 248–249
Simms, Eva-Maria, 224
Smith, Andrea, 222
Smith, Barbara, 222
space (*see* Spatiality)
spatiality, 88, 92–93, 108, 113, 204, 222, 238–239
Spelman, Elizabeth, 73
Spiegelberg, Herbert, 222
spiritual activism, 36–37, 42, 46, 226–227
spirituality, 42–43
Spivak, Gayatri Chakravorty, 235, 244
standpoint theory, 34, 71, 177–178, 230–231
Stawarska, Beata, 224
Steele, Shelby, 175
Stein, Edith, 221, 224
Stoller, Sylvia, 224
Stone-Mediatore, Shari, 8, 38
streetwalker theorizing, 89–90, 97, 100, 102, 106–109, 112–114, 168, 203–205, 240–241
subjecthood. *See* intersectionality; multiplicitous selfhood; new *mestiza*; *la nepantlera*
subjectivity. *See* active subjectivity; Cartesian subjectivity; Chicana identity; intermeshedness; intersectionality; Kant and Kantianism; Latina identity; lesbian identity; multiplicitous selfhood; *nepantlera*; new *mestiza*; queer identity; world-traveling
Sullivan, Shannon, 138, 244
Sushytska, Julia, 231

Sylvester, Christine, 140–141

Tabuenca Córdoba, María Socorro, 29–31
tactical strategies, 89, 107–108, 112, 203–205, 236
temporality, 12, 13, 50, 57, 78–80, 84, 98, 178, 180–182, 187, 252–253
Torres, Lourdes, 222
transcendence, 55, 175, 240, 254
transformation. *See* active subjectivity; hometactics; coalitional politics; deep coalition; consciousness, differential; consciousness, *mestiza*; *nepantla*; *la nepantlera*; spiritual activism; streetwalker theorizing; tactical strategies; world-traveling
Trujillo, Carla, 222
Truth, Sojourner, 72, 225
Turner, Victor, 134

unity and plurality, 18, 41–44, 91, 237–238

Vallega, Alejandro, 224
Vasconcelos, José, 25, 231
Vasterling, Veronica, 224
Velazco y Trianosky, Gregory, 35

Weir, Allison, 13, 146–148, 155, 159–162, 168, 244–245, 247–249
Weiss, Gail, 138–139, 222, 245–246
Wilkerson, William, 79, 252
Wilson, Tarika, 247
Wolff, Janet, 90
Wolin, Richard, 222
world-traveling (*see also* existential pluralism; Lugones, María; multiplicitous selfhood; ontological pluralism)
and authenticity, 129–130, 196–197

critical world-traveling, 13, 120,
    131–139, 141–142, 168, 207–208
and curdling, 103
definition of, 88
and dominant groups, 136–142, 254
and double-consciousness, 119–123
epistemic aspects, 87–88, 90, 95,
    97, 100–101, 103, 105, 111, 115,
    120, 126, 140, 154, 235
and Heidegger, 12–13, 49, 62
limitations of, 13, 91–95, 97–100,
    127–129, 153
and memory, 97, 109–111

as method, 140–141
and not being-at-ease, 66–67, 70
self-traveling, 75, 89, 97–98, 109,
    116

Yarbro-Bejarano, Yvonne, 32
Young, Iris Marion, 222, 244, 248
Young, Julian, 222

Zamir, Shamoon, 242
Zaytoun, Kelli, 100, 104, 114, 239
Zeiler, Kristin, 224
Zerilli, Linda, 244